Mid-Atlantic

GARDEN GUIDE

TOP 10

Edited by Mike MacCaskey, Lynn Ocone, and the Editors of Sunset Books

Principal Photography by Susan A. Roth

MENLO PARK • CALIFORNIA

D1362438

SUNSET BOOKS, INC.

VICE PRESIDENT, GENERAL MANAGER: Richard A. Smeby
VICE PRESIDENT, EDITORIAL DIRECTOR: Bob Doyle
PRODUCTION DIRECTOR: Lory Day
OPERATIONS DIRECTOR: Rosann Sutherland
MARKETING MANAGER: Linda Barker
ART DIRECTOR: Vasken Guiragossian
SPECIAL SALES: Brad Moses

STAFF FOR THIS BOOK·

PROJECT EDITORS: Mike MacCaskey and Lynn Ocone
COPY EDITOR: Vicky Congdon
DESIGN & PRODUCTION: Linda M. Bouchard
ILLUSTRATORS: Erin O'Toole, Lois Lovejoy, Jenny Speckels
MAP DESIGN AND CARTOGRAPHY:
Reineck & Reineck, San Francisco
PREPRESS COORDINATOR: Danielle Javier
PROOFREADER: Joan Beth Erickson
INDEXER: Mary Pelletier-Hunyadi

COVER: Photograph by Susan A. Roth.
Design by Vasken Guiragossian.

10 9 8 7 6 5 4 3 2 1
First printing January 2006

Library of Congress Control Number: 2005929635
ISBN-13: 978-0-376-03532-5
ISBN-10: 0-376-03532-3

Printed in the United States.

For additional copies of *Mid-Atlantic Top 10 Garden Guide*
or any other Sunset book, call 1-800-526-5111 or visit
our web site at **www.sunsetbooks.com**.

CONSULTANTS

Brent and Becky Heath are third-generation bulb growers
and daffodil hybridizers in Gloucester, Virginia.

Adrian Higgins writes about horticulture for *The Washington
Post*. He has an extensive ornamental garden at his home, and he
maintains a fruit and vegetable garden in Washington, D.C.

Alan R. McDaniel is an Associate Professor at Virginia
Polytechnic Institute and State University. He also assists with
horticulture programs in Virginia high schools.

Carole Ottesen is an award-winning garden writer and
photographer who has spent the last 25 years developing a 2-acre
organic garden at her home in Potomac, Maryland.

Rita Pelczar holds degrees in horticulture from the University
of Maryland, and has worked as an extension agent, horticulture teacher,
public garden director, and writer.

Holly Shimizu is the executive director of the U.S. Botanic Garden
in Washington, DC. Currently she is helping to implement the new
National Garden on the National Mall that will feature a rose garden.

PHOTOGRAPHERS

ALL PHOTOGRAPHS EXCEPT THOSE NOTED BELOW ARE BY
SUSAN A. ROTH.

BRENT AND BECKY'S BULBS: 62; DAVID CAVAGNARO: 14T, 236, 241B,
249L; ALAN & LINDA DETRICK: 5, 45R; ROGER FOLEY: 128; SAXON
HOLT: 95L, 124T, 246; MICHAEL MACCASKEY: 89T; JERRY PAVIA: 61T,
63T, 166, 193L, 193R, 239B, 244B, 245T, 247T, 249R, 255T; SPC PICTURE
COLLECTION: 58T, 63B, 154, 169, 192, 234T; THOMAS J. STORY: 242T;
CONNIE TOOPS: 155; TOM WOODWARD: 36T, 190T, 212T.

GARDEN DESIGNERS

BEN PAGE ASSOCIATES: 191, 227T; ANNE BROOKS: 9; DUNCAN
CALLICOT: 219BL; CONNIE CROSS: 15, 28T, 72, 106, 183B, 206, 214, 226,
232; KATHY FLEMING: 147, 263; GAIL GEE: 4, 7, 156, 261T; BENJAMIN H.
HAMMONTREE: 262R; IRELAND GANNON ASSOCIATES: 221BR;
LANDCRAFT ENVIRONMENTS: 264T; 265; LANDSCAPES BY ATLANTIC
VERTICAL: 98; BOB LANE AND ROBERT WARREN: 76; LOUISE MERCER:
225B; TOM PELLETT: 231T; ROBYN'S NEST: 12B; JOANNA SACCUCCI: 235;
SUBURBAN WATER GARDENS: 18; BUNNY WILLIAMS: 208.

OUR THANKS TO THE FOLLOWING PUBLIC GARDENS

Brookside Gardens, Wheaton, MD; Colonial Williamsburg, Williamsburg, VA;
Dumbarton Oaks, Washington, DC; Katerine Dulin Folger Rose Garden, Smithsonian
Institution, Washington, DC; Green Spring Gardens Park, Alexandria, VA; Longwood
Gardens, Kennett Square, PA; Mary Livingston Ripley Garden, Smithsonian Institution,
Washington, DC; National Gallery of Art Sculpture Garden, Washington, DC; The
New York Botanical Garden, Bronx, NY; Planting Fields Arboretum State Historic
Park, Oyster Bay, NY; The United States Botanic Garden, Washington, DC; The United
States National Arboretum, Washington, DC; Washington National Cathedral,
Washington, DC; Winterthur Museum & Country Estate, Winterthur, DE.

Contents

4   Gardening in the Mid-Atlantic Region

14   Perennials

36   Annuals·

58   Bulbs

80   Roses

102   Flowering Shrubs

124   Flowering Trees

146   Evergreens

168   Shade Trees

190   Vines

212   Ground Covers

234   Edibles

256   Seasonal Chores

268   Climate Zones

270   Index

Gardening in the Mid-Atlantic Region

After a quarter century of gardening in the Mid-Atlantic region, I can't think of anywhere else I would rather pursue my favorite hobby. Sure, there are moments when the bugs are exasperating, days when the winter seems endless, or summer's heat and humidity too sapping. But on balance, this is one of the most rewarding spots I know for creating deeply satisfying landscapes. The soils, while typically heavy, have a welcoming, slightly acidic pH range; the rainfall is abundant; the seasons varied; and the growing season long.

In my northern Virginia garden, I can count on 210 days between the last frost of spring and the first one of fall, plenty of time for the border annuals and potted tropicals to outdo themselves. The soil warms rapidly in early May and nurtures root growth well into November. I cut salad greens at Thanksgiving and dig carrots in late December. Typical winter low temperatures range from 0° to 15°F (–17 to –9°C), but the winter seems to be ever more fleeting each year, not because of global warming, but because it is so much fun to push the envelope at both ends of the growing season.

OPPOSITE PAGE: *A shade garden that features the green of hostas and burgundy of coral bells is accented by a pair of painted chairs and red-flowered hibiscus.*

"Average" numbers are, of course, tricky benchmarks in so dynamic a place. Here we see not just the confluence of many rivers great and small into the Chesapeake Bay, but the blending of northern and southern climates, the convergence of continental, Gulf, and maritime weather systems, and a rich, cosmopolitan array of plants to boot. We get about 40 inches of rainfall most years, and about half of that falls in summer. While gardeners out West can only dream of this much rainfall, there have nonetheless been years here when weeks of dryness have turned to months of drought. It pays to be prepared for atypical conditions.

You'll find a map of the Mid-Atlantic region and its five pertinent climate zones on pages 268 and 269. But note that within it, there are marked differences between the localized climates. South of the Rappahannock River in northeast Virginia, spring comes a little sooner and summer lingers a bit longer, as a rule. Gardens close to the Chesapeake Bay and the Atlantic Ocean, while in hotter growing zones, see spring arrive a little later and the fall depart later too, because of the way these large bodies of water store energy. Gardeners there may not believe this, but Richmond, Virginia, registers slightly cooler summer temperatures, on average, than the surrounding counties, and that same part of central Virginia tends to be in a rain "shadow" that makes for drier gardening.

Before the age of air-conditioning, people didn't flee to the mountains of the Virginias and Maryland just for the fun of it: At 2,000 or 3,000 feet above sea level, the dog days are agreeably bearable, with lower temperatures, more breezes, and the prospect of cooler nights. These conditions allow for fabulous garden making and a broader selection of plants, particularly conifers. At these higher elevations, however, the growing season is a month or more shorter than in the lowlands.

DESIGNING WITH PLANTS

It is currently fashionable to hire a landscape contractor to design and install a showcase garden. These instant gardens not only dramatically alter your landscape, they quickly change the contours of your bank account as well. There can be great value and satisfaction in skillfully designed "hardscape" features such as patios, retaining walls, or stairs and landings. Indeed, they create a skeleton to be fleshed out with plants. But when a new landscape is also stuffed with oversized trees and shrubs, there are problems for plants and gardener alike. You gain in instant gratification, but you lose out in other ways. An instant landscape suggests that a garden is a product, not a process, and that it won't change. Nothing could be further from the truth. Also, the immediate garden takes the homeowner out of the picture, robbing you of your chance

to learn to choose and care for a variety of plants successfully.

No garden, however well designed and implemented, is perfect. Pieces of it need constant adjustment for various reasons. Perhaps the soil and light conditions aren't right, and various plants grow too little or too much. Sometimes the situation changes dramatically: If a big tree comes down in a storm, for example, your shade garden becomes a planting in full sun overnight.

When you allow yourself a long-range view of your garden, you give yourself time to understand that plants form the garden's structure just as much as a stone wall does. You learn to see the architecture of an ornamental tree, or the horizontal lines of an informal hedge, and the various textures and shades of green in leaves. You create a garden that is less reliant on flowers for show, and one that is somehow deeper and more soothing.

A few salient points about designing with plants:

■ If an unremarkable tree of modest age is too large for its environment and is standing in the way of a garden makeover, don't be afraid to remove it.

■ The appropriate selection of a plant is dependent on the scale of its setting. In a small city garden I designed, I used three Japanese silver grasses (*Miscanthus,* page 29), each 8 feet tall and 3 feet across, to screen the patio from the adjacent sidewalk. Nearby, I planted a drift of giant hyssop, a perennial that will grow to 5 feet in good soil. The grasses were fulfilling the same role that a tall row of cedars or hollies might in a suburban setting; the hyssop, on the same diminished scale, performed as a bank of lilacs might.

■ A visit to a garden center can be a risky thing. You may end up buying on impulse, usually something in flower. When you get the plant home, you may find that you have no room for it, you cannot meet its growing conditions, or, out of bloom, it's dull. Also, just because a variety is sold at a local nursery doesn't mean that it will grow well here. Plants are shipped from greenhouses and fields across the country.

■ There are a number of top-notch public display gardens throughout the region where you can learn about varieties of ground covers, perennials, grasses, shrubs, and trees that grow well in the Mid-Atlantic zones. You'll see their light requirements and eventual size, and, so

LEFT: *'Morning Light' Japanese silver grass is an attractive screen.*
OPPOSITE PAGE: *A backyard with a brick patio and landscaped with evergreens creates an all-season sanctuary.*

noted, you can seek them out from garden centers and local and mail-order nurseries.

■ Some northern plants don't grow well in this region, although the farther west you are and the higher your elevation, the better your chances of success. Heaths and heathers are useful as container plants in every season but summer; they rarely establish in beds, however. Common or French lilacs are popular shrubs, but hot weather in April damages their flowers. In our region, Korean spice viburnum (page 108) or oakleaf hydrangea (page 112) are better choices. Similarly, European and native paper birches struggle, while 'Heritage' river birch (page 183) excels. Unfortunately, many varieties of rhododendrons sold locally look handsome

in their nursery pots but are not well suited to the heat and humidity of our climate, which induces root rots and stem blights. A few carefully selected rhododendrons will do well, however. Look for royal azalea (page 114), or alternatively, the flame azalea (page 115).

These missteps are all part of the long learning curve of gardening and are endured by even the most seasoned gardeners. But by avoiding obvious pitfalls, you'll be better able to cope with the ones that creep up on you. Fortunately, the successes always outpace the failures and in a few short years, your blank yard will become a rewarding landscape. Your accumulated knowledge of and love for plants will make for a richer life as a gardener, too.

10 years, the witch hazel, purchased as an upright stick, will become a spreading shrub 12 feet across. But you must.

As we move toward more natural gardens with less clipping, accounting for a tree or shrub's mature size becomes ever more important. And re-member, the heat and moisture in the Mid-Atlantic induces rampant growth in woody plants that is unmatched in much of the rest of the country.

In time, all trees and shrubs benefit from trimming, shaping, and pruning, but a plant that has to be continually cut back because it has outgrown its space was probably not the right choice for that location.

The natural urge to compensate for the small-ness of nursery plants is to overcrowd them.

TAKING THE LONG VIEW

One of the most important and least consid-ered elements in a garden is the effect of time. Granted, it is difficult to look at a 6-foot-tall hornbeam in a 5-gallon pot and imagine it as a 30-foot-tall tree, or to consider that after

Perennials and dwarf shrubs can be shifted about, but bigger plants don't move so well nor do they develop fully in crowded plantings. It is better to give your shrubs adequate room to start, and fill in temporary voids with annuals or ground covers or simply mulch them.

As housing developments place larger homes in closer proximity to each other, the need to screen becomes ever more pressing. Here again, the impulse is to plant large specimens of fast-growing evergreens, such as the Leyland cypress. Apart from its problems here with pests and diseases, it is also a conifer that over-powers its space, not just with its vigor but its density as well. If you need a screen 12 feet tall, the Leyland cypress will reach that in four years, but it won't stop there. Better to plant, say, a holly osmanthus (page 156). You'll wait three or four extra years for the screen you want but ultimately, you'll have an evergreen you can live with.

VEGETABLE GARDENING

The rewards of the vegetable garden are many, but high on the list is the soul-satisfying process. In our climate, you can get two to three crops from the garden between May and December. Veggies loosely fall into two types: warm season and cool season. Warm-season choices include peppers (pages 244), tomatoes (page 254), and the entire range of cucurbits, from cucumbers (page 240) to pumpkins (page 248). Probably the most popular cool-season crops are lettuce and other salad greens (page 246). Some vegetables can be harvested for much of the season, including potatoes, chard (page 246), parsnips, and successive crops of beans (page 236). I sow onion and leek seeds in late August for harvest the following summer, and I plant garlic cloves in October, to be harvested the following July. Vegetable gardens need tending, but the results are unbeatable.

For a vegetable garden, you need a location that is sunny, with lots of enriched soil, and either raised beds or a network of paths to keep feet out of the growing areas. Rabbits can be a problem for some gardeners. Groundhogs and deer frustrate others. In those cases, a serious barrier or fencing may be in order.

shade-loving perennials, including ferns (page 20), hellebores (page 22), and hostas (page 24).

For shade-gardening inspiration, visit the March Bank at Winterthur near Wilmington, Delaware, or Peirce's Woods at Longwood Gardens in Kennett Square, Pennsylvania. Or explore the Asian and Fern Valley plant collections at the National Arboretum in Washington, D.C. In these locations, you will see that a woodland garden is not the same as a neglected wooded lot.

SOIL BUILDING

There may be places where gardeners can plunge a shovel into the ground and turn over naturally rich soil, but here we must

SHADE GARDENING

In a place where trees grow quickly, which they do here, shade is an issue. Many people see shady lots as a liability because of their desire to grow grass or to raise roses. Actually, shade is an asset, and the most soulful gardens are those in shade, or at least in partial shade. Why? Because the gardener is forced to diminish the role of blooms and compose with leaf textures and colors.

Once you are ready to plant, the array of shade-tolerant ornamental trees, shrubs, ground covers, and bulbs is large and exciting. And the choices are even more inspiring for perennials—whole books have been written on

work for it. In the Delmarva and Tidewater regions of Virginia, gardeners contend with sandy or silty soil that drains quickly and leaches desirable nutrients—organic enrichment is a must. But gardeners in most of the Mid-Atlantic region find the topsoil to be predominantly clay.

Soil supports an amazing realm of life—earthworms and other beneficial animals, but also a universe of microbial life which, as we are only beginning to understand, plays a vital role in the health and vigor of our plants. In a healthy soil, there exists a world of beneficial fungi and bacteria that bolster plants' immune systems and improve their nutrient uptake. This is why many gardeners minimize the use of chemical fertilizers, believing the better long-term approach is to "feed the soil, not the plant." This approach requires a lot of effort at the start of your gardening adventure, but it's one that will pay dividends for years.

If you're gardening in a new location, you may find that the soil has been neglected and depleted. Buyers of new homes, or owners of existing ones that have been added on to, face a worse prospect: the dense subsoil that was once buried a few feet down now constitutes the topsoil. Don't be in a rush to plant until you have improved the soil.

There are several techniques for soil improvement. You can till in large quantities of organic matter, or add a few inches of shredded leaves or finely ground mulch and allow it to decompose before working it into the soil. On hardpan or weedy grass destined to become a plant bed, you can layer sheets of newspapers and cover them with a couple inches of organic matter. Again, allow it to break down for several months before planting.

Furthermore, it is necessary with any cultivated bed to replenish the organic matter at least annually. I like to use a mulch of either shredded and partially composted leaves or finely ground pine bark and let the earthworms work it into the soil.

While you're getting the soil ready for plants, you'll learn more about your gardening environment and have the time to contemplate the layout of your landscape. Later, you'll learn just as I have: plants thrive in the Mid-Atlantic, and gardeners don't do so badly here, either.

—ADRIAN HIGGINS

Perennials

Like faithful friends, perennials come back to our gardens year after year. *Perennials* are plants that live for more than two years, as opposed to *annuals*, which complete their life cycle in only one season, or *biennials*, which live no longer than two seasons. In our moderately cold climate, most soft-stemmed, or *herbaceous*, perennials die back to the ground when winter comes, their roots remaining dormant until longer, warmer days nudge them awake.

Perennials with foliage that is cut down by frost, such as astilbes (page 16) and hostas (page 24), remain dormant over the winter months. Tucked safely underground, their roots are alive and well, but there is no hint of their presence beyond the tattered vestiges of last year's growth. Others, like cardinal flower (page 18), are visible all winter as a rosette of foliage close to the ground. All perennials produce fresh new foliage in the spring.

Most perennials reproduce by dropping fertile seeds from spent flowers, some quite vigorously, and their offspring rise up every

spring for years after the original plants have died. Many spread via underground runners, or by gradually expanding in size with new shoots while the center may or may not die out.

ORCHESTRATING A SHOW

The trick to designing a perennial garden is timing the different bloom periods to have flowers throughout the season. A garden of just annuals is colorful but static, whereas a well-planned perennial garden is constantly changing, even in winter. Growing a perennial garden is a bit like conducting an orchestra; it can take awhile

ABOVE: *A bed of perennials bursts with color even in fall. Plants include rusty red 'Autumn Joy' sedum, and several flowering grasses.* OPPOSITE PAGE: *Purple flowers of hellebore rise above the lustrous leaves in late winter or very early spring.*

to get all the plants in tune, but it is gratifying when the colors and textures create a pleasing composition.

DIGGING IN

Perennials can live for many years, so proper soil preparation is essential. Perennials generally have long roots and need good soil at least 1½ feet deep. Before planting, amend it with plenty of rotted organic matter, such as compost, decayed leaves, aged manure, or peat moss, and apply more as a mulch in spring and fall. Roots, earthworms, and microorganisms will do more soil conditioning.

Over the years, a plant may lose vigor, flower less, or develop a hole in its center. In that case, it's time to dig it up and split the root mass into two or more chunks before replanting. Dividing plants is a good way to expand your garden—and to make new friends. Who wouldn't be charmed by the offer of a free plant?

In general, here in the Mid-Atlantic, late August through September is a good time to plant or divide perennials that bloom in summer. Those that bloom late in fall, such as asters (page 26) or toad lilies (page 34), are best planted or divided in spring.

Pay attention to these simple tasks and your perennials will be trouble free—or at least, my Top 10 perennials will.

—CAROLE OTTESEN

Astilbe
Astilbe chinensis

Like most perennials, astilbes have a prescribed period of bloom. Most begin blooming in late May, but *Astilbe chinensis* blooms in late summer. Astilbes are attractive before and after bloom by virtue of foliage so attractive that it is useful in bouquets. The foot-long, horizontally branching leaf stems bear numerous small leaflets that give the foliage a ferny appearance, and they would make this plant worth growing even if it did not flower. But it does bloom and when that happens, the long-lasting, feathery plumes in shades of white, pink, salmon, lavender, and red are truly spectacular.

Both foliage and flowers lend themselves to mass plantings, creating a lovely and long-lived summer ground cover that ages gracefully. After frost, the leaves wither, but rust-colored seed stalks remain on the plants through the winter and are especially attractive poking up through snow.

Hybrid astilbes come in a range of colors, including lavender, white, red, pink, and various shades of each, thus providing a wide range of color combinations for gardeners to explore.

PEAK SEASON

Spring or late summer, depending upon the type

MY FAVORITES

'Pumila' is a very dwarf astilbe with pink flowers that doesn't mind clay soil and takes more sun than most other varieties.

'Purple Candles' is a very late-blooming astilbe that sends up 3-foot-tall, deep purple flowers in July.

'Visions' has scented foliage, and the raspberry red flowers wait until late June to appear. Plants tolerate drier soil than many other astilbes.

RELATED SPECIES

Hybrid astilbe, *Astilbe × arendsii,* are widely available. Of the many varieties available, my favorites are 'Bridal Veil' (2-foot-tall, pure white flowers in June) and 'Fanal' (blood red flowers that reach 30 inches in height in June).

Japanese astilbe, *Astilbe simplicifolia,* grows 16 inches tall. Leaves are lobed, not divided. 'Sprite' is a charming 10-inch-tall, pink-flowered plant that blooms in July.

GARDEN COMPANIONS

Astilbes are one of the best plants to follow spring bulbs in the garden because their beautiful foliage fans out and over the sprawling leaves of daffodils and the yellowing after-bloom leaves of tulips.

When Plant container-grown nursery plants in the fall to give astilbes time to establish for the following spring's bloom. If plants aren't available in fall, set them out as early as you can get them in spring.

Where Most important, choose a place that won't dry out in summer. Plant astilbes in partial shade and in rich soil that is consistently moist but well drained. They will grow in full sun if they have sufficient moisture.

How Astilbes prefer rich soil. Incorporate plentiful compost into a generous planting hole. Gently loosen the roots and spread them out in the hole. Make sure the plant is growing at the same depth that it was in the container. Backfill and water deeply. Space plants 18 inches apart and add a 4-inch layer of mulch between them.

TLC Astilbes are relatively carefree, but will languish if they don't have sufficient moisture. Keep their roots cool and moist by replenishing the layers of mulch each year.

RIGHT: Astilbe chinensis *'Pumila' blooms in late summer.*
BELOW: Astilbe × arendsii *'Fanal' combines dark red flowers and bronzy leaves.*

Cardinal Flower
Lobelia cardinalis

Cardinal flower blooms when little else does: in the hazy, hot, and humid days of July and August for which the Mid-Atlantic is notorious. The flowers are a brilliant red, held on sturdy, very upright stalks that rise from rosettes of evergreen foliage. Depending upon age, sun, and moisture, the plants can range from 1 to 4 feet tall when in flower.

In the wild, you can often find cardinal flowers growing in moist woods near streams in places where the overhead canopy parts to let in some sunshine. Take a cue from nature and try to provide similar conditions in the home landscape. Cardinal flower makes a colorful subject for the dappled shade of a woodland garden. It self-sows into great, riveting red colonies when its needs are met. Be sure to plant cardinal flowers near a window so you can watch the hummingbirds flock to the tubular red blossoms.

PEAK SEASON

Cardinal flower is at its best in July and August when the bright red flowers draw wildlife into the garden.

MY FAVORITES

'Alba' is similar to the species form, but bears pure white flowers on 3-foot-tall spikes.

'Bee's Flame' has bright red flowers that contrast attractively with its dark purple foliage.

'Queen Victoria' is a beautiful combination of bright red flowers and bronze foliage. It is less hardy than other species and cultivars, surviving only in zones 31 and 32.

'Ruby Slippers' bears big, buxom flowers that are a velvety ruby red rather than the bright clear red of the species.

GARDEN COMPANIONS

Cardinal flowers make good companions to astilbes and toad lily (Tricyrtis), which also prefer moist soil and partial sun. For months of bloom, plant cardinal flowers behind an early-flowering astilbe, such as 'Bridal Veil', and in front of the toad lilies.

OPPOSITE PAGE: *A pond or streamside plant in the wild, cardinal flower thrives adjacent to this koi pond.*

When Sturdy cardinal flowers can be planted in either spring or fall, when container-grown plants are available, but they bloom better the first summer in the garden when they were planted the previous fall.

Where Cardinal flowers love moisture. In fact, they can grow in full sun if plentiful moisture is available. In partially shaded areas they will be somewhat more tolerant of dry soil, though even there prefer moisture.

How Before planting, amend the soil with plenty of organic matter. Gently tease the roots to loosen them and spread them out in the planting hole. Space plants 18 inches apart. Backfill and water deeply. Carefully mulch between plants to keep the soil cool and moist, but make sure the mulch doesn't cover the foliage rosettes.

Brilliant red cardinal flower is a potent summertime attractor of hummingbirds.

TLC Cardinal flowers are relatively carefree. Divide big clumps every 3 years and transplant volunteers to appropriate new homes. After leaves drop in the fall, keep matted, wet leaves from smothering the evergreen rosettes.

*'Queen Victoria' is limited to zones 31 and 32.

Ferns
Dryopteris, Polystichum

Most people admire ferns growing in the woods but would never think to plant them in the garden. Perhaps one reason for this is that ferns look delicate and don't seem like garden plants. The truth is that ferns are some of the oldest plants on the planet and as such, have had to be real survivors. They are tough plants that can take heat and cold and will even withstand the occasional drought. They are generally not bothered by the ailments and insects that pester other plants. And deer usually pass them right by.

Ferns can do just about any job around the garden. A number of them are evergreen and long-lived. They will stay in place for years, getting better with time. They make good ground covers and accent plants, and will even fill a spot in the border if conditions are right. All they ask for in return is partial shade and moderately moist soil.

LEFT: *Young fronds of autumn fern blend several colors.*
ABOVE: *Christmas ferns begin to unfurl their long, dark fronds.*

LEFT: *In fall, autumn fern fronds change again to an attractive rust color.*
RIGHT: *A clump of Christmas fern is fronted here by bishop's hat (Epimedium) and backed by hosta.*

PEAK SEASON

Ferns never flower. They just look refreshingly cool and green throughout the year.

MY FAVORITES

Autumn fern *(Dryopteris erythrosora)* is an evergreen aristocrat, sending up broad new fronds that are a bronzy orange color before they turn a lustrous green, then darken to rust in fall. It grows about 2 feet tall and equally broad. Autumn fern is a superb ground cover, sophisticated enough for an entrance garden.

Christmas fern *(Polystichum acrostichoides),* an evergreen native, grows to about 2 feet high and 30 inches wide. The low, broad clumps are terrific for edging a shady path. This fern also makes a good ground cover for a shady slope.

Tassel fern *(Polystichum polyblepharum)* grows about 18 inches high and about 2 feet wide. A clump of tassel fern, with its long, subtly lustrous, arching, evergreen fronds, serves as a fine accent in a shady border.

GARDEN COMPANIONS

Ferns are the perfect companions to wildflowers such as Dutchman's breeches *(Dicentra cucullaria)* and trilliums. After the ephemeral wildflowers disappear, the ferns keep their spot in the garden looking lush.

When Plant container-grown ferns in fall or spring.

Where Plant ferns in partial to full shade in rich, moist, loamy soil. Spray on a foliar fertilizer the first spring after planting.

How Incorporate plentiful compost into a bed that has been cleared of weeds or turf. Space large ferns 18 to 24 inches apart. Mulch around them, but leave their crowns—the raised portion from which the fronds emerge—free of debris. Water well until the plants establish.

TLC Once established, ferns are carefree. Sometimes, however, seeds of other plants land in the center of the clump and sprout there. Check your ferns twice each year and pull out any weeds that have taken up residence.

Hellebore
Helleborus orientalis

Hellebores, also called "Lenten roses," are simply the best, the longest-lasting, and the easiest-to-grow perennials available. Unless your yard is a dry, sun-baked field, buy yourself a hellebore and plant it in moist soil in partial shade. It will change what you think about perennials. Planting a hellebore is more like planting a flowering evergreen shrub that never outgrows its place. It will develop slowly into a lovely dark green, attractively rounded plant that blooms dependably in March, and sometimes as early as February. The older the clump gets, the more flowers you will have. Colors are shades of white, pink, rose, and yellow, often brushed or speckled with a contrasting dark maroon. The flowers are followed by very attractive seedpods. These last well into May and look enough like flowers that you will want to leave them on the plants.

Hellebores also qualify as foliage plants. A mature plant reaches about 18 inches in height and spreads to 30 inches wide, with lobed leaves of a rich, dark, lustrous green. It is the perfect edging for a shrub border.

Hellebore flowers bloom reliably in early spring and sometimes even in late winter.

PEAK SEASON

Hellebores are good-looking through-out the year, but are outstanding at peak bloom time in late winter and early spring.

MY FAVORITES

'White Lady' bears absolutely pure white flowers that are held upright on handsome plants.

RELATED SPECIES

Christmas rose *(Helleborus niger)* is similar to the Lenten rose but is smaller and less robust. It grows to about 14 inches and has white petals around a pale yellow center.

Stinking hellebore *(Helleborus foetidus)* has a horrible name for such a lovely plant. This perennial grows to about 24 inches tall and has beautifully divided leaves in a deep, glossy green. It sends up cup-shaped, chartreuse flowers in winter, sometimes even in early December.

GARDEN COMPANIONS

Hellebores are wonderful in masses under trees with shapely limbs such as deciduous magnolias. They are also lovely in combination with azaleas, especially the deciduous ones.

When Buy and plant container-grown plants in spring while they're in bloom so that you can chose according to the colors you prefer. You can also plant hellebores in fall.

Where Hellebores thrive in partial shade in rich soil that is consistently moist but well drained.

How Before planting, enrich the soil with organic material such as compost. Gently remove the hellebore from its container. Tease out any roots that are encircling the root ball. Spread the roots out into the planting hole. Backfill the hole, tamp the soil, and water thoroughly. Mulch to conserve moisture.

TLC Hellebores are rarely bothered by disease or insects. They do require neatening in late winter for them to look their best at bloom time. Cut off old, damaged, discolored leaves and discard. Top-dress with compost and renew or replace the mulch.

TOP: *'White Lady', a cultivar of* Helleborus × hybridus.
CENTER: *Delicate veining is apparent in this close-up of a hybrid hellebore.*
BOTTOM: *White flowers of Christmas rose* (Helleborus niger) *typically first appear in late December.*

Hosta

Hosta

The large, heart-shaped leaves of Hosta sieboldiana 'Elegans' are each over a foot long. The plant gradually spreads to about 4 feet wide.

Unless your neighborhood is infested with deer (who, unfortunately, seem to prefer hostas over many other succulent choices), hostas are some of the toughest, longest-lasting, and handsomest shade lovers you can plant. Although they do bloom, they are primarily foliage plants that bring color and texture into the garden with their beautiful leaves. Hostas come in all sizes, and the leaves are available in many shades and permutations of green, yellow, and white. Their shape—generally a mounding clump that spreads wider than it is tall—seems to work just about everywhere in the garden. Plants are attractive in containers, where they will grow for years. Further, hostas make fine ground covers under trees, where they prosper even in dry shade. And when a clump of hosta is planted as an accent, the shape is reminiscent of a bow of beautiful green ribbon.

Hostas bloom in summer, sending up tall flower stalks with often fragrant, lily-like bells in shades of lavender and white. Hostas ask little and give a lot. They live for years and years, gradually forming ever larger clumps.

When The best time to buy hostas is in the spring when you can see their foliage, but you can plant container-grown plants in fall.

Where When hostas are given a place in the garden that suits their preferences—part shade in rich, slightly acid soil that's moist but well drained—they mature swiftly into dense, leafy, full-size plants. They are such tough plants, however, that they will grow almost anywhere—just not as quickly or as large.

How Prepare the soil by adding organic matter such as compost. Remove plants from their containers and gently uncoil any roots that encircle the root ball. Spread the roots out in a hole big enough to accommodate them, making sure the plant is set at the same depth that it was growing in its container. Space larger hostas at least 4 feet apart and smaller ones between 2 and 3 feet apart, depending on the variety. Mulch around the plants. Water deeply at planting time and weekly thereafter until the hostas are established.

TLC Slugs can disfigure hostas. Spreading crushed eggshells, sand, or perlite around the plants affords some protection. Slugs are also attracted to beer and will crawl into a shallow dish of it and drown. Nontoxic slug baits are also available.

LEFT: *In August, a flower spike of 'Frances Williams' rises above the clump of leaves.*
RIGHT: *The white leaf margins of 'Patriot' ensure this hosta will brighten shaded areas.*

PEAK SEASON

Foliage is showy all season. Flowers appear in summer.

MY FAVORITES

Hosta 'Frances Williams' is an old favorite of great beauty. Its round gray-green leaves are edged with yellow. It forms a big, spreading mound that can reach 3 feet tall by 4 feet wide. The flowers are white.

Hosta 'Krossa Regal' is a truly sculptural hosta. Its gray-green leaves are firm and elegantly formed, and they stand strongly upright, forming a vase shape about 2½ feet tall by almost 4 feet wide. Lavender flowers top stems that can reach 5 feet.

Hosta 'Patriot' has green leaves that are edged in white, giving it a very neat appearance. It grows about 20 inches tall by about 2 feet wide. The flowers are lavender.

Hosta sieboldiana 'Elegans' is a classic hosta with gray-green "seersucker" leaves. It is a giant, growing to 2½ feet tall by 4 feet wide. The flowers are white.

GARDEN COMPANIONS

Hostas are the perfect plants to follow bulbs such as daffodils or tulips because they fill out in May after the bulbs have bloomed. They are also natural companions to ferns such as the tall ostrich fern (*Matteuccia pensylvanica*).

New England Aster

Aster novae-angliae (Symphyotrichum novae-angliae)

Next fall when you go to the garden center and are tempted to buy chrysanthemums, consider the New England aster instead. Every fall in the Mid-Atlantic, the fields are carpeted with their cheerful starlike flowers. This North American native blooms beautifully in the wild here without help from anyone because it has had eons in which to adapt to the conditions in our region. Its acclimatization to local soil types, temperatures, and rainfall ensures plants will be carefree additions to your perennial border. In fact, when these plants don't have to compete in a crowded field or meadow and are given the cushy conditions of an average garden, they outdo themselves. They grow taller—to 5 feet high and wide—and cover themselves with hundreds of 2-inch flowers in pink, white, and purple-blue for several weeks in fall, a time of year when colorful blossoms are particularly welcome. As border plants, asters are tough to beat.

New England aster produces bright purple flowers from late summer into fall.

PEAK SEASON

Asters bloom for weeks in the late summer and fall.

MY FAVORITES

'Alma Poetschke' is the most unusually colored of all the New England asters, flowering in an unforgettable bright salmon pink.

'Purple Dome' is a wonderful dwarf New England aster that grows into a compact mound about 15 inches tall; it bears purple blossoms.

RELATED SPECIES

Tatarian aster (*Aster tataricus*) grows in a very upright manner and is one of the latest asters to bloom. 'Jindai' reaches 4 feet in height and bears purple flowers.

White wood aster (*A. divaricatus*) is good in partly shaded places. It bears white blossoms on 2-foot-tall plants.

GARDEN COMPANIONS

Like asters, many ornamental grasses are fall bloomers and at their best during fall's crisp, sunny days, so are good companions. Feather reed grass (*Calamagrostis × acutiflora* 'Stricta') is an upright plant that can serve as an attractive foil to New England aster's billowing form. Prairie dropseed (*Sporobolus heterolepis*) has shiny seeds that sparkle in the autumn sunlight, as well as a mounding form that complements aster's growth habit.

ABOVE: *Flowers of 'Purple Dome' are 2 inches wide.*
RIGHT: *Flowers of Tatarian aster are 1 inch wide.*

When Plant container-grown asters in the early spring so they'll be well established by the time fall bloom time rolls around.

Where New England asters require full sun. They are not fussy about soil, are tolerant of wet soils and, once established, are fairly drought tolerant.

How Plant container-grown asters in ordinary garden soil that has been amended with compost. Allow about 9 square feet per plant. Tease out any circling roots and spread them out in a hole that will accommodate them. Water deeply after planting and for the first several weeks thereafter. Spread a 3-inch layer of mulch to conserve moisture.

TLC Pruning to control size, shape, and sprawl is the secret to beautiful asters in the garden. In June, cut the plants back by a third to a half. The resulting plant will be more compact and the blooms more abundant. Asters grow quickly and need division every fourth year.

Ornamental Grasses

Miscanthus, Molinia

Ornamental grasses are invaluable in a sunny garden. Their fine but dense foliage provides much-needed volume, and their quiet greens moderate the effect of potentially clashing colors. And grasses also add sound and movement to the garden. Smaller ornamental grasses serve as wonderful fillers around leggy roses or other angular plants. Large grasses,

such as Japanese silver grass *(Miscanthus sinensis),* reach 6 feet or more and act as screens or bold accents. Those with early-blooming flowers on tall, delicate stalks, such as moor grass, are in constant motion, swaying even in the absence of a breeze.

All summer long, ornamental grasses are the hardworking supporting cast for the flowering stars of the garden. But in autumn, the grasses take center stage. Some wait until September and October to bloom. After frost, grasses take on lovely shades of wheat and almond and retain their "bulk" while other plants wither into sticks and dried stems. Most grasses remain showy far into winter.

ABOVE: *A lacy screen of moor grass fronts a low wall.*
RIGHT: *'Morning Light' Japanese silver grass.*

LEFT: *Even in midwinter 'Gracillimus' Japanese silver grass adds interest to a garden.*
RIGHT: *Leaves of flame grass (Miscanthus sinensis 'Purpurascens') turn red in fall.*

PEAK SEASON

In fall the late-blooming flowers dazzle in the autumn sunlight.

MY FAVORITES

Japanese silver grass

Miscanthus sinensis 'Gracillimus', maiden grass, has an upright shape and very narrow, medium green foliage. Flowers come in October, emerging magenta and lightening to pink.

Miscanthus sinensis 'Morning Light' has finely striped green and white foliage. Smaller than the species form, 'Morning Light' grows only about 5 feet tall by about 2 feet wide.

Miscanthus sinensis 'Purpurascens', flame grass, grows 3 to 4 feet tall. Leaves become orange red in fall, then fade to reddish brown.

Moor grass

Molinia caerulea arundinacea 'Windspiel' is like a piece of kinetic sculpture. The summer flowers, in constant motion on even windless days, are held on impossibly fine, 5-foot stems that rise out of 2-foot foliage clumps.

GARDEN COMPANIONS

Tall, upright Tartarian aster *(Aster tataricus)* or compass plant *(Silphium laciniatum)* combine well with the shape of the wide-spreading Japanese silver grass.

When Plant container-grown grasses in spring.

Where Ornamental grasses grow best in full sun in moist but well-drained soil.

How Remove weeds and turfgrass from the bed and incorporate organic matter into the soil. Set grasses into generous holes at the same depth that they were growing in their containers. Water well and mulch to conserve moisture and prevent weeds. All ornamental grasses grow wider with age and should be spaced accordingly. Plant shorter grasses about 3 feet apart; allow 6 feet between larger grasses.

TLC Grasses are easy-care additions to the garden, but they do require a yearly cutting back to look their best, especially if spring blooming bulbs are planted nearby. Cut the grasses back to about 4 to 10 inches above the ground in early spring. In April, the grasses will begin to send out new growth. Once established, grasses rarely need fertilizing. Soil that is too rich can cause rank, floppy growth.

Purple Coneflower
Echinacea purpurea

Coneflowers are some of the best all-around perennials to be had. They are carefree, thriving "on the economy". Once established, they withstand drought or deluge and intense heat or cold. These are tough natives that bloom despite the intense heat of July and August. The big, showy flowers derive their common name from the prominent orangey-green cones in the center of the purple-pink daisy petals. Great candidates for perennial borders or stylized meadows, coneflowers are also some of the longest-lasting cut flowers that you can grow.

These are popular wildlife plants too. When in blossom, coneflowers are invariably hosts to clouds of hovering butterflies. In fall, finches and other birds come for the seeds.

Coneflowers respond enthusiastically to the right growing conditions. If they have rich, moist soil and full sun, they may grow more than 4 feet tall. In ordinary soil, they usually stand about 30 inches tall. Clumps spread outward, and volunteers appear where conditions are favorable.

Native purple coneflower has everything: it's tough, hardy, and it blooms all summer.

LEFT: *Petals of 'Magnus' purple coneflower spread out flat, not downward as is typical.*
RIGHT: *'White Swan' differs from the species in its slightly smaller size as well as color.*

PEAK SEASON

Coneflowers are at their best in July when they first come into bloom.

MY FAVORITES

'Kim's Knee High' bears a rose-purple flower on a very compact plant that grows only about 2 feet tall.

'Magnus' has big, flat, rosy red flowers on a 30-inch plant.

'White Swan' is a lovely white coneflower that is slightly smaller than the species, growing only about 28 inches tall. You can grow it from either seeds or plants.

RELATED SPECIES

'Sunrise' is a pale yellow coneflower, and 'Sunset' has an orange blossom. Both are among the Sunrise Big Sky hybrids, which are crosses between the purple coneflower *(Echinacea purpurea)* and its yellow-flowered relative, yellow coneflower *(E. paradoxa)*. Plants in this series resemble purple coneflower in height, flower, and leaves, but the flower colors reveal the yellow-flowered parent.

GARDEN COMPANIONS

Plant coneflowers in the middle of the perennial border. They combine well with plants that are lower growing and spreading, such as tickseed *(Coreopsis verticillata),* which makes a good edger. Plant taller perennial sunflowers *(Helianthus)* behind them.

When Plant and divide coneflowers in the fall or early spring. If grown from seed started indoors in March, they will bloom the first year in the garden.

Where Plant coneflowers in full sun in moderately moist soil with good drainage.

How Prepare the soil by adding organic matter such as compost. Remove the plants from their containers and gently loosen the roots so they will grow outward. Spread the roots out in the planting holes. Backfill the holes, water, and mulch around the plants to prevent weeds and keep the soil moist.

TLC Coneflowers are tough plants, but will appreciate a yearly topdressing with compost. Cut off spent flowers to keep new ones coming, but save a few at the end of the summer. Finches love coneflower seeds!

Sedum 'Autumn Joy'
Sedum (Hylotelephium)

For one of the most carefree and longest-lived perennials you can grow, plant *Sedum* 'Autumn Joy'.

'Autumn Joy' sedum begins to bloom by midsummer and looks good right into fall.

For these reasons, it is often planted as an 18-inch-tall deciduous ground cover. The new growth first appears in March and forms a low mound of succulent, round, lettucelike green by April, making 'Autumn Joy' a great choice for interplanting with bulbs. Crocuses bloom just before the new growth begins to rise up. Daffodils bloom between the low mounds of sedum that soon grow large enough to camouflage the sprawling after-bloom foliage of the bulbs.

In late June, the flowers appear—flat clusters of the same lettuce green as the foliage. Very slowly, they turn first to a pale pink, then later to a rose color. But it is in late August and September, when the flowers deepen to a spectacular rusty red, that this plant lives up to its name. That performance alone would more than guarantee a welcome spot in any garden, but 'Autumn Joy' does more. The attractively faded flowers remain well into winter and look good, especially against the snow.

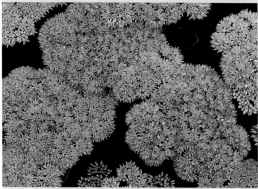

Sedum 'Autumn Joy' moves through each season with color and character: spring (top), summer (center), and winter (bottom).

PEAK SEASON

'Autumn Joy' sedum is spectacular from August through October.

RELATED PLANTS

'Frosty Morn' is similar in habit and size to 'Autumn Joy', but it has variegated leaves of white and pale green. Pink flowers appear in September.

'Matrona' is similar to 'Autumn Joy' but is larger, growing to about 24 inches tall. It has succulent, purple-tinged foliage.

Mountain sedum (*Sedum ternatum*) is a low-growing, native succulent that grows and blooms in light shade. It is evergreen and produces showy white flowers in May. There is a pink form called 'Larinem Pink'.

'Vera Jameson' is a low-growing variety, reaching only about 8 inches tall. The leaves are a beautiful blue-gray, and the flowers bloom a bright rose color.

GARDEN COMPANIONS

In addition to combining well with bulbs such as crocuses, alliums, and daffodils, 'Autumn Joy' sedum is splendid partnering with ornamental grasses such as fountain grass (*Pennisetum alopecuroides*) or prairie dropseed (*Sporobolus heterolepis*).

When Plant container-grown 'Autumn Joy' sedum in spring as early as it is available.

Where 'Autumn Joy' sedum thrives in full sun and moderately moist but well-drained soil. It is extremely cold tolerant, but may be knocked over by hard, driving rain so some shelter from wind is often beneficial.

How Prepare a bed for 'Autumn Joy' by removing weeds and turf and adding organic matter such as compost. Tip the plant out of the container and gently tease out any roots that encircle the root ball. Dig a hole that accommodates the roots and plant at the same depth that the sedum was growing in the container. Space plants about 15 inches apart. Water well after planting. Mulch to conserve moisture and discourage weeds.

TLC Unfortunately, deer eat 'Autumn Joy.' To discourage deer from browsing, try one of the many barriers or repellents that deter them. Leave the flower stalks on the plants throughout the winter or until they cease to please.

Toad Lily

Tricyrtis

Toad lilies are a shade gardener's dream come true. But they are not nearly as commonly planted as they deserve to be. These graceful plants not only bloom in the shade, they also bear some of the latest flowers of the year, opening their orchidlike blooms in late September and October and flowering even after light frosts. The flowers, borne on long, arching stems that reach 3 feet in height, are white with bright purple spots. They make excellent cut flowers that would be appreciated at any time, but they are all the more valuable because they appear when little else is blooming.

One-inch-wide purple- and white-speckled flowers cover 'Sinonome' toad lily in late summer.

In rich, loose, moist soil, toad lilies will quickly (in 2 years) form large clumps with many flowering stalks. Their tall, arching forms are a good choice for a graceful transition from taller shrubs to low ground covers. They are perfect along a woodland path or in an entrance garden in dappled shade.

PEAK SEASON

Toad lily blooms in late September and flowers into November, tolerating light frost.

MY FAVORITES

Tricyrtis hirta 'Miyazaki' has pale purple blossoms with darker purple spots. It flowers in September.

Tricyrtis 'Sinonome' produces clusters of 1-inch-wide purple- and white-speckled flowers. The plant grows 3 feet tall and is very drought tolerant.

GARDEN COMPANIONS

Tall toad lilies make great companions to the 1-foot tall running fern *(Thelypteris decursive pinnata)*. Or use them to follow early-blooming wildflowers such as the native wake robin *(Trillium grandiflorum)*.

When Plant nursery-grown containers of toad lilies in the spring.

Where Toad lilies perform best in half to full shade in moist but well-drained soil that is very rich in organic matter.

How Plant toad lilies in soil that is rich and loose in shady areas of your garden. If necessary, amend the soil with plenty of compost and leaf mold. Space the plants at least 3 feet from other plants so they will be able to spread. In placing them, remember that the stems will arch toward the light. Mulch with rotted leaves, if available, or shredded hardwood. Water well.

TLC Deer will eat toad lilies. If you live in deer territory, use some kind of deer barrier or repellent spray or risk losing your plants. Cut the plants back after a hard frost. In spring, top-dress with compost unless the soil is very rich in humus.

ABOVE: *A close-up of 'Sinonome' flowers.*
LEFT: *Tricyrtis hirta 'Miyazaki' are brighter in shady areas.*

Annuals

To a botanist, an *annual* is a plant that completes its entire life cycle in a single growing season. That definition fits many garden annuals like marigolds (page 46) and zinnias (page 56). But the definition of an annual has a purely practical aspect too. Other plants that we treat as annuals in our Mid-Atlantic gardens, such as coleus (page 38) and impatiens (page 42), would actually live much longer in warmer climates. But because they flower quickly even when grown from seed and last only a single season in our region, we consider them annuals too.

GETTING STARTED

If you need only a few annuals, or you don't have the time or space to grow them from seed, purchase plants at a garden center. Look for sturdy plants with healthy color.

Growing annuals from seed requires a bit of patience and careful tending, but the selection available from seed catalogs is far more extensive than what you'll find at most garden centers. Some annuals can be sown directly in the garden; others need extra growing time and should be started indoors.

Refer to the seed packet for directions. Grow seeds indoors in a sterile potting mix, and unless you have a greenhouse, you'll need artificial lights.

Before transplanting young plants to the garden, dig the soil to a depth of 10 to 12 inches, adding organic matter such as compost or leaf mold. If possible, wait for a cloudy day with little or no wind to transplant; these conditions will reduce stress on the seedlings. Water thoroughly and pinch off any flower buds to encourage root and leaf growth.

RIGHT: *Annuals 'Pineapple Beauty' coleus, orange cosmos, and purple mealycup sage complement 'Purpureum' fountain grass and lantana.*
OPPOSITE PAGE: *Cosmos sulphureus 'Orange Ladybird'.*

ANNUAL OPTIONS

Annuals fit into lots of different planting schemes. A walkway flanked with brightly colored, low-growing annuals is a great way to greet visitors. A "hedge" of tall annuals can temporarily enclose a patio or screen a work area. Sprinkle annuals among plantings of perennials or shrubs to significantly extend the flowering season of those beds.

Many annuals make great cut flowers. You can plant annuals specifically for cutting in rows—as you would vegetables—or simply plant enough in your flower beds so you can snip a few for indoors now and again. I like to plant a few rows of "cutting annuals" alongside my vegetable garden where they do double duty, providing an attractive border and plenty of material for flower arrangements.

One of my favorite ways to grow annuals is in containers. Window boxes and hanging baskets bring the garden right up to the house. I combine two or three different annuals in large pots to flank my front door. When combining plants, be sure to select those with similar requirements for light and water. Use anything from an old boot to a hollowed-out stump to create your own brand of garden art. And remember that in summer, plants in containers may need daily watering.

Annuals appeal to anyone who embraces change. In just a few weeks, these fast-growing plants can transform a landscape, and if properly tended, most will perform all season long. They only last one season, so you can alter your planting scheme each year, sampling new varieties and experimenting with different combinations. If you are like me, a few favorites will find a spot in your garden year after year. But I always save some space to try something new.

—RITA PELCZAR

Coleus

Solenostemon scutellarioides

For those of us who like to paint the landscape with bold strokes, coleus is just the plant. Coleus are grown not for their flowers but for their exotic foliage, available in a wide range of colors, patterns, and textures on upright plants that grow from 1 to 3 feet tall. They are among the easiest annuals to grow and, in a partially shaded spot, will thrive with little care.

Purple leaves of 'Dark Star' coleus produce a dramatic contrast to the silvery leaves of Plectranthus argentatus.

Mixing their wild colors and patterns in a bed can look messy, so I prefer growing a single variety to create a sweep—that bold stroke—of color. Coleus also make great container plants, either alone or mixed with more subdued flowering annuals like pink or white impatiens or browallia.

Pinch off the flowers as they form so that the plants will put all their energy into growing leaves. I take cuttings of my coleus in late summer; they root easily in water or potting soil. When cold weather threatens, I bring the new plants indoors. Placed in a sunny window, they provide indoor color for months.

When Coleus is extremely sensitive to cold; plant it in the garden after all danger of frost has passed. To grow plants from seed, sow indoors 8 to 10 weeks before the last frost date.

Where Most coleus grow best in partial shade. New varieties, particularly those with deep red and purple foliage, will tolerate more sun as long as you supply adequate water. Moist, well-drained soils, supplemented with organic matter, are best.

ABOVE: *'Sunset'*
BELOW LEFT: *'Inky Fingers'*
BELOW RIGHT: *'The Line'*

How Dig the garden soil to a depth of 10 to 12 inches, incorporating 2 to 3 inches of compost or leaf mold. Acclimate indoor-grown seedlings to the outdoors by placing them in a protected, shady location for a few days and, if possible, transplant on a cloudy day with little or no wind. Space plants 8 to 12 inches apart and pinch out the top pair of leaves to encourage bushiness. Fertilize new plants with a dilute solution of a complete liquid fertilizer. For container plantings, incorporate a slow-release fertilizer into the growing mix.

TLC Keep the soil evenly moist, but not soggy. Mulching with shredded bark, leaf mold, or pine needles will inhibit weeds. Fertilize every 2 to 3 weeks with a complete liquid fertilizer at half strength. When flowers appear, pinch or cut them back to channel growth to the leaves.

PEAK SEASON

Late spring to first frost

MY FAVORITES

'Black Dragon' develops two-toned leaves of deep pink and dark purple. They are heavily crimped, giving them a puffy, quilted texture.

'Dark Star' has dark purple, slightly shiny leaves with scalloped edges. It's very sun tolerant.

'Inky Fingers' is a very tidy, compact selection that grows about a foot tall with a slightly greater spread. Its irregularly lobed, deep burgundy leaves are broadly edged with lime green.

Kong Series coleus make large, mounding plants in several colors and patterns, all with huge leaves.

'Limelight' has chartreuse leaves with slightly darker veins.

'Sunset' is orange-red in the center, blending to dark red; the leaves are outlined in yellow.

'The Line' is chartreuse but with a dark maroon midrib.

GARDEN COMPANIONS

Coleus are at their best in a mass planting, but they also make an effective accent in a mixed bed or container planting with flowering companions like impatiens, browallia, or *Petunia integrifolia.*

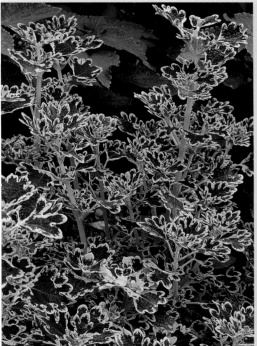

Cosmos

Cosmos

The dainty flowers and fine-textured leaves of cosmos may look delicate, but this summer bloomer has an iron constitution. It thrives in hot weather, producing flowers nonstop from midsummer until frost. Cosmos are wonderful fillers for mixed beds, where their flowers attract birds and butterflies, and they are ideal for cutting.

Cosmos *(Cosmos bipinnatus)* bears flowers that range from white to pale pink and deep magenta. Its leaves are threadlike. The leaves of yellow cosmos *(C. sulphureus)* are a bit coarser, but the main difference is its flower colors: they are clear yellow, orange, or scarlet.

Cosmos can grow 6 feet tall, although dwarf varieties that top out at 12 to 24 inches are also available. I prefer these smaller ones—they fit easily among other annuals or perennials, and, unlike the tall types, they don't need staking.

Plant your cosmos in a sunny spot in your leanest soil and chances are, you'll have lots of flowers for both your garden and your vases. Don't fertilize the plants; if the soil is too rich, you'll likely see many leaves but few flowers, and these won't appear until very late in the season.

Flowers of 'Ladybird Mix' come in scarlet, yellow, and orange.

PEAK SEASON
Midsummer to frost

MY FAVORITES
'Bright Lights' bears its yellow, gold, orange, and red semidouble flowers on 3-foot plants. Flowering begins earlier than with most varieties.

'Cosmic Orange' is a 12-inch dwarf type that produces clear orange flowers with yellow centers.

'Ladybird Mix' grows about 16 inches tall and blooms early with orange, yellow, or red flowers.

'Sea Shells' grows 3 to 3½ feet tall and bears white, pink, and carmine flowers with quilled petals that are pale on the outside and more deeply colored within.

The Sonata Series ranges from 18 to 24 inches tall, and rarely requires staking. The flowers are white, rose, pink, and cherry pink.

'Sunny Red' grows 14 inches tall and is deep red with yellow streaks in the center.

GARDEN COMPANIONS
Annuals or perennials with a contrasting texture or growth habit, like lamb's ear, *Plectranthus*, floss flower (*Ageratum*), or alyssum, work well with cosmos. Use white and pink cosmos with other pastel-colored flowers; yellow and orange selections complement blue flowers.

ABOVE: *'Sonata White'*
TOP RIGHT: *'Sonata Pink'*
BOTTOM RIGHT: *'Sea Shells'*

When Sow seed directly in the garden after the last spring frost, or indoors 6 weeks earlier. Transplant young plants in late spring.

Where Grow in full sun, in lean, well-drained soil, supplemented with organic matter.

How Dig the garden soil to a depth of 10 to 12 inches, incorporating 2 to 3 inches of compost or leaf mold. Sow seed directly or carefully transplant young plants, with minimal root disturbance, on a cloudy day with little or no wind. Space plants or thin seedlings 12 to 18 inches apart.

TLC Keep the soil evenly moist, but not soggy. Don't fertilize or flowers will be few and late. Removing spent blooms and cutting flowers for indoor use will encourage the production of more flowers. Cosmos will self-sow, but seedlings from hybrids may have different traits. Tall types will need staking; otherwise they may get top-heavy and flop over.

Impatiens
Impatiens walleriana

N othing adds summerlong color to a shady garden more effectively than impatiens. A tropical perennial that we grow as an annual, its neat, compact, mounding habit is compatible with both formal and informal landscaping styles. Depending on the variety, plants grow 4 to 24 inches tall and they surpass their height in spread.

Impatiens are ideal for edging a shaded perennial bed.

Impatiens are very easy to grow—just provide some shade and sufficient water and they flourish. In a mass planting under trees or in front of shrubs, or edging a bed, they provide a broad band of color. They are equally at home sprinkled here and there among perennials and shrubs in a woodland garden. They excel in containers, but when it gets very hot in the summer, keeping them adequately watered may become a chore.

These simple flat-faced flowers, available in shades of pink, white, red, orange, lavender, and bicolor, remind me of childhood—they have a look of innocence, and I'm sure impatiens inhabited the woods around Snow White's cottage. There are new varieties with double or semidouble blooms, but I find the simple single form to be the loveliest.

PEAK SEASON

Late spring to first frost

MY FAVORITES

Bruno Series are large and vigorous plants that grow from 12 to 16 inches tall. Both the leaves and the flowers are somewhat thicker than is typical, making these more sun tolerant.

Super Elfin Series grows to 10 inches tall, and the well-branched plants have a considerably greater spread. Flower colors include white, pink, violet, orange, and red.

Tempo Series tops out at 9 inches. This series offers a wider range of flower colors than Super Elfin, and includes bicolors and picotees.

RELATED SPECIES

New Guinea hybrids are grown both for their colorful, often-variegated foliage and their large flowers in all the typical impatiens colors, plus yellow. They make terrific container plants, and grow well in sun or light shade.

GARDEN COMPANIONS

Impatiens are spectacular massed, either as a single variety or a mixture. They provide a low skirt of color beneath shade-loving shrubs. In woodland gardens, they combine well with hosta, trillium, hardy begonia, and ferns.

When Transplant young plants in late spring, after the soil has warmed. To grow impatiens from seed, sow indoors 10 to 12 weeks before the last frost by pressing them gently onto the surface of the growing mix and keeping them moist.

Where Grow in full to part shade, in a fertile, moist, well-drained soil supplemented with organic matter. New Guinea hybrids can be grown in sun or light shade.

How Prepare the planting area by mixing 2 to 3 inches of compost or leaf mold into the upper 10 to 12 inches of soil. Transplant young plants on a cloudy day with little or no wind spacing plants 12 to 18 inches apart and watering them well.

TLC Fortunately, there is no need to deadhead impatiens—they just keep blooming until frost. And their low-growing habit covers the soil surface so that no mulch is required under mass plantings. Conscientious watering, particularly during periods of hot weather, and regular applications of a complete liquid fertilizer will keep plants vigorous.

RIGHT: *Pink flowers of New Guinea impatiens are 2½ inches wide.*
BELOW: *Flowers of 'Super Elfin Mix' come in a wide range of pastel and bright colors.*

Madagascar Periwinkle
Catharanthus roseus

Madagascar periwinkle is a tender perennial from—where else?—Madagascar. Grown as an annual in temperate climates like ours, it begins flowering in late spring on very young plants and continues without pause until frost. In the tropics, it becomes a somewhat rangy shrub, but you'd never know that from its well-mannered habit in our gardens.

The plants form neat, dense mounds of dark green leaves and pretty inch-wide flowers, each with five petal-like lobes. Flower colors include white, shades of pink from pale to hot, lilac, and red; many sport a contrasting eye. Varieties range in height from less than 6 inches to 1½ feet. Madagascar periwinkle combines easily with other annuals or perennials in mixed beds. The more spreading types are perfect for hanging baskets or planters.

The quality I find most endearing about Madagascar periwinkle is that the plants are absolutely unfazed by hot weather. I also appreciate their tendency to self-sow—not to the point of becoming a nuisance, mind you, but just enough so I can always find a few seedlings where last year's plants grew. These volunteers transplant quite easily.

Madagascar periwinkle grows and flowers well during hot weather.

ABOVE: *Plants of aptly named Cooler Series are more tolerant of cool and wet weather than other varieties.*
RIGHT: *These pale flowers of Madagascar periwinkle are accented by a white center.*

PEAK SEASON

Flowering begins soon after planting in spring and continues into fall.

MY FAVORITES

Cooler Series plants grow upright reaching 12 to 14 inches in height. 'Grape Cooler' has lavender pink flowers with a rose eye and 'Peppermint Cooler' produces red-eyed white flowers.

Mediterranean Series plants have a cascading, spreading habit that is ideal for hanging baskets, window boxes, and containers. Plants grow only 6 inches tall, but spread to 2 feet.

Pacifica Series plants are well branched and extra early blooming. They are available in white, pink, rose, and light purples with or without contrasting eyes. 'Pacifica Red' was the first red-flowered variety. The large plants grow about a foot tall and have bold, 2-inch-wide flowers with overlapping petals.

GARDEN COMPANIONS

Combine Madagascar periwinkle with blue mealycup sage, French marigolds (*Tagetes patula*), petunias, or sweet alyssum in a mixed annual bed. Or sprinkle them among sun-loving perennials, such as lamb's ear, catmint, and daylily (*Hemerocallis*).

When Madagascar periwinkle grows easily from seed, but it takes a long time, so sow it indoors in mid-February for spring planting. Plants are widely available at garden centers, where you will often find them blooming precociously in their cell-pack or pot, so you can easily select the flower colors you prefer. Transplant them to the garden after the soil has thoroughly warmed in the late spring. Planting in cool weather may stunt plants and reduce flowering.

Where Grow in full sun in well-drained soil; wet soil may cause plants to rot. They will, however, tolerate some drought.

How Prepare the garden soil by mixing 2 to 3 inches of compost or leaf mold into the upper 10 to 12 inches of soil. To use as an edging, space plants 8 to 12 inches apart. Spreading types can be planted 14 to 24 inches apart. Space plants closer in containers. Water well, but avoid wetting the leaves more than necessary.

TLC The flowers of Madagascar periwinkle drop off on their own, so there is no need for deadheading. Avoid overwatering, especially in heavy clay or poorly draining soil. Do not overfertilize; a monthly application of a dilute complete liquid fertilizer is sufficient. Potted plants can be brought indoors for winter blooms.

Marigold
Tagetes

Combined here with creeping zinnia, 'Little Hero Yellow' marigold takes hot Mid-Atlantic summers in stride.

Some folks don't like the smell of marigolds, but I find it refreshing. Regardless of what you think of their fragrance, these cheery plants are well worth growing for their brightly colored flowers, fernlike foliage, and robust disposition.

Marigolds range in size from a dainty 6 inches to a towering 4 feet, and although they are all native to Mexico and Central and South America, the taller types are known as African marigolds *(Tagetes erecta)*. This species is an excellent background plant, and it is terrific for cutting. The daintier, low-growing types include French marigolds *(T. patula)* and Signet marigolds *(T. tenuifolia)*. These work well at the front of a border, as edgings, or in containers.

Flowers may be single, double, or somewhere in between, and they are 1 to 5 inches across. Most are yellow, gold, or orange; some have maroon accents. All are edible, though some taste better than others.

Their tolerance for heat and drought recommends marigolds for places in the yard where regular watering is inconvenient. They can provide a blast of color all summer around a mailbox or along a driveway, even if you rarely water them.

When Sow seed indoors 6 to 8 weeks prior to the last frost. Transplant or direct-sow in the garden after danger of frost has passed.

Where Plant marigolds in a sunny spot. They thrive in a moist, well-drained soil but tolerate drought well.

How Turn soil to a depth of 10 to 12 inches, incorporating 2 to 3 inches of compost or leaf mold. Acclimate indoor-grown seedlings by placing them in a protected location for a few days before transplanting (on a cloudy day, if possible). Space plants 6 to 18 inches apart, depending on the variety. Pinch off the flower buds and top leaves to promote bushiness. Fertilize new plants with a dilute solution of a complete liquid fertilizer.

TLC Marigolds are among the easiest annuals to grow. Avoid overfertilizing or you will have lots of leaves and few flowers. Deadhead spent blooms to promote flower production. Tall varieties may need staking.

RIGHT: *Flowers of the African type 'Inca Orange' are 3 inches wide; plants grow 16 inches tall.*
BELOW LEFT: *'Disco Flame' is a red and gold member of the Disco Series.*
BELOW RIGHT: *These African marigold hybrids produce both orange and yellow flowers.*

PEAK SEASON

Early summer into fall; marigolds are somewhat tolerant of light frosts.

MY FAVORITES

African marigolds

Their large flowers, though wonderful, often turn mushy and black once spent, so require deadheading. Still, these varieties deserve mention:

Perfection Series and especially 'Vanilla', with its creamy white flowers, are outstanding. They grow 14 inches tall. The Inca and Climax Series are similar but taller, the former to 16 inches, the latter to 3 feet.

French marigolds

Disco Series grows 8 to 10 inches tall and bears single flowers atop stocky plants.

Little Hero Series plants grow 8 inches tall and have 2-inch-wide flowers. Colors include gold, red, yellow, and orange.

'Queen Sophia' has 2-inch, double russet orange flowers. Each petal is tipped with gold. A uniform 10 inches tall, its neatly rounded form makes it a perfect choice for edging a walkway or drive.

GARDEN COMPANIONS

Marigolds combine well with other brightly colored annuals like mealy-cup sage, zinnia, cockscomb (*Celosia*), and yellow cosmos.

Mealycup Sage
Salvia farinacea

Some plants are stars of the garden; others are the critical supporting cast. And no plant fills the latter role better than mealycup sage. Interspersed with boldly colored or dramatically textured plants, it offers a soft, cool, subtle element, contrasting with and balancing its more flamboyant neighbors. Despite its delicate appearance, this sage has a very sturdy nature, standing up to the heat and humidity so typical of our summers.

A perennial in its native Texas, mealycup sage is not reliably hardy in the Mid-Atlantic region, although it will occasionally survive a mild winter. As an annual, it performs well in sunny gardens and containers. The flowers are exceptional candidates for both fresh and dried indoor arrangements.

The plant grows from 1½ to 2 feet tall, with an erect, shrubby habit. Silvery hairs cover its gray-green leaves, giving them a soft, dusty appearance. The foot-long flower stems that rise above the leaves support whorls of small blue, white, or bicolored flowers that are incredibly long lasting.

The cool color of 'Silvery White' mealycup sage is welcome in the heat of midsummer.

PEAK SEASON

Flowers appear in early to midsummer and continue into fall.

MY FAVORITES

'Silvery White' are silvery white.

'Sizzler Purple' flowers are red-purple.

'Strata' is compact and bears clear blue flowers with silvery bases that emerge along silvery stems.

'Victoria' has deep violet-blue flowers.

'Victoria White' is white.

RELATED SPECIES

Scarlet sage (Salvia splendens) grows 8 to 30 inches tall and produces large, showy flower spikes that are held above dark green, heart-shaped leaves. Flowers are typically red, but may be purple, pink, or white. 'Red Hot Sally' grows to a stocky 10 inches; 'Rambo' reaches a height of 24 inches. Both bear red flowers.

Texas sage (S. coccinea) is a less dense plant than scarlet sage and grows 2 feet tall and wide. Selections are available in red, white, salmon, and pink. It often self-sows.

GARDEN COMPANIONS

Mealycup sage is a comfortable companion to everything from roses to marigolds. In containers, it looks great with trailing petunias and 'Profusion Orange' zinnia.

When Purchase plants in cell-packs or 4-inch pots and transplant them into the garden after all danger of frost has passed and the soil has warmed. To grow from seed, sow indoors 10 to 12 weeks before the date of the last expected frost.

Where Plants do best in full sun but will tolerate light shade. Mealycup sage performs well in a mass planting on a sunny bank.

How Prepare soil by incorporating organic matter such as compost or leaf mold to a depth of 10 to 12 inches. Set plants 12 to 14 inches apart. Apply a dilute complete liquid fertilizer after planting.

TOP LEFT: *Blue and 'Sizzler Purple' mealycup sage combine well.*
TOP RIGHT: *'Lady in Red' is a variety of Texas sage.*
BOTTOM: *Scarlet sage makes a fiery addition to a summer garden.*

TLC Fertilize at 2- to 3-week intervals throughout the summer. Although plants tolerate some drought, they will benefit from occasional watering during dry periods. To dry the flowers, cut the stems when the blossoms are fully open, tie them in loose clusters, and hang them upside down in a dry, dark area for several weeks.

Pansy and Viola
Viola

Pansies and violas are wonderful season extenders. Unlike most other annuals, they thrive in chilly temperatures and fade as summer heats up. Despite their diminutive stature—most are less than 8 inches tall—they dominate garden centers in early fall, as well as in early spring when there is little else in flower. Their cheerful five-petaled flowers are easy to recognize—they're the ones that look like faces.

'Sorbet Sunny Royale' is a supercharged Johnny-jump-up.

The flowers are 2 to 4 inches across and come in a wide array of colors. They make a big impact massed in a bed or sprinkled through a mixed border. And they are precious in containers. What's more, the flowers are edible—they really brighten a spring salad.

Our modern-day pansies *(Viola × wittrockiana)* were developed from several alpine species, so it's no surprise they like cool weather. They are actually short-lived perennials, but are best treated as annuals, given that they rarely survive a Mid-Atlantic summer. Violas *(V. cornuta)* are closely related to pansies, but they generally produce smaller flowers in greater quantity and they are somewhat more tolerant of heat.

PEAK SEASON

Fall-planted pansies and violas may bloom from early fall until late December. After a short winter break, their flowering resumes with the first hint of spring. Spring pansies and violas last until summer's heat.

MY FAVORITES

Pansies

'Imperial Antique Shades' has large flowers in subdued shades of yellow, pink, creamy white, lilac, and peach.

'Beaconsfield' produces bicolored flowers of pale and deep blue.

Majestic Giant Series boasts 4-inch flowers in many colors.

Violas

The Sorbet Series blooms early and prolifically. Its flowers are a mixture of solids and bicolors with whisker-like markings.

'Yesterday, Today, and Tomorrow' produces petite blooms that go through a series of color changes from nearly white to light blue to deep blue.

GARDEN COMPANIONS

Pansies and violas are naturals for pairing with spring-flowering bulbs. They also combine well with Virginia bluebells (Mertensia), bleeding heart (Dicentra), and forget-me-nots (Myosotis).

When Plant pansies and violas in late summer or fall, as soon as plants become available. You can also plant in early spring, but get plants in as early as possible so they will mature and flower before hot weather sets in.

Where Plant in full sun or part shade in a rich, moist, well-drained soil. Pansies and violas planted in part shade may last longer when the warm weather arrives. Plant them near a walkway where their intricate markings can be viewed at close range.

How Incorporate organic matter, such as compost or leaf mold, into the top 10 to 12 inches of soil and space plants 6 to 8 inches apart—closer in containers. Water thoroughly and apply a dilute low-nitrogen liquid fertilizer.

TLC Water plants regularly, but don't let the soil become soggy or plants may rot. Fertilize at 2- to 3-week intervals through the season. Remove spent blossoms to encourage further blooming. Keep an eye out for seedlings—violas in particular tend to self-sow and may provide some plants for next season.

RIGHT: *A pansy in lavender shades*
BELOW LEFT: *An antique-style pansy*
BELOW RIGHT: *Multicolored pansy*

Petunia
Petunia × hybrida

Today's petunias are a tribute to the efforts of plant breeders. Older petunias produced floppy flowers on often-scraggly plants that had no stamina. Even so, they've been top-selling bedding plants since the 1930s. New hybrids are far more deserving of their popularity; they bear oodles of flowers that are often smaller and, frankly, far more charming, than the floppy old-fashioned hybrids. These tough garden performers fill many roles: some grow in neat mounds for use in beds, others display a trailing habit, ideal for spilling out of planters and window boxes or for creating a border at the front of a flower bed. And petunias bloom continuously all summer.

The flowers come in almost every color and include soft, pale shades as well as bold, intense tones. Flowers may be plain, frilly, or crimped, and single or double, and they range from less than an inch to nearly 5 inches across. I find the small single varieties most appealing and easiest to incorporate into mixed plantings. With their flower-laden stems that extend several feet below the pot, cascading types are among the most spectacular for hanging baskets.

Petunia integrifolia is the sprawling ancestor of most hybrid petunias.

Wave Series petunias, such as 'Lilac Wave' (left) and 'Pink Wave' (right), spread very rapidly, forming a low, solid mat studded with flowers.

PEAK SEASON

Late spring until first frost

MY FAVORITES

Cloud Series petunias bear large, 4- to 5-inch flowers. They are great in containers and hanging baskets.

Supertunias are weather-tolerant hybrids that bear 2- to 3-inch flowers. They are another excellent choice for containers and hanging baskets.

Wave Series of low-growing, spreading hybrids with 2½-inch flowers is ideal for a flowering ground cover or for containers. The plants spread from 3 to 5 feet.

RELATED SPECIES

Petunia integrifolia, with its more open, sprawling habit, is useful in mixed container plantings for its ability to weave among other plants. The flowers are only an inch across, and are rose red on the outside, deepening to dark purple at their centers.

GARDEN COMPANIONS

Petunias provide color in the foreground of mixed beds of other sun-loving annuals or perennials. In containers, they combine well with zinnias, browallia, mealycup sage, heliotrope, and sweet potato vine.

When Growing petunias from seed is a rather difficult and lengthy process, so purchase young plants in cell-packs or 4-inch pots and transplant to the garden or to containers after all danger of frost has passed.

Where For best flowering, plant petunias in full sun and in fertile, moist, well-drained soil. Plants will grow in partial shade but they will produce fewer flowers. If your soil is heavy clay, grow petunias in containers. Protect them from strong winds.

How Prepare the soil by incorporating organic matter, such as compost or leaf mold, into the top 10 to 12 inches of soil. Space plants about a foot apart for mounding types, 2 feet apart for spreading types, and closer together in containers. Fertilize plants with a complete water-soluble fertilizer at planting time.

TLC Fertilize at 2- to 3-week intervals throughout the season. Water as needed to keep soil evenly moist. Petunias are easy to transplant even when they are large, and are valuable for filling in bare spots in the summer garden, so it's worth keeping a few extra petunia plants handy. Be sure to provide these late-season transplants with plenty of water.

Sunflower
Helianthus annuus

One of the most familiar and most endearing summer annuals, the common sunflower charms all ages and tastes.

One of the easiest annuals to grow, sunflowers are a great introduction to gardening for children. The seeds of this North American native are large and easy to handle, the plants are not choosy about where they grow as long as they are planted in full sun, and their flowers are big and beautiful.

Depending on the variety, sunflowers grow from 1½ to 12 feet tall. Taller types work well as screens, temporary hedges, or background border plants; shorter selections brighten the middle or foreground of a bed. Flowers are typically yellow, but white, red, mahogany, and bicolored flowers are also available. Sunflowers grown primarily for seed bear large flowers atop straight stalks. Those grown for cutting are bushy with many branches and smaller flowers.

Planting a row or two along one side of a vegetable garden provides both a cheerful edging and a source of some of the best cut flowers you can grow. Additionally, sunflowers attract lots of birds, particularly goldfinches, which you will see dancing from flower to flower as they sample the seed—reason enough to include these cheery plants in your garden.

When Sow sunflower seed in the garden where you want plants to grow after all danger of frost has passed.

Where Sunflowers will adapt to most soils as long as they are planted in full sun. Short varieties look great and perform well in large tubs in a sunny spot, either by themselves or mixed with other flowering annuals.

How Although sunflowers are adaptable to most soils, they will perform best in a moist, well-drained, moderately fertile site. Sow sunflower seed by pressing it into the soil about ½ inch deep. Thin plants when they are 3 or 4 inches tall so that they stand about 2 feet apart.

TLC Fertilize at monthly intervals with a complete fertilizer. Plants tolerate some drought, but will benefit from watering during dry spells. To dry sunflower seeds for snacks or for feeding the birds, cut the flower heads, leaving several inches of stem, when seed is ripe but before it begins to fall. Hang the stalks upside down in a dry, well-ventilated area. Or just leave them in the garden; the birds will pick them clean.

RIGHT: *'Teddy Bear' flowers are 4 inches wide.*
BELOW: *'Evening Sun' flowers are 7 inches wide.*

PEAK SEASON

Midsummer to fall. Multistem (branching) varieties continue flowering over a much longer period than single-stem types.

MY FAVORITES

'Chianti' produces deep red, 3- to 4-inch flowers on well-branched plants that grow 4 to 5 feet tall. The flowers are pollenless, so make tidy and attractive indoor arrangements.

'Evening Sun' grows 6 to 8 feet tall and produces many flowers in colors of red, mahogany-red, burgundy, and gold.

'Italian White' is a free-flowering, bushy, selection that grows 5 to 7 feet tall. Its flowers—which are wonderful for cutting—are 4 inches across, and have creamy white petals with chocolate brown centers.

'Mammoth Russian' is a heavy seed producer with huge yellow flower heads on plants up to 12 feet tall.

'Teddy Bear' is a dwarf that tops out at 2 to 3 feet and bears double yellow flowers.

GARDEN COMPANIONS

Sunflowers are bold additions to mixed borders. They combine well with other casual annuals like zinnias, cockscomb (Celosia), cosmos, and nasturtium.

Zinnia

Zinnia

Zinnias, not surprisingly, are Mexican natives—their brilliantly colored flowers deck out a garden like a fiesta. *Zinnia elegans,* the most commonly grown species, has an upright habit and grows from 6 inches to 4 feet tall. It has broad leaves and solid or bi-colored flowers in yellow, white, red, pink, orange, green, or magenta. Flower size ranges from slightly bigger than an inch to a full 6 inches across, and the blossoms display a variety of forms, from tiny buttons to large cactus types that have rolled or quilled petals. Tall varieties, with their straight, sturdy stems and long-lasting flowers, are ideal for cutting. Shorter varieties are useful in the foreground or the middle of a bed.

Narrow-leafed zinnias (*Z. angustifolia, Z. haageana, Z. peruviana,* and hybrids) make terrific flowering ground covers or additions to window boxes or planters. They bear small, daisylike flowers that, depending on the variety, are gold, orange, or white. These selections are particularly well suited to our climate because they are resistant to powdery mildew, which can be a problem with other zinnias, and they tolerate heat and drought.

Hot colors of 'Dreamland Mix' zinnias are backed here by cool mealycup sage.

LEFT: *An unexpected color in a tall zinnia, white provides interest and creates intriguing design possibilities.*
RIGHT: *The narrow leaves of spreading zinnias are mildew resistant.*

PEAK SEASON

Midsummer until the first frost

MY FAVORITES

Broadleaf zinnias

Dreamland Series is compact and grows 10 to 12 inches tall. It bears showy, 4-inch, dahlia-type flowers.

State Fair and Oklahoma Series both produce large flowers on 30- to 40-inch stems that are excellent for cutting.

Thumbelina Series includes selections with 1¼-inch, single or semidouble flower heads on 6-inch plants that are great for edging sunny beds.

Narrowleaf zinnias

Spreading zinnias grow in loose mounds to about 12 inches high and bear 1½-inch flowers in white, gold, or orange. 'Crystal White' and the Star Series are notable.

Profusion Series zinnias grow 12 to 18 inches tall and are disease resistant and weather tolerant. Their single flowers come in shades of orange, cherry red, and white. They are great for beds or containers.

GARDEN COMPANIONS

Zinnias pair well with foliage plants like dusty miller and sweet potato vine, or with flowering annuals like nasturtium. Orange-flowered varieties contrast with mealycup sage and purple petunias.

When Sow zinnia seed indoors 4 to 6 weeks before the last expected frost, or sow directly in the garden after the soil warms in June. Don't transplant the seedlings in cool weather or the plants will be stunted.

Where Plant zinnias in full sun in rich, moist, well-drained soil that has been improved with organic matter. Choose a site with good air circulation.

How Prepare soil by incorporating organic matter, such as compost or leaf mold, into the top 10 to 12 inches. Sow seed, barely covering it with soil. Or, transplant young plants into the garden, disturbing the roots as little as possible to prevent damage. Purchase plants when conditions are right for transplanting—leaving plants in containers too long will weaken them. When transplanting, pinch off flowers, flower buds, and the top pair of leaves to encourage bushy growth and more flowers.

TLC Water during dry spells and fertilize at 2- to 3-week intervals with a dilute water-soluble fertilizer. Tall varieties may need staking. Deadhead or cut flowers for indoor use to encourage continuous flower production.

Bulbs offer a burst of color, often just when our gardens need it most. In this chapter, you'll learn about bulbs that bloom in late winter, spring, summer, and fall. In addition, you'll discover that, according to botanists, not all the plants we call bulbs are, technically, bulbs.

Crocuses are corms, for example, and dahlias and alstroemeria are tuberous roots. But daffodils, tulips, and lilies are really and truly bulbs. These technical terms refer to the underground parts of these plants. True bulbs contain the minute beginnings of stems, roots, leaves, and flowers—these compact packages lie dormant underground until spring when the soil warms and they can realize their full potential. Corms are actually thickened stems, and tuberous roots are swollen roots.

A BULB'S LIFE

For the most part, all bulbous plants are grown the same way: You plant a dormant portion underground, then wait for green growth to appear aboveground. Much the same as most perennials, the blossoms of spring-flowering bulbs typically last about 2 weeks, longer if the spring weather is cool, and not as long in hot weather.

Choose the right ones, and bulbs can supply color when your garden is desperate for it. Daffodils and grape hyacinths are especially lovely in spring when carpeting the sunny edge of a woodland before the trees have leafed out. Lilies bloom in the summer when most gardens are in the doldrums; caladiums add summer color to shady places. Dahlias provide lots of flowers in early summer, a few blooms during the hottest weather, and then huge numbers of flowers when it gets cooler in the fall.

RIGHT: *'Purple Prince' tulip at peak bloom.*
BELOW: *Fiery colors of dahlia flowers echo the summer sun.*
OPPOSITE PAGE: *An orange Asiatic lily combined with blue larkspur.*

AFTER-BLOOM CARE

Don't cut back bulb leaves until they've lost about half of their green color. That's your signal that their productive life is ending and you can remove them without stunting next year's flowers. In spring, clumps of forget-me-nots, unfurling fern fronds, emerging hostas, and bushy astilbes can easily hide the fading bulb leaves. Crocuses and grape hyacinths are small enough that their leaves wither away inconspicuously, but the fading leaves of some larger bulbs, such as tulips, can look unkempt. Use larger perennials, such as daylilies, to camouflage them. Lilies bloom in early to mid-summer, when the garden has filled out, so their withering leaves aren't as obvious.

After flowering, bulbs such as daffodils, crocuses, and grape hyacinths perennialize, meaning they'll come back year after year. Some actually set seed, increasing their colonies as if they were native wildflowers. Others, such as dahlias, must be dug up for winter storage in colder regions and replanted the following season. Or you can treat them as annuals, in much the same way you grow impatiens each year.

Bulbs are like push-button plants, programmed to perform on schedule, but designing with them takes planning. Choose and time planting correctly, and bulbs will add an element of life and color to your garden.

—BRENT AND BECKY HEATH

Alstroemeria, Peruvian lily
Alstroemeria

A hybrid evergreen alstroemeria blooms generously through summer once plants are well established.

Native to South America, alstroemerias produce clusters of azalea- or orchid-like flowers. While the beautiful flowers are reason enough to add these plants to your garden, their real claim to horticultural fame is their capacity to look good up to two weeks after cutting. It's one reason alstroemerias are so often used in vases on restaurant tables.

Alstroemerias are generally either "deciduous" or "evergreen." The former type develop long stems in early spring. As those shoots begin to fade and turn brown, flowering shoots appear. Lasting into midsummer, the flowers range from orange, peach, and red to near white, and are usually flecked with darker colors. Many of these types can be grown from seed.

Evergreen alstroemerias include two species and many hybrids, and compared with the deciduous kinds, produce somewhat larger, showier flowers.

Alstroemerias start slowly. Don't plant them expecting instant gratification. The first time we planted alstroemeria, we didn't see one leaf the entire summer. By the third summer, the plants bloomed prolifically, and today those same plants provide cut flowers almost all summer long, which is why alstroemeria is so high up on our list of favorites.

ABOVE: *'Sweet Laura' has bright yellow flowers.*
BELOW: Alstroemeria aurea, *an evergreen type*

PEAK SEASON

Summer

OUR FAVORITES

Deciduous

Ligtu Hybrids are a bit shorter than other alstroemerias. They provide a long season of bloom in a wide range of pastels, often with veins of dark red or black. Leafy shoots reach 2 feet tall in late winter and spring. As they mature and brown, flowering shoots appear. Start from bulbs or seeds; plants will self-sow.

Evergreen

'Freedom' has medium pink flowers with freckled white areas. It is heat tolerant but needs water and fertilizer to stay in bloom. It grows 2½ feet tall and about 1 foot wide.

'Sweet Laura' sports 9 to 12 yellow flowers per stem. Well-established plants begin to flower by late spring or early summer and continue until frost. This variety is hardy throughout the Mid-Atlantic region. The plant grows 2½ feet tall and spreads slowly by underground stems.

GARDEN COMPANIONS

Any plant that loves full sun and well-drained soil should get along beautifully with alstroemeria. Taller lilies or cannas make a nice background for them, and the shorter rain lilies (Zephyranthes) add another layer of color around the edges of a border.

When Plant in spring after danger of frost has passed. Handle the tuberous roots carefully, as they tend to be brittle. Or sow seeds of Ligtu Hybrids in fall, winter, or early spring.

Where Plant in full sun; in zone 31, provide some shade to prevent bleaching of the flowers. Provide humus-rich soil that is moist but well drained. Alstroemerias grow well in containers.

How Plant the white, fleshy roots about 6 to 10 inches deep and 12 inches apart. Sometimes pots of growing alstroemeria are available that you can plant just like any container plant.

TLC Alstroemeria will survive drought, but growth and blossoming will be increased if you water deeply and regularly during the growing season. Flowering may slow down or stop in the hottest weather; prolong bloom in summer by applying a thick layer of mulch to help keep the roots cool. In zones 34, 35, and 36, mulch heavily in late fall. You can take potted alstroemeria inside in the fall. Keep the plants dry and water to restart them in spring. Alstroemeria takes a year or two to acclimate, especially when it is planted late in the spring.

Amarcrinum
× *Amarcrinum*

Amarcrinum is one of those rare hybrids resulting from a cross between plants from two similar plant genera: *Crinum moorei* and *Amaryllis belladonna,* the belladonna lily. Much more dependable in the Mid-Atlantic region than belladonna lily, amarcrinum features 2-foot blossom stalks, each one carrying six to 10 buds. In mid- to late summer, these open into waxy, long-lasting, fragrant pink flowers with white throats. Each individual flower is 2½ to 4 inches across. As one flower dies, another opens at the top of the stalk, and this process continues until the first hard frost. Strap-shaped glossy green leaves that reach 1½ feet in length provide a pleasing backdrop for the blossoms. The plant is nearly evergreen in mild winters and prefers lean, sandy soil. It's not bothered by rodents or deer.

Pink flowers of amarcrinum poke up through a shrub to reach daylight.

Amarcrinum is a marvelous pest-proof plant, but it isn't one to choose for instant gratification. These plants start slow but get better every year. We planted them at the south-facing edge of a mature pine grove where they get some protection from the colder winter winds and benefit from a summer baking. They are thriving in this location, and the display improves steadily each year.

When Plant either in the fall after the first frost or in the spring when danger of frost has passed.

Where Amarcrinum prefers a protected location in full sun to partial shade. Plant in well-drained but rich soil. In colder interior regions (zones 34–36), plant where there is a bit of protection from early frost to ensure a long blooming season and mulch for added protection from a hard freeze. Or, plant in a container that can be protected from the harsh winter temperatures and winds.

TOP: Crinum × powellii 'Album'
BOTTOM: Close-up of the trumpet-shaped flowers of amarcrinum.
BELOW LEFT: Long, strap-like leaves of amarcrinum grow nearly as high as flowers.

PEAK SEASON

Late summer until frost

RELATED PLANTS

Crinum × powellii bears up to 15 trumpet-shaped, rich pink, fragrant flowers on 2- to 3-foot stems; once established, it often blooms twice during the summer.

Crinum 'Ellen Bosanquet' is a classic bulb found in many old gardens. It has trumpet-shaped flowers of a rich rose color and almost lime green leaves.

GARDEN COMPANIONS

Asiatic lilies, which are planted much deeper, make their way up through the foliage of amarcrinum and put on a show earlier in the summer. Shorter, bush-forming dahlias with lower-growing oxalis look lovely around the base of amarcrinum.

How Plant these bulbs in spring or fall, spacing them 1 to 2 feet apart. In zones 34 and 36, cover the bulbs with 3 inches of soil; in zones 31 and 32, cover just to the neck of the bulb with soil. This bulb is also a good container plant; figure one bulb per 8-inch pot. In pots, leave the top third of the bulb exposed.

TLC If planted in the spring, the foliage may not appear for 2 to 8 weeks, so if you live where the season is shorter (zones 34–36), pot up the bulbs as soon as you receive them in early spring and transplant them to the garden later. This will give them a head start and a longer growing period. Amarcrinum likes to get settled and be left alone. They need a full season to become established after planting or transplanting, and will continue to thrive thereafter if left undisturbed. Once roots are established, plants are drought tolerant.

Crocus
Crocus

Crocuses are among the earliest plants to bloom, so are one of the first to signal that spring is on the way. Here, they flower in February and March in a range of bright colors. They're so modest in price that it's no great investment to scatter them around the garden in quantity, plugging them into a lawn where the grasslike leaves are not a problem as they wither and fade away. We look forward to seeing their dark, slender leaves poking up through the snow, followed by the fat buds and the vivid purple, yellow, and white flowers later in the month.

The most common kind of crocus are the so-called Dutch crocuses, which are hybrids of *Crocus vernus*. These plants and flowers are larger than the other species, and they bloom a bit later. They add a burst of vivid color in the lawn, in the front of a border, or in a rock garden, where even just a few in a clump will catch your eye.

ABOVE: *An heirloom, 'King of the Striped' is one of the most planted crocuses.*
LEFT: *The best crocus for naturalizing in lawns is* Crocus tommasinianus.

When Plant crocus corms in the fall after the first frost.

Where Crocuses prefer full sun and well-drained, sandy loam. Plant where the inconspicuous leaves can be left to mature. (Crocuses will naturalize in lawns that aren't treated with herbicides, and in which leaves are allowed to mature.) You'll get to enjoy the flowers in spring well before the lawn needs mowing, and afterward, the grasslike crocus leaves will hardly be noticeable. Set your lawn mower blade at the very highest setting for the first few times you cut the lawn to let the crocus foliage mature before being mowed.

How If your garden soil is heavy, hard, or wet, amend it with organic matter such as compost. Plant the corms 2 to 3 inches deep and 1 to 2 inches apart. To plant, use a trowel with a small, narrow (1 to 1½ inches wide) blade. Stab down into the soil, then pull the trowel toward you—the "slot" created is just large enough for one crocus corm. Stab 2 inches away, pull toward you, and the first hole is covered as you open a hole for the next crocus. By using this "stab-pull-drop" planting method, you can plant hundreds of crocuses in a short time. Alternatively, you can lift the turf with a spade, plant, and place the sod right back on top.

TLC Water established crocuses in the spring only if weather is dry, and avoid watering in summer when plants are dormant, if possible. Sprinkle slow-release fertilizer high in potash (10-10-20) on top of the soil in the fall right after planting and every fall thereafter. (If soil is well amended with compost, fertilization may not be necessary.)

PEAK SEASON

Late winter and early spring

OUR FAVORITES

Crocus flavus 'Golden Yellow' is one of those "55 mph" colors that can be seen from great distances (or when traveling at highway speed).

C. sieberi sublimis 'Tricolor' is a beautiful and colorful crocus. It stops people in their tracks with its lilac blue, yellow, and white colorations. Blooms as early as January in zone 31.

C. tommasinianus tolerates some shade and will do fine under trees. 'Ruby Giant' has rich, reddish purple flowers; 'Barr's Purple' is a medium purple. They naturalize beautifully. Peak bloom is in February.

Dutch crocus (*C. vernus*) is the most common species and many hybrids are available. Many are excellent, but our favorite is 'King of the Striped'. An heirloom, it has grayish white flowers striped in lilac blue. 'Yellow Mammoth' flowers are clear gold.

GARDEN COMPANIONS

Crocuses look best when grown in masses. Combine them with violas and other small flowers at the front of a flower bed. They also come up through dwarf periwinkle (*Vinca minor*), where they pop out against the dark foliage.

LEFT: *'Yellow Mammoth' is a brightly colored variety of Dutch crocus.* RIGHT: *'Ruby Giant' has reddish purple petals and a white center.*

Daffodil

Narcissus

Daffodils are the bulbs everyone knows and loves. What's not to like about a plant that's not only good-looking in gardens and as a cut flower but is also pest resistant and comes back year after year?

Their bright colors and perky shapes make daffodils the most ebullient of plants—the perfect antidote to winter doldrums. In addition to yellow, daffodils come in orange, red, pale pink, peach, salmon, white, and combinations thereof, and in many shapes and sizes, as well as in early, midseason, and late bloom times. The classic daffodil flower has a cup-like center surrounded by petals, but there are also double-flowering daffodils as well as varieties with multiple flowers on each stem. Some daffodils are nicely fragrant, which is an added value. Right after flowers fade the slender, straplike leaves are attractive linear accents in the garden, but you'll want to cut them back once they're mostly faded.

Flowering time varies widely. Read plant descriptions and catalog information carefully, and by combining the very early, midseason, and late-blooming types, you can have daffodils blooming for up to 3 or 4 months.

Petals of 'Jetfire' are bent back as if by wind.

PEAK SEASON

Early to midspring

OUR FAVORITES

'Accent' has a fade-proof salmon pink cup that stands out against its crisp white petals. The flowers of this reliable perennial face up and seem to look right at you.

'Ceylon' is particularly showy, with its up-facing yellow and orange flowers. It is one of the most reliable and longest-lasting daffodils.

'Jetfire' is very brightly colored; its early bloom time makes this yellow and orange flower a lovely daffodil to grow in pots or to force.

'Pink Charm' is an elegant flower with pure white petals and a vivid pink-banded cup that stops people in their tracks. One of the best pinks, it often bears two flowers per stem.

GARDEN COMPANIONS

Daffodils share the same space happily with other sun-loving plants that need moisture in the fall and spring and prefer dry conditions in the summer. Even when combined with plants that are planted at a shallower depth (astilbe, daylilies, and peonies, for example), the daffodils normally manage to come up around or through the other perennials.

LEFT: *'Accent'*
CENTER: *'Ceylon'*
RIGHT: *'Pink Charm'*

When Plant bulbs in the fall after the first frost but early enough for bulbs to make roots before the ground freezes. In our area (Gloucester, VA; zone 32), the best time to plant is between mid-October and Thanksgiving. Before then, the ground temperature may be too warm, and warm, wet conditions may cause the bulbs to rot.

Where Daffodils do best in full sun, although they tolerate light shade. They require loamy, well-drained soil, and will rot in soggy soil. We don't recommend daffodils for lawns. Grasses grow too fast here, making it almost impossible to avoid mowing the foliage too early. As an alternative, plant the outskirts of the lawn area as a meadow where early bulbs are the first to bloom, followed by other perennials, biennials, and annuals for the rest of the gardening season.

How If your soil is too wet or too heavy, amend it with organic matter. Or, build a raised bed and use a mixture of compost and soil to fill it. Water the bulbs thoroughly and, if planted late, cover them with a 6-inch layer of mulch. As soon as the weather begins to warm in spring, water generously if the weather is dry. Before growth appears, top-dress with a slow-release bulb fertilizer that is high in potash (10-10-20). Place an organic mulch, such as shredded leaves or bark, around the plants when they are 3 to 4 inches tall, but keep it away from the leaves.

TLC Cut back on watering as foliage dies down after blooming. Do not remove daffodil foliage until its green color begins to fade, usually about 8 weeks after the last flowering. Begin regular watering again in the fall if the weather is dry, and apply bulb fertilizer.

Dahlia

Dahlia

Native to Mexico and Central America, dahlias add more to our summer garden than any other summer bulb. Throughout early summer and again in late summer until frost, they produce an abundance of bold flowers that are perfect for arrangements.

Dahlias come in a myriad of shapes and sizes from the tiny pompon types to the huge dinner plate sizes. Some are tall and long-stemmed (great for large flower arrangements); others are short and bushy.

It's usually recommended in our region that dahlia tubers be dug up and stored over the winter. But they've overwintered here in Gloucester, Virginia, for years. To help them survive the winter, however, we do plant them a bit deeper than is normally necessary, to about 3 inches deep, and we add a bit of extra winter mulch.

ABOVE: *Cactus types 'Park Princess' and similar yellow-centered 'Twiggy'.*
FAR LEFT: *'Fascination' has notably dark green foliage.*
LEFT: *'Crichton Honey' flowers are a formal type.*

PEAK SEASON

Early to midsummer until frost

OUR FAVORITES

'Crichton Honey' grows 3 to 4 feet tall and has golden ball-like flowers that are 3 to 4 inches in diameter.

'Edinburgh' bears long-stemmed, 3-inch-wide flowers that are a variable mixture of white and burgundy. The plant grows 2 to 3 feet tall and has dark green leaves.

'Fascination' bears 6-inch-wide, semi-double flowers in various shades of lilac pink that are surrounded by luscious greenish black foliage. The plants grow 18 to 24 inches tall.

'Night Queen' has deep claret (almost black-colored) ball-shaped blossoms on burgundy stems. The leaves are dark green on plants that grow 1 to 2 feet tall. Flowers are particularly long-lasting.

'Park Princess' has tightly rolled, blush pink petals on flowers that are 4 inches wide. It flowers heavily and is an excellent cut flower. The plants grow 2 to 3 feet tall.

GARDEN COMPANIONS

Dahlias make wonderful companions to any sun-loving annual, perennial or bulb. Try them with amarcrinum, lilies, cannas, artemisia, cleome, larkspur, and roses.

When Plant dahlias outdoors after all danger of frost has passed and the soil has warmed to 50°F/10°C in the spring (about the time you'd plant tomatoes). Inland and at higher elevations (zones 34, 35, and 36), get a jump on the shorter season by starting tubers indoors in pots or deep flats 4 to 6 weeks before the last frost date. If planted outside too early, the buried tubers will survive, but new growth could be damaged by frost.

TOP: *Cactus-type flower*
BOTTOM: *Ball-type flower*

Where Dahlias are happy in full sun or partial shade, although they produce more flowers in full sun. Plant in rich, well-amended soil that stays evenly moist.

How Plant the dwarf cultivars 1 to 1½ feet apart; plant taller types 1½ to 2 feet apart. Plant so the crown is about 1 to 3 inches below the soil level. Tall varieties and those with large flowers will likely need staking.

TLC Dahlias require regular summer watering. Frequent cutting for flower arrangements and deadheading spent blossoms will encourage new blooms. Placing a 2-inch layer of organic mulch around the plants helps to conserve moisture and suppress weeds. When plants have two or three sets of leaves, pinch out the growing tips just above the upper set of leaves to encourage bushy growth. A light application of bulb fertilizer in midsummer is beneficial.

Grape Hyacinth
Muscari armeniacum

Grape hyacinths are probably the most popular of all the small bulbs that bloom in early spring. The nearly universal appeal of this diminutive plant is for the stunning effect that masses of them can produce. At the famous Keukenhof Gardens in the Netherlands, thousands of grape hyacinths are planted in long beds that curve along paths and between trees. The effect of all those cobalt blue flowers blooming at once in spring is nearly blinding. Admittedly, we don't plant them in the same quantity (and you probably won't either). We do plant many, however, and always in clumps of a dozen or so.

Low growing (we call them a "shoes-and-socks" bulb), they reach about 8 inches tall, and spread only 2 inches wide. The leaves are slender and almost grasslike. The "grape" in the name is from their fragrance (which, given the size of the bulbs, is easy to miss): It's reminiscent of the scent of grape juice. All grape hyacinths are Mediterranean and western Asia natives. They are frost hardy and prefer cool areas, so are ideal for inland and higher elevation areas of the Mid-Atlantic.

Another, more practical virtue of grape hyacinths is their habit of producing leaves in the fall while most bulbs are hidden under the soil. That's why we use them as markers that remind us with their foliage where to not dig or where to top-dress with fertilizer.

'Valerie Finnis' grape hyacinth is blooming here with 'Peach Blossom' tulip.

PEAK SEASON
Early through late spring

OUR FAVORITES
'Blue Spike' is a double form. The flowers are sterile and cannot be pollinated, which means they last somewhat longer. The plants reach 4 to 6 inches in height.

'Christmas Pearl' looks just like the species but blooms much earlier and stays in bloom for much longer. It's also great for forcing in pots. The plants grow 4 to 6 inches tall.

'Valerie Finnis' has charming pale lavender blue flowers that are very desirable for garden artists who juxtapose colors carefully. The plants grow 6 to 8 inches tall.

RELATED SPECIES
Muscari botryoides 'Album' is a 4- to 6-inch-tall heirloom grape hyacinth with dense spikes of pure white pearl-like flowers that bloom in mid- to late spring. These look especially lovely with other grape hyacinths, violas, or anemones.

GARDEN COMPANIONS
Muscari combines well with all types of midspring-blooming bulbs, as well as early annuals, early perennials, ground covers, and flowering trees and shrubs.

When Plant in the fall after the first frost but before the ground freezes.

Where Plant in rich, well-drained soil around the edges of flower beds, on top of larger spring-flowering bulbs, or around flowering trees and shrubs.

How Use the stab-pull-drop method (see How, page 65) of planting these small bulbs; set them 3 to 5 inches deep. Or, place the bulbs on top of a 6-inch layer of compost and cover with about 4 inches of compost, soil, or sand.

TLC Water well at least once after planting and top-dress with a slow-release fertilizer high in potash (10-10-20). If spring is relatively dry, water at least once a week. Don't cut the foliage until it begins to turn yellow.

TOP: *'Blue Spike' produces long-lasting double flowers in a tight cluster.*
BOTTOM: *The pure white flowers of 'Album' are an excellent companion to many other bulbs and flowers.*

Lily
Lilium

'Stargazer' lilies rise above hostas and the strawberry-like flowers of globe amaranth.

Gardeners love lilies for their large, showy, and fragrant flowers. The most common lilies for gardens are hybrids: the June-blooming Asiatic varieties and the July- and August-blooming oriental lilies. Though flowers are less dramatic, the species lilies have their own subtlety and charm.

Asiatic lilies have both wide and narrow funnel-shaped, six-petaled flowers that bloom on long straight stems, decorating the early summer garden like no other plant. Some face up, some out, and others down.

Oriental lilies are similar to the Asiatics, but are often larger and have petals that curve back, called recurved. They bloom in mid- to late summer. They have large white, pink, or yellow flowers, often spotted with gold or banded with red, and are fragrant. Oriental lilies grow on tall stems whose leaves fan out from top to bottom; they sometimes need staking. These lilies are best in the back of the border, where their flowers have no trouble attracting attention.

The many wild species lilies and their history in gardens goes back thousands of years. Highly variable and less formal in effect, they generally require less space than hybrid lilies and many make good blooming partners with other bulbs and perennials.

PEAK SEASON
Summer

OUR FAVORITES

Asiatics
'Clubhouse' has luscious, soft yellow-orange color. Growing 2 to 3 feet tall, it is hardy and disease resistant.

'Lollipop' petals are creamy white and brushed with rose color at their tips. Plants grow 2½ feet high.

Orientals
'Black Beauty' is not really black, but it comes close: The dark raspberry petals are edged with a tiny white line and a matching white heart. The plants reach 3 to 4 feet in height.

'Casa Blanca', with its pure white flowers atop 4-foot stems, is easily one of the most dramatic and sought-after lilies.

'Stargazer' has fragrant, upright, and large rose-red flowers that are show-stoppers. In full sun and good soil, plants grow to 2½ to 3 feet.

GARDEN COMPANIONS
Lily bulbs reside deep in the soil, so they're able to share garden space with many other types of plants with similar requirements that are planted at a shallower depth. Plant tall lilies with other strong, tall plants, like cannas, which will provide support.

When Plant lilies in fall after the first frost to ensure the soil has cooled. If bulbs are available in the spring, plant them as soon as the ground can be worked.

Where Lilies do best in full sun in well-drained soil that is at least slightly acidic, about pH 6.5. They will tolerate partial shade but normally produce more blooms in sunlight. Plant taller varieties at the back of the border so that the branches of shrubs and other perennials help support them.

How Lily bulbs are not hard and firm like daffodils, but are formed of many layers of scales. This often makes them appear soft or pithy, but that is normal. Lilies form stem roots, so it's important to plant them deep enough so that those roots will help to hold the plants upright without staking. Plant 8 to 10 inches deep in well-drained soil; mulch after planting.

TLC Lilies like their roots cool and require moisture during the growing season. When picking flowers, remove as little of the stem as necessary; at least one-half of the foliage is required to nurture the bulb. Also, when you cut the flower, snip off the pollen-bearing parts to avoid staining tablecloths and clothes.

RIGHT: *'Casa Blanca'*
BELOW LEFT: *'Clubhouse'*
BELOW RIGHT: *'Lollipop'*

Snowflake

Leucojum aestivum 'Gravetye Giant'

Once you experience the sheer quantity of white flowers you'll understand the reason for the common name, snowflake. This variety, 'Gravetye Giant', is slightly taller and produces larger flowers than the species.

Snowflake is one of the most under-utilized spring-flowering bulbs for our region. Nicknamed "snowflake" for its many white flowers, *Leucojum* has a list of virtues that begins with being extremely easy to grow. 'Gravetye Giant' is slightly larger than the species, growing 12 to 18 inches high. It also produces more and larger flowers, sometimes up to nine per stem. Widely available, it is superior in every way to the species.

None of the common burrowing or browsing bulb pests bother snowflake, and you only need to plant it once. The bulbs will increase in number year to year by both division and seeds. The nodding, bell-shaped, white flowers are dainty-looking but very sturdy. And each petal is accented by a small green dot near the tip.

Snowflake prefers mostly sunny conditions during growth and bloom but it requires little light during its summer dormancy. It is among the very few spring bulbs that will tolerate damp growing conditions. These bulbs are perfect for naturalizing among deciduous shrubs and trees.

PEAK SEASON

Early to late spring

RELATED SPECIES

Leucojum vernum, often called "spring snowflake," usually blooms very early, along with snowdrop *(Galanthus), Iris reticulata,* and species crocus. It performs best in cool, moist soil that's rich in organic matter. Its leaves appear when or just after its fragrant flowers open in early spring. Plant height is 4 to 6 inches.

GARDEN COMPANIONS

Snowflake is very charming alone or planted with other perennials. Daffodils, tulips, grape hyacinth, scilla, anemone, and violas all make good companions.

ABOVE: *This bed of 'Gravetye Giant' covers the bare lower stems of rhododendrons.*
BELOW: *Snowflake blooms at the same time as flowering dogwood.*

When Plant snowflake in fall after the first frost but before the ground freezes.

Where Plant in well-drained soil. In hotter areas, planting in light shade is beneficial. Snowflake is charming at the front of a casual flower bed or tucked among stones at the edge of a woodland site. It is very moisture tolerant and can be planted on the edge of a pond or stream.

How Plant bulbs 4 to 6 inches deep and about 5 to 6 inches apart. Dig one hole for each bulb, excavate an area for a larger planting, or place the bulbs on top of 6 inches of compost, then cover with 4 to 6 inches of soil, sand, or more compost. Water well after planting.

TLC Snowflake requires moisture throughout the year, especially during the growing season. Water regularly until foliage dies down in late spring.

Spider Lily

Lycoris

It's the long stamens and narrow, wavy-edged, backward-curving flower segments that lend the flowers of this lily a "spidery" look and have garnered it its common name. When gardeners grow spider lily for the first time, they see why it's also called "surprise lily" (because of how the flowers appear, seemingly overnight, on naked stems). This plant has other curious names as well. In the Williamsburg, Virginia area, spider lilies are called "British soldiers" because the flowers are the same color as the Revolutionary War redcoats. And in coastal areas, they're known as "hurricane lilies" because they bloom during hurricane season.

Spider lily produces narrow, strap-shaped leaves in spring that then die down and disappear in early to mid-summer. Later in the summer, red or pink flowers appear on bare, 2-foot-tall stems. These flowers are very long-lasting in the garden and in a vase.

One unusual characteristic of spider lilies is that they actually bloom better once their roots are dense and crowded, so it's best to not disturb plantings for several years. It's also why, when growing them in containers, they perform better in pots where the bulbs are crowded than in larger ones where they have more room.

Spider lilies, like their amaryllis relatives, are not bothered by browsing

Red flowers of Lycoris radiata contrast attractively with the dark green picket fence.

pests like deer or burrowing ones, such as voles. Not instant-gratification plants, once spider lilies are settled in their new home, they will get better and better each year.

ABOVE: *Close-up of* Lycoris radiata *flowers shows the long, curved stamens that characterize these bulbs.*
BELOW: *The wider, pink flower petals of* Lycoris squamigera *resemble other members of the amaryllis family.*

PEAK SEASON

Midsummer and early fall

OUR FAVORITES

Lycoris radiata is the most common spider lily. Its flowers are red with a golden sheen. Flowering stems are 1½ feet tall. Leaves that appear in winter benefit from the protection provided by a ground cover such as periwinkle *(Vinca minor)*.

L. squamigera is the hardier spider lily. Also known as naked lady lilies, they produce clusters of fragrant, funnel-shaped, 3-inch-wide pink or rosy lilac flowers on 2-foot stems. The foliage grows in spring during milder weather.

GARDEN COMPANIONS

Lycoris radiata looks wonderful with *Rhodophiala, Sternbergia,* amarcrinum, autumn crocus *(Colchicum),* chrysanthemum, and dahlia. *Lycoris squamigera* is outstanding with asters, floss flower *(Ageratum),* and wormwood *(Artemisia).*

When Plant spider lilies as soon as they are available in late spring; they are happier and perform better if their roots don't dry out.

Where Plant spider lily in rich, well-drained soil in partial shade.

How Set the spider lily bulb in a shallow hole, leaving the narrow top exposed. After planting, top-dress with a controlled-release fertilizer high in potassium (10-10-20).

TLC Don't cut the foliage until it begins to turn yellow.

*Lycoris radiata is hardy in zones 31, 32, and 34.

Tulip

Tulipa

T he peacocks and parrots of the bulb world, tulips offer more sizes, shapes, and colors than you can imagine for any type of garden design scheme. An incredible source of inexpensive color for the garden, they are available in almost every color (except blue). Intensity of the colors sometimes varies according to climate and even from one season to another.

Huge plants and flowers of 'Pink Impression' are a garden focal point.

There are many kinds of tulips. Some are grouped together because of their shape, others because of their bloom time, and still others by heritage. The most practical way to narrow the selection is to focus on bloom-season categories. Early bloomers, such as some species tulips and early single and double types, normally bloom in March and help to announce the arrival of spring. Late-blooming types, such as the tall-growing single and double late types, usually bloom in April and mark the transition from spring to warmer summer weather.

When Plant tulip bulbs in the fall after the first frost; here in the Mid-Atlantic region, they are remarkably tolerant of planting as late as early December.

Where Plant tulips in very well-drained soil and in full sun. Don't plant tulips in flower beds that are heavily irrigated all summer, as the combination of moisture and heat will cause the bulbs to rot.

How Amend heavy soil with compost. For best results, plant tulip bulbs about 8 to 10 inches deep. You can either dig individual holes or, for a mass planting, dig up a swath of soil. If you're planting tulip bulbs in a brand-new area, spread 6 inches of compost on top of the soil, place the tulip bulbs on top, and cover them with 6 to 8 inches of soil, sand or more compost. Top-dress with a 9-9-6 bulb fertilizer, water well, and mulch lightly. If you have problems with voles or similar burrowing pests, add a layer of sharp crushed gravel below and above the tulip bulbs to deter these critters. Before we plant, we sometimes spray the bulbs with a bitter-tasting repellent that helps deter the voles. (Be sure to let the repellent dry before planting.) You can find animal repellents at garden centers.

TLC If the fall and spring are dry, provide ½ inch of water per week to help the roots develop in the fall and the flowers form in the spring. It's best to deadhead the spent flowers and remove them from the garden; letting them go to seed consumes the bulbs energy that's needed to develop the next year's flower. Also, if dead tulip flowers are allowed to continually fall to the ground in the flower bed, the deterioration of those petals could encourage disease.

LEFT: *The yellow, orange, and rose color blend of 'Blushing Lady' is a soothing combination.*
RIGHT: *'Princess Irene' is a bold bright orange accented by purple streaks.*

PEAK SEASON
Spring

OUR FAVORITES
Midseason bloomers
'Blushing Lady', one of the tallest lily-shaped tulips, is long-stemmed and graceful. The yellow and buff orange flowers, with washes of blushing rose, sit atop 3-foot stems. The result is a real knockout.

'Pink Impression' produces very large flowers that are deep pink. Stems grow to 3 feet tall and more.

Late bloomers
'Princess Irene' is one of our all-time favorites. It has the unusual color mix of bright orange with purple streaks, called flames. Nicely fragrant, it grows 12 inches high.

GARDEN COMPANIONS
Tulips combine well with all types of spring-flowering bulbs that also like full sun and moisture in the fall and spring. Combine them with bulbs and perennials that emerge early, prefer lots of sun, and don't require daily watering in the summer. Dahlias, lilies, bachelor's button (*Centaurea cyanus*), cosmos, bleeding heart (*Dicentra*), painted daisy (*Chrysanthemum coccineum*), and hellebore are examples.

Roses

Success with roses comes from knowing the best types to plant in your particular region. Roses are often seen as being difficult to grow, a reputation earned largely because of breeding and our own desire for perfection from this most generous of flowering plants.

Wild roses grow throughout the temperate regions of the Northern Hemisphere without any help from us, however, blooming freely in early summer and setting fruit abundantly through the fall. The growth habits, leaves, flowers, and hips of the many forms of wild roses remind us of the strong and beautiful ancestries of our garden roses.

Old garden roses (page 96), primarily European, were notable for their soft, open flowers borne on handsome plants that fit well into gardens. Asian roses, both wild kinds and the ones cultivated in gardens for centuries, offered a larger range of colors on repeat-flowering plants. Rose breeders began crossing these Asian and European roses, along with species roses (page 100), creating new

kinds of roses for generations of home gardeners. These crosses have resulted in our large-flowered climbers (page 82), floribundas (page 84), and hybrid teas (page 88), all of which are valued for their ability to bloom repeatedly through the season and for their amazing array of strong colors and subtle shadings.

The downside is that many of our modern roses inherited disease susceptibility along with their improved blooms. And some of the grace, fragrance, and romance of the old garden roses was sacrificed. With that in mind, there has been an increasingly successful movement in the last several years to reintroduce older roses into our gardens. There has also been a focus by plant hybridizers on introducing new types

of roses that are disease resistant and easy to care for, have better growth habits, flower nearly continuously, and feature colorful, fragrant blossoms. We want our roses perfect, and with some help, they do come close.

ROSE CARE

The major problems with roses here in the Mid-Atlantic region are powdery mildew and black spot diseases. Exactly when the symptoms will appear each year varies with weather conditions and with the specific rose variety. Good cultural practices are your best insurance against diseases. Most roses require a good garden soil with plenty of compost or composted manure added to it. To maintain good air circulation, don't overplant around roses. Protect leaves of particularly desirable and susceptible roses with fungicidal soap or garden sulfur combined with an antitranspirant (a foliar spray that reduces water loss through foliage and aids in disease control) as soon as leaves emerge in early spring. Mites can be a problem during a heat spell. The best way to get rid of them is to blast the undersides of the leaves with a hard spray of cold water. Removing old blossoms will help give more energy back to the plant, but if you are growing a rose for its hips, stop cutting back by July 4th to allow enough time for the hips to develop.

—HOLLY SHIMIZU

Climbing Roses

Climbing roses are at the heart of many gardens, rambling over fences, mailboxes, pillars, or arches. They disguise boring perimeter walls and fences and attractively frame entryways.

Climbers may be large or small, and the various kinds assume different shapes and have different habits. Some produce long, flexible stems from the ground each year, and can grow into the upper branches of a tree or cover a beach cottage. Others, including all of my favorites noted here, have a more permanent woody framework. They may bloom once or repeatedly, but they can have either large single flowers or smaller clustered ones.

Choose a climbing rose that will grow to the height you have available, and then provide suitable support. Choosing a variety that fits well in your garden's color scheme and overall design is also important, especially given that climbers will be part of your landscape for many years.

Two plants of 'America' easily reach this arbor's top and cover it in blooms.

PEAK SEASON

Spring into fall

MY FAVORITES

'America' has large, fragrant, salmon pink, very double blossoms that reliably repeat-bloom. They make excellent cut flowers. One of the short climbers, this rose reaches a height of 8 to 10 feet and can be trained on a wall, fence, or trellis. Cut off spent blooms to encourage reblooming.

'Dortmund' has flashy single blossoms of an intense red, each with a small white center adorned with gorgeous yellow stamens. It is a vigorous grower that provides recurrent, although not continuous, bloom, so be sure to cut off the old blossoms to encourage reblooming. The flowers have a slightly spicy fragrance. The plant is thorny and has attractive leathery, shiny leaves.

'New Dawn' is a robust rose that grows 18 to 20 feet high and is absolutely tough and hardy. It is probably the best pink rose for our region. There is also a white-flowering form known as 'White Dawn'.

GARDEN COMPANIONS

In full sun, consider planting 'Grosso' hedge lavender (*Lavandula* × *intermedia* 'Grosso') or mealy-cup sage 'Victoria' (*Salvia farinacea* 'Victoria') near the base of climbing roses.

When Plant bare-root roses during the cold season (usually in December, January, and February). Plant container-grown roses in spring as soon as the ground is workable, but don't plant roses with leaves if frost threatens.

Where Choose a location with enough space for the roots to stretch out and for the branches to reach full size. Plants need at least 5 or 6 hours of full sun daily. Good air circulation will help minimize disease and pest problems.

How Amend soil with organic matter before planting. Soak the roots of bare-root plants in a bucket of water for a few hours before planting. Space fan-trained climbers about three-fourths of their mature height apart; upright growers about one-fourth of their mature height. Ideally, choose climbing roses that are growing on their own roots, not grafted. If your rose is grafted, plant it so that the graft union is 1 to 2 inches below the ground level.

TLC When weather is dry, water new roses approximately twice a week and established roses once a week. Water established roses deeply, preferably in the early morning. In spring, place a 1-inch-thick layer of mulch around the plants. In late fall, once weather is reliably cold, cover the base of each plant with an inch of mulch to protect it from severe cold. In late winter, prune the roses, removing any dead, diseased, or damaged branches and then thin and shape as desired. Cut off the oldest canes at their base; cut back lateral growth of stiff-stemmed roses to 4 or 5 buds. Aim to have canes of one-, two-, and three-old-year wood. In early spring, as soon as the new growth is emerging, remove the protective mulch and fertilize.

TOP: *'Dortmund' is hardy and disease free.*
BOTTOM: *'New Dawn' blooms continuously throughout the season.*

Floribunda Roses

The nearly white open flowers of 'Gruss an Aachen' contrast nicely with blue milky bellflower.

Floribundas are bush roses, like hybrid teas (page 88), and they are as abundantly flowerful and come in an equally wide range of colors. But compared with hybrid teas, floribundas tend to be somewhat shorter, and their flowers are a little smaller and more typically arranged in clusters instead of borne singly. Flowers of some floribundas have the classic high-centered flower shape of a hybrid tea. Others are flatter and more informal.

Floribundas were originally bred in Denmark, and gardeners there call them bedding roses because they are so effective in mass plantings. You can grow them as a large-area ground cover, as well as individually in rose beds or in borders. Some floribundas are well suited to growing in containers.

These roses are very prolific bloomers, and some of the cultivars bloom almost continuously from June until November, with only a relatively short hiatus during the height of summer's heat.

As with hybrid teas, there are climatic and disease challenges for some floribundas in our region. My recommendations are for cultivars that are relatively easy and suc-

cessful in this area; they also represent the range of what is available from this wonderful group of roses.

PEAK SEASON

Late spring into fall

MY FAVORITES

'Betty Prior' has been popular for decades because it is reliable and tough. Single, medium pink blooms are produced in clusters and have a mild fragrance; this rose is almost always in bloom. It reaches a height of 3 to 4 feet and about 3 feet in width.

'Gruss an Aachen' has lovely red-tinged buds that open to double flowers that are blushed with white; they become pure white as they age. Growing to a height of about 3 feet, this long-blooming and fragrant rose is a treasure.

'Nearly Wild' earned its name for its single, clear pink blooms with distinct stamens that resemble those of a species rose. Its everblooming quality and dependability make it a superb plant for mixed borders and in a variety of landscapes. The height and width are about 3 feet.

GARDEN COMPANIONS

Germander (Teucrium chamaedrys) makes an ideal low green hedge surrounding a bed of floribunda roses. Also consider white-flowering perennial candytuft (Iberis semper-virens) or blue milky bellflower (Campanula lactiflora).

When Plant bare-root roses during the cold season (usually in December, January, and February). Plant container-grown roses in spring as soon as the ground is workable, but don't plant roses with leaves if frost threatens.

Where Choose a location with enough space for the roots to stretch out and for the branches to reach full size. Plants need at least 5 or 6 hours of full sun daily. Good air circulation will help minimize disease and pest problems.

How Amend soil with organic matter before planting. Soak roots of bare-root plants in a bucket of water for a few hours before planting. Space plants about three-fourths of their mature height apart. Ideally, choose roses that are growing on their own roots, not grafted. (Ask your nursery, or check for the bulbous, swollen graft union just below the stems.) If your rose is grafted, make sure to plant the graft union 1 to 2 inches below ground level.

TLC When weather is dry, water new roses approximately twice a week and established roses once a week. Water established roses deeply, preferably in the early morning. In spring, place a 1-inch-thick layer of mulch around the plants. Remove spent blooms to encourage repeat flowering. In late fall, once weather is reliably cold, cover the base of each plant with mulch to protect it from severe cold. In early spring, remove mulch, fertilize, and prune back to approximately half the normal height of the rose. Remove weak and inward-facing canes, as well as any damaged by winter cold or pests.

LEFT: *Carmine pink 'Betty Prior' blooms profusely and continuously through the season.*
RIGHT: *Flowers of 'Nearly Wild' have a sweet and fruity scent.*

Hybrid Musk Roses

Hybrid musk roses have a complex and clouded history. They were developed in the early twentieth century from, most experts agree, the multiflora rambler rose 'Trier', which is a distant descendant of the distinctively scented musk rose *(Rosa moschata)*. But these hybrids did not generate much interest in those early years, and few records documenting their origins have survived. Despite this false start, hybrid musks were rediscovered in the 1960s and created a huge sensation in the rose world at that time.

Hybrid musks are large, 6- to 8-foot shrubs, small climbers, or, in a few cases, ramblers that can grow up into trees or on trellises. They perform well in dappled or partial shade as well as in sun. In fact, among all roses, the hybrid musks are the most tolerant of shade. They are nearly everblooming, producing large clusters of flowers in red, white, yellow, buff, or pink. Most have a musky or apple scent that is reminiscent of old roses and attractive dark green foliage, and many have the bonus of bright orange hips in autumn and early winter.

White-flowered 'Moonlight', with its prominent yellow stamens, complements striped leaves and blue flowers of 'Zerba' iris.

PEAK SEASON

Late spring into fall

MY FAVORITES

'Ballerina' is a truly great garden plant that covers itself in hydrangea-like masses of single pink blossoms along graceful stems all season. It is usually grown as a 4- to 5-foot-high shrub.

'Buff Beauty' bears ruffled apricot to buff yellow, sweetly scented flowers in June and again in fall. It's a medium-sized, 4- to 5-foot shrub with arching canes, dark semiglossy green leaves, and dark red new growth.

'Lavender Lassie' is covered with fragrant powderpuff-like, lilac pink blooms in spring, followed by good repeat bloom. Plants grow to about 5 feet tall and are well branched. The plant is effective as a specimen or hedge, or trained as a pillar.

'Moonlight' will grow 20 feet up into a tree. Its small, white semidouble flowers with prominent yellow stamens are simply beautiful and abundant. The blossoms also have a true musk fragrance.

GARDEN COMPANIONS

Plant hybrid musk roses with lady's-mantle (Alchemilla mollis) for its airy, yellow-green summer flowers, or with Russian sage (Perovskia atriplicifolia) for its gray leaves and long-lasting spikes of blue flowers in late summer.

When Plant bare-root roses during the cold season (usually in December, January, and February). Plant container-grown roses in spring as soon as the ground is workable, but don't plant roses with leaves if frost threatens.

Where Choose a location with enough space for both roots and branches to reach full size, and where plants will receive the optimum 5 or 6 hours of full sun daily. Hybrid musk roses can repeat bloom even when growing in dappled shade, however. Good air circulation will help minimize disease and pest problems.

TOP: *Small, delicate pink flowers of 'Ballerina' are followed in fall by orange hips.*
BOTTOM: *'Buff Beauty' flowers are 4 inches wide and fragrant.*

How Amend soil with organic matter before planting. Soak roots of bare-root plants in a bucket of water for a few hours before planting. Space plants about three-fourths of their mature height apart. Look for roses that are growing on their own roots, not grafted. If your rose is grafted, make sure the graft union is 1 to 2 inches below ground level.

TLC When weather is dry, water new roses approximately twice a week and established roses once a week. Water established roses deeply, preferably in the early morning. In spring, place a 1-inch-thick layer of mulch around the plants. In late fall, once weather is reliably cold, cover the center of each bush with mulch to protect it from severe cold. In spring, remove this mulch and fertilize. Cut out older and spindly canes, and remove suckers to restrain spreading.

Hybrid Tea Roses

Hybrid teas are the fancy show roses of our time. They have long been the most popular type of rose because they do a lot of what most gardeners want: produce large flowers in a range of colors on long, strong, single stems. Hybrid teas make stunning bouquets.

Dark velvety red 'Mister Lincoln' is one of the most fragrant roses available.

The first true hybrid teas were bred in the 1860s. By the 1880s, they had gained broad recognition, and by the turn of the century, hybrid teas were widely seen to be a huge improvement over most other kinds of roses. They were by far the dominant group of roses to emerge during the early twentieth century, and for more than a century now, they have dominated the imaginations of most rose gardeners.

Along with their obvious beauty and other virtues, hybrid teas have also gained a reputation for needing attention, which is justified. Most hybrid teas need regular spraying and I don't recommend them to anyone without the time and energy to care for them. The varieties listed at right give the most for the least effort. Nevertheless, others may be worth the extra effort they require for their beauty.

ABOVE: *Maroon stamens of 'Dainty Bess' contrast with the delicate pink petals.*
BOTTOM: *The white petals of 'Pristine' are brushed with pink.*

PEAK SEASON

Late spring into fall

MY FAVORITES

'Dainty Bess' has been a favorite hybrid tea for 80 years. It has fragrant, silvery pink-lavender flowers with showy dark, wine-colored stamens, and it blooms continuously through the growing season. The foliage is attractive and disease resistant.

'Mister Lincoln' is perhaps the ideal red rose: the deep red buds open to well-formed, dark red flowers that are deeply fragrant. The leaves are large, glossy, and dark green.

'Pristine' is unmistakably elegant, even when compared with many other elegant hybrid teas. Large, pointed crimson buds open to sweetly scented white flowers that are blushed pink.

GARDEN COMPANIONS

Good companions for hybrid teas include germander *(Teucrium chamaedrys),* 'Grosso' hedge lavender *(Lavandula × intermedia* 'Grosso'), 'Victoria' mealy-cup sage *(Salvia farinacea* 'Victoria'), Mexican bush sage *(Salvia leucantha),* and 'Blue Beauty' rue *(Ruta graveolens* 'Blue Beauty').

When Plant bare-root roses during the cold season (usually in December, January, and February). Plant container-grown roses in spring as soon as the ground is workable, but don't plant roses with leaves if frost threatens.

Where Choose a location with enough space for both roots and branches to reach full size, and where plants will receive at least 5 or 6 hours of full sun daily. Good air circulation will help minimize disease and pest problems.

How Amend soil with organic matter before planting. Soak roots of bare-root plants in a bucket of water for a few hours before planting. Space plants about three-fourths of their mature height apart. Ideally, choose roses that are growing on their own roots, not grafted. If your rose is grafted, plant so that the graft union is 1 to 2 inches below ground level.

TLC When weather is dry, water new roses approximately twice a week and established roses once a week. Water established roses deeply, preferably in the early morning. In spring, place a 1-inch-thick layer of mulch around the plants. Remove faded flowers to encourage repeat bloom. In late fall, once weather is reliably cold, cover the center of each plant with mulch to protect it from severe cold. In early spring, remove this mulch, fertilize, and prune. Cut back to half the normal height of the rose, cutting just above an outward-facing bud. Remove weak, inward-facing canes, and damaged canes.

Miniature Roses

Miniature roses are very similar to modern bush roses, except in size—few ever exceed 18 inches in height!

These diminutive roses can provide elements of structure and spots of color at the front of borders, as bedding plants, in rock gardens, climbing over small features and spilling over fences, in containers, and even as miniature standard, or tree, roses. These last-mentioned forms are like garden sculptures, and many gardeners have discovered that they are the perfect finishing touch in their gardens.

The original miniature roses were raised from a dwarf China rose (*Rosa chinensis* 'Minima') and were commonly grown on cottage windowsills, especially in Switzerland, where they were rediscovered in 1922 by a plant breeder.

For gardeners with limited outdoor space, the pleasure of enjoying rose colors and forms on a smaller scale is a real bonus.

The climbing miniature 'Jeanne Lajoie' covers itself in 1-inch-wide pink flowers.

ABOVE: *'Rise 'n' Shine' produces its fragrant blooms continuously through the season.*
BOTTOM: *Rich red flowers of 'Black Jade' look like red candy.*

PEAK SEASON

Spring through fall

MY FAVORITES

'Black Jade' is very distinctive, thanks to its extremely deep red buds and flowers and attractive foliage. Plants grow about 2 feet tall.

'Green Ice' has whitish blooms that change to green as they age. The flowers are slightly fragrant. Plants grow 18 to 24 inches tall.

'Jeanne Lajoie' has small leaves and flowers, but the plant is vigorous enough to cover smaller structures, such as an arch over a doorway, with double pink flowers for many months. Moreover, it is totally hardy and easy to grow.

'Popcorn' bears buds as beautiful as its fragrant white flowers. The plants are known to be free of disease and insect problems. This 18- to 24-inch rose is excellent for a container or as a low accent in a border.

'Rise 'n' Shine' covers itself with pure yellow, fragrant, double blooms. Plants reach 18 to 24 inches tall.

GARDEN COMPANIONS

Good companions include 'Victoria' mealy-cup sage (*Salvia farinacea* 'Victoria'), perennial candytuft *(Iberis sempervirens),* and 'Blue Beauty' rue (*Ruta graveolens* 'Blue Beauty').

When Plant container-grown plants in spring as soon as the ground is workable, but don't plant roses with leaves if frost threatens.

Where Choose a location with enough space for roots and branches to reach full size, and where plants will receive at least 5 or 6 hours of full sun daily. Good air circulation will help to minimize disease and pest problems.

How Amend soil with organic matter before planting. Space plants about three-fourths of their mature height apart. To grow indoors, use soilless potting mix and a 6-inch or larger container.

TLC Roots of miniature roses are shallow, so you'll need to water, fertilize, and mulch frequently. This is especially true if plants are growing in containers. Though hardy, miniatures still need some winter protection in our region; cover plants with mulch or surround with burlap in late fall, or move container plants to a protected location, such as a garage. In early spring, rake the mulch back and prune the rose back to approximately half its normal height, cutting just above outward-facing buds. Remove weak and inward-facing canes, as well as any damaged by winter weather or pests.

Modern Shrub Roses

Compared with the hybrid teas (page 88), which are cultivated for their near-perfect flowers, modern shrub roses are bred to be all-around garden plants. Rose breeders listened to gardeners' requests for hardy, good-looking, low-maintenance roses, and for the last several years, that's where many of the more exciting breeding break-throughs have occurred. The result is this growing and diverse group of roses, which has many uses in gardens.

Among the most popular shrub roses are those that look and smell like old-fashioned roses, but are much more disease resistant and flower repeatedly through the season. The trademarked David Austin roses are the leading example of this type.

Superior resistance to all rose diseases and continuous bloom through the season make 'Knock Out' one of the best roses for low maintenance.

The ultimate toughness test for any flowering shrub is a median strip, and modern shrub roses such as 'Knock Out' pass the test, blooming all season long.

Many of these newer shrub roses are ideal for gardeners in the Mid-Atlantic region who desire an easy-care rose. If you can relate to that, roses in this category won't disappoint you.

When Plant bare-root roses during the cold season (usually in December, January, and February). Plant container-grown roses in spring as soon as the ground is workable, but don't plant roses with leaves if frost threatens.

Where Choose a location with enough space for roots and branches to spread out. Plants need at least 5 or 6 hours of full sun daily. Good air circulation will minimize disease and pest problems.

How Amend soil with organic matter before planting. Soak roots of bare-root plants in a bucket of water for a few hours before planting. Space plants about three-fourths of their mature height apart. Ideally, choose roses that are growing on their own roots, not grafted. If your rose is grafted, make sure to plant the graft union 1 to 2 inches below ground level.

TLC When weather is dry, water new roses approximately twice a week and established roses once a week. Water established roses deeply, preferably in early morning. In spring, place a 1-inch-thick layer of mulch around the plants. In late fall, once weather is reliably cold, cover the center of each bush with mulch to protect it from severe cold. In early spring, remove this mulch and fertilize. Little pruning is needed. Remove some of the oldest canes, along with weak growth. Prune repeat-flowering kinds in early spring; prune plants that bloom only in late spring after blooms fade.

RIGHT: *'Heritage' is deeply fragrant.*
BELOW LEFT: *A row of 'Bonica' makes a flowerful hedge.*
BELOW RIGHT: *'Alchymist' has an old-fashioned look.*

PEAK SEASON

Spring through fall

MY FAVORITES

'Alchymist' blooms only once a year, in spring, and the flowers take a long time to open. But when they do, they cover the plant with apricot yellow flowers that are divinely scented. It grows 8 to 12 feet in height and is often trained as a pillar rose.

'Bonica' is an tough and versatile shrub that bears sprays of rose pink flowers in dainty clusters all season. The 4-foot-tall plants have an attractive growth habit and perform reliably with minimal care.

'Heritage' is my favorite rose because of its fragrance, everblooming habit, and many-petaled blossoms. Its scent is similar to an old rose, with strong lemon overtones. Growing to 6 feet, it is effective in a border, cottage garden, or as a specimen.

'Knock Out' has single cherry red flowers in clusters that come non-stop all season long. The leaves are very resistant to black spot disease. The plant grows about 3 feet tall.

GARDEN COMPANIONS

Plant with germander *(Teucrium chamaedrys)*, 'Grosso' hedge lavender *(Lavandula × intermedia* 'Grosso'), Mexican bush sage *(Salvia leucantha)*, or Russian sage *(Perovskia atriplicifolia)*.

Noisette Roses

Noisettes are best known for their generous production of silky, perfumed flowers. They are a group of hybrids that were produced in the early nineteenth century by John Champney, a farmer in Charleston, South Carolina. He crossed a China rose called 'Old Blush' with a hybrid musk (page 86), called it 'Champneys' Pink Cluster', and gave some plants to a friend and nurseryman, Philip Noisette, who in turn sent plants to France. The new hybrids shortly became popular and it was Noisette's name that stuck.

The success of 'Champneys' Pink Cluster' induced more hybridization. Crossed with itself and other China roses, it led to a strain of similar roses in white, pink, and red; crossed with tea roses (page 88), it yielded large-flowered, climbing tea-Noisettes.

Noisettes come in shades of white, cream, yellow, orange, and sometimes red. They are also notable for creating orange and yellow shades of modern climbing roses.

All Noisettes are best in milder Mid-Atlantic climates, such as Georgetown or Richmond, and in north-facing locations around the house where winter temperatures are less subject to extreme swings.

PEAK SEASON
Spring to fall

MY FAVORITES
'Champneys' Pink Cluster', the original Noisette, is loved for its clusters of beautiful pink buds that open throughout the growing season to become fragrant blooms. This rose grows well up through trees or along fences, reaching 6 to 9 feet in height. It is very disease resistant.

'Mme. Alfred Carrière' is known as one of the best white climbers. It reaches 12 to 15 feet in height, spreading free-flowering creamy white blooms along its branches well into autumn and filling the air with luscious fragrance.

'Mary Washington' bears white flowers with a tinge of pink on almost thornless stems; the cupped double blossoms are delightfully fragrant.

GARDEN COMPANIONS
Complement Noisettes with germander *(Teucrium chamaedrys)*, lady's-mantle *(Alchemilla mollis)*, 'Grosso' hedge lavender *(Lavandula × intermedia 'Grosso')*, 'Victoria' mealy-cup sage *(Salvia farinacea 'Victoria')*, Russian sage *(Perovskia atriplicifolia)*, or southernwood *(Artemisia abrotanum)*.

OPPOSITE PAGE: *'Champneys' Pink Cluster' is loosely trained along a post-and-rail fence.* ABOVE LEFT: *'Mary Washington'* ABOVE RIGHT: *'Mme. Alfred Carrière'*

When Plant bare-root roses during the cold season (usually in December, January, and February). Plant container-grown roses in spring as soon as the ground is workable, but don't plant roses with leaves if frost threatens.

Where Choose a location with enough space for both roots and branches to reach full size, and where plants will receive at least 5 or 6 hours of full sun daily. Good air circulation will help minimize disease and pest problems.

How Amend soil with organic matter before planting. Soak roots of bare-root plants in a bucket of water for a few hours before planting. Space plants about three-fourths of their mature height apart. Ideally, choose roses that are growing on their own roots, not grafted. If your rose is grafted, make sure to plant the graft union 1 to 2 inches below ground level.

TLC When weather is dry, water new roses approximately twice a week and established roses once a week. Water established roses deeply, preferably in the early morning. In spring, place a 1-inch-thick layer of mulch around the plants. In late fall, once weather is reliably cold, cover the base of each plant with mulch to protect it from severe cold. In early spring, remove this mulch and fertilize. Prune to remove older canes and weak growth. Prune repeat-flowering kinds in early spring, spring-blooming kinds after bloom.

Old Garden Roses

The "old garden roses" are primarily those that were grown in Europe before the hybrid teas (page 88) came along. Typically, these roses have gentle flower and plant shapes, very fragrant blossoms, and a kind of nostalgic charm that provides a perfect counterpoint in modern rose gardens.

Some old garden roses bloom only once a year, in spring, but others are repeat bloomers. The bushes are handsome, and many produce showy hips in fall.

Several of these roses earn a place in the garden just for their heady fragrance. With one of these roses nearby, the long days of June signal not just the beginning of summer, but the onset of a particular sort of olfactory pleasure as well, one that can evoke memories and feelings otherwise lost to our normal perceptions. Perhaps that is why rose attar, the distilled oil of rose fragrance, was once nearly priceless.

Old garden roses are all-around garden plants with many qualities to charm you and to enhance your garden.

Thornless 'Zéphirine Drouhin' is a good choice for planting near paths and entryways.

PEAK SEASON
Spring

MY FAVORITES
'Ispahan' is known for its long period of midseason bloom and its large, pink, fragrant blossoms. The 3-foot-tall plants are hardy and disease free.

Rosa chinensis 'Mutabilis' has silky flowers that flutter above the leaves, a quality that inspired the name "butterfly rose." Single flowers combining yellow, orange, red, and crimson are set off by reddish leaves on maroon stems. A trouble-free rose, it grows 3 to 5 feet tall. (Especially in the case of this rose, plants that are not grafted but are growing instead on their own roots perform best.)

Rosa rugosa 'Alba' is cold hardy, disease resistant, and tolerant of salt spray. The white flowers in spring are followed by attractive hips in the autumn. Plants spread by underground roots, and this rose makes an excellent dense barrier hedge.

'Zéphirine Drouhin' is an almost thornless 8- to 10-foot-tall large shrub or climber with strong full pink blooms that are sweetly scented. It looks superb growing against a wall.

GARDEN COMPANIONS
Use Mexican bush sage (*Salvia leucantha*), Russian sage (*Perovskia atriplicifolia*), or southernwood (*Artemisia abrotanum*) with any of these roses.

When Plant bare-root roses during the cold season (usually in December, January, and February). Plant container-grown roses in spring as soon as the ground is workable, but don't plant roses with leaves if frost threatens.

Where Choose a location with enough space for both the roots and branches to reach full size, and where plants will receive at least 5 or 6 hours of full sun daily. Good air circulation will help minimize disease and pest problems.

How Amend soil with organic matter before planting. Soak roots of bare-root plants in a bucket of water for a few hours before planting. Space plants about three-fourths of their mature height apart. Choose roses that are growing on their own roots, not grafted. If your rose is grafted, make sure to plant the graft union 1 to 2 inches below ground level.

TOP: Rosa rugosa 'Alba' is very hardy.
CENTER: 'Ispahan' flowers are 2½ inches wide.
BOTTOM: Flowers of Rosa chinensis 'Mutabilis' have one set of petals.

TLC When weather is dry, water new roses approximately twice a week and established roses once a week. Water established roses deeply, preferably in the early morning. In spring, place a 1-inch-thick layer of mulch around the plants. In late fall, once weather is reliably cold, cover the base of each plant with mulch to protect it from severe cold. In early spring, remove this mulch and fertilize. Prune to remove older canes and weak growth. Prune repeat-flowering kinds in early spring, spring-blooming kinds after bloom.

Polyantha Roses

Polyantha roses are generally considered the precursors of the floribundas (page 84) and have many characteristics in common with them.

Individual polyantha flowers are small, even insignificant, and they are usually not fragrant. But the overall effect from the masses of blooms can be amazing. For long periods beginning in June and continuing well into fall, these small plants are covered with clusters of colorful blossoms.

Polyanthas provide a casual but colorful look not offered by many other garden plants. They are typically small, bushy plants ideally suited for borders and as bedding plants. Many are also good in containers—even indoors. They bloom nonstop in clusters and are among the most beloved of smaller-flowered roses. 'Cécile Brunner', the sweetheart rose, is probably the best known, and no other rose makes a more perfect boutonniere.

Polyanthas are easy to grow, relatively disease resistant, and hardy. Most are small, so when they are in mixed borders, they need to be in front of other plants. Give a polyantha a spot in your garden with good soil, nutrition, light, and water, and given its prolific flowering, it will be an incredibly rewarding plant.

The informal growth and flowers of low-maintenance 'The Fairy' complement this picket fence.

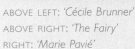
ABOVE LEFT: *'Cécile Brunner'*
ABOVE RIGHT: *'The Fairy'*
RIGHT: *'Marie Pavié'*

PEAK SEASON

Spring to fall

MY FAVORITES

'Cécile Brunner' produces perfectly formed, thimble-sized light pink flowers held in open sprays. The 3-foot-high plants are very easy to grow, though winter protection is required.

'Marie Pavié' grows 2 to 3 feet high. It has a rounded habit and stems are nearly thornless. Plants are covered with small, fragrant white-pink flowers set atop attractive foliage. Little pruning is necessary.

'The Fairy' blooms profusely from June through November and is a charming blush pink. The dainty pink buds are borne in clusters. Left untrained, it has a rounded, flowing shape. It is also an excellent border or container plant. This rose is disease resistant and winter hardy.

GARDEN COMPANIONS

Combine polyanthas with germander *(Teucrium chamaedrys)*, lady's-mantle *(Alchemilla mollis)*, 'Grosso' hedge lavender *(Lavandula × intermedia* 'Grosso'), 'Victoria' mealy-cup sage *(Salvia farinacea* 'Victoria'), perennial candytuft *(Iberis sempervirens)*, 'Blue Beauty' rue *(Ruta graveolens* 'Blue Beauty')*, southernwood *(Artemisia abrotanum)*, and violets *(Viola odorata)*.

When Plant bare-root roses during the cold season (December, January, and February). Plant container-grown roses in early spring, but not if plants have leaves and frost threatens.

Where Choose a location that provides space for roots and branches to spread and reach full size. Plants need at least 5 or 6 hours of full sun daily and good air circulation.

How Amend soil with organic matter before planting. Soak bare-root plants in a bucket of water for a few hours before planting. Space plants about three-fourths of their mature height apart. Ideally, look for roses that are growing on their own roots, not grafted. If your rose is grafted, make sure to plant the graft union 1 to 2 inches below ground level.

TLC Water new roses approximately twice a week and established roses once a week. Water established roses deeply, ideally in early morning. Mulch the plants in late spring. In late fall, once weather is reliably cold, cover the center of each bush with mulch to protect it from severe cold. In early spring, remove this mulch, fertilize, and prune to reduce the size of the plant by half. To prune, remove weak and inward-facing canes, as well as any damaged by winter weather or pests.

Species Roses and Their Hybrids

Harison's yellow rose covers itself in yellow, licorice-scented blooms from May into June.

If "honor thy parents" were a truism among roses as it is among people, the species roses would be the most honored type. Various individuals from this group have been crossed and then recrossed hundreds or thousands of times in order to produce the vast array of roses that we have today. Moreover, rose breeders go back to the species roses all the time, crossing them into hybrids, hoping to add their vigor, disease resistance, and hardiness to new offspring.

But the most important thing to know is that the species roses (including their cultivars) are outstanding roses in their own right. They are often more beautiful than almost any other kind of shrub when used appropriately. While most of them bloom only once, in spring, the red-ripening rose hips are frequently spectacular, and because they last for months, are more than enough incentive to add these roses to your garden. Use species roses as specimen or foundation plants, wherever they can take center stage in spring.

PEAK SEASON

Spring

MY FAVORITES

Rosa glauca is prized for its distinctive blue-green leaves and round, red hips. The small pink flowers are charming. With its large size (mature plants often reach 10 by 10 feet), and stunning mauve-colored foliage, it's an excellent background plant.

Rosa × harisonii, or Harison's yellow, traveled west with the settlers and is the namesake of the "yellow rose of Texas". Its flowers are a bright lemon yellow, and it can thrive in mediocre soil and with no care. Mature plants are 6 feet high and 4 feet wide.

Rosa × roxburghii, the chestnut rose, is a 5- to 6-foot-tall plant with an attractive arching habit. Pink flowers come in early spring and occasionally again, later in the season. The bark peels attractively from older canes.

GARDEN COMPANIONS

Accent species roses with Mexican bush sage *(Salvia leucantha)*, Russian sage *(Perovskia atriplicifolia)*, or southernwood *(Artemisia abrotanum)*.

When Plant bare-root roses during the cold season (usually in December, January, and February). Plant container-grown roses in spring as soon as the ground is workable, but don't plant roses with leaves if frost threatens.

Where Choose a location with enough space for both roots and branches to reach full size, and where plants will receive at least 5 or 6 hours of full sun daily. Good air circulation will help minimize disease and pest problems.

How Amend soil with organic matter before planting. Soak roots of bare-root plants in a bucket of water for a few hours before planting. Space plants about three-fourths of their mature height apart. Ideally, choose roses that are growing on their own roots. If your rose is grafted, make sure the graft union is 1 to 2 inches below ground level.

TLC When weather is dry, water new roses approximately twice a week and established roses once a week. Water established roses deeply, preferably in the early morning. In spring, place a 1-inch-thick layer of mulch around the plants. In late fall, once weather is reliably cold, cover the base of each bush with mulch to protect it from severe cold. In spring, remove this mulch and fertilize. Cut out older and spindly canes, and remove suckers to restrain spreading.

RIGHT: *Blossoms of chestnut rose.*
BOTTOM LEFT: *Simple flowers of* Rosa glauca *come in spring.*
BOTTOM RIGHT: *Orange-red fruits of* Rosa glauca *provide winter color as well as food for birds.*

Flowering Shrubs

Trees provide a garden with a tall vertical and overhead presence. Closer to ground level, annuals and perennials decorate with seasonal color and texture. But in the midground, it's shrubs that dominate. They provide a framework for the landscape: delineating areas, directing traffic, highlighting the architecture of your home, and providing a graceful transition between towering trees and low-growing plants.

Shrubs with ornamental flowers add seasonal color to your garden, and often fragrance as well, and they are adaptable to many garden styles and to varied uses. A flowering shrub can be grown individually as a specimen; in groupings of a single kind to create a hedge or mass planting; or in mixed beds with other shrubs, annuals, and perennials.

thrive in sun; others prefer shade. Some need moist conditions, while others do well in drier sites. Mature size is another important consideration. Don't plant shrubs too close together or in locations they will outgrow, or pruning will become an onerous chore and the shrubs may be more pest prone.

By grouping shrubs with perennials that bloom at the same time, you can create intriguing flowering vignettes. To highlight various areas of the garden as the season progresses, plant shrubs that bloom during different times of the year.

CHOOSING THE BEST SHRUBS

To select flowering shrubs, compare their growth requirements and habits with the specific conditions of your site. Some shrubs

RIGHT: *White flowers of oakleaf hydrangea appear in early summer.* OPPOSITE PAGE: *Golden petals of witch hazel signal winter's retreat in March.*

Many shrubs provide ornamental displays beyond their flowers. Evergreens like Japanese pieris (page 106) and mountain laurel (page 110) add color to the winter landscape. Many viburnums (page 108) produce colorful fruit that attracts birds and other wildlife. The fall foliage of fothergilla (page 104), royal azalea (page 114), and witch hazel (page 122) rivals their flowers for showiness.

PURCHASING AND CARE

Shrubs can be purchased as bare-root, balled-and-burlapped, or container-grown plants. Bare-root shrubs must be planted in early spring while they are still dormant; soak them for 2 hours before planting. Container-grown and balled-and-burlapped stock can be planted year-round, but early spring and fall are best.

On the whole, flowering shrubs look best when pruned to simulate their natural growth habits. While formal affects can be achieved by shearing shrubs into geometric forms, this style requires constant maintenance and often sacrifices the flowers.

To reduce size, to remove damaged branches, or to thin for improved air circulation, cut branches either back to a side branch or all the way to the ground. Many shrubs flower most prolifically on vigorous younger stems. Periodically removing the oldest stems all the way to the ground—a technique called renewal pruning—helps promote flowers.

But timing is critical: if you prune at the wrong time, you may remove an entire season's flowers. Shrubs that bloom in summer and fall generally flower on the current season's growth and can be pruned in winter or early spring. Shrubs that bloom in spring, such as Japanese pieris, develop their flower buds the previous season. Prune these shrubs immediately after flowering before the new flower buds are set.

—RITA PELCZAR

Dwarf Fothergilla

Fothergilla gardenii

White flowers cover dwarf fothergilla for several weeks in spring.

Native to the southeastern United States, dwarf fothergilla is a deciduous shrub that deserves broader use in landscapes. In spring before its leaves emerge, the 1- to 2-inch, bottlebrush-shaped flowers appear. They open a soft green, and mature to milky white, releasing a delicate honey scent. In summer, the plant's leaves are blue-green. But this shrub really comes into its own in fall when those leaves turn red, yellow, and orange, lighting up a bed with color. Once you encounter a fothergilla in autumn, you'll want one for your garden.

This shrub is native to coastal areas. Its habit is somewhat variable. It usually grows 2 to 3 feet tall and wide, although it may reach 5 feet. Some specimens are neatly rounded, while others spread by suckers to form large clumps.

PEAK SEASON

In spring when flowers appear; in fall when the leaves turn brilliant shades of yellow, orange, and red.

MY FAVORITES

'Blue Mist' is notable for its bluish gray leaves, which provide an interesting backdrop for many summer-blooming perennials.

'Mt. Airy' has large flower clusters and consistently outstanding fall color. It grows 5 to 6 feet tall.

RELATED SPECIES

Large fothergilla (*Fothergilla major*) is native to mountainous regions. It usually grows to 10 feet in height, but may reach 15 feet. It bears 2-inch flower clusters that appear slightly later than those of dwarf fothergilla, often in tandem with its expanding leaves.

GARDEN COMPANIONS

Fothergilla harmonizes with other spring-flowering shrubs like azaleas, rhododendrons, Japanese pieris, and viburnums. It complements the golden leaves of summersweet (*Clethra*) and the deep burgundy leaves of Virginia sweetspire (*Itea virginica*). Grow perennials such as: Virginia bluebells (*Mertensia*), green and gold (*Chrysoganum virginianum*), catmint (*Nepeta*), or hardy geranium at the base of the shrub.

LEFT: *The crimson fall color of dwarf fothergilla is the equal of any sugar maple.*
BELOW: *White, 2-inch-long, scented flowers of dwarf fothergilla.*

When Plant balled-and-burlapped or container-grown plants in early spring or fall.

Where Fothergilla can grow in full sun or part shade, but it needs at least 2 to 3 hours of sun a day to bloom well and to develop good fall color. It thrives in moist, well-drained, acid soils. It is a perfect choice for the edge of a woodland bed or near a walkway where its unusual honey-scented flowers can be enjoyed close at hand.

How Plant in soil that has been enriched with organic matter. For balled-and-burlapped plants, remove as much of the burlap as possible without injuring the roots. Water thoroughly and mulch with a loose organic material like shredded bark or wood chips. Water regularly for the first two growing seasons until the shrub is well established.

TLC Fothergilla rarely needs pruning, but if it produces suckers and you want to limit its spread, simply remove those that develop beyond the desired area.

Japanese Pieris
Pieris japonica

For a shrub with year-round interest, you can't do better than Japanese pieris. Its whorls of glossy, leathery leaves are evergreen, so it provides garden color all winter. In early spring, urn-shaped, fragrant white or pink flowers open, dangling in 3- to 6-inch "chains." New leaves emerge apple green, bronze pink, or red. By mid- to late summer, the dainty buds for next year's flowers have formed and, like the flowers, hang gracefully from the stems, persisting until they open the following spring.

Very early in spring, Japanese pieris covers itself in fragrant flowers.

The species form of Japanese pieris grows 9 to 12 feet tall and 6 to 8 feet wide, although smaller varieties are available. It has a compact, irregularly mounded outline, with stems that arch to the ground. Japanese pieris belongs to the same family as azaleas and rhododendrons and is well suited to the same sort of naturalized woodland setting, but it also makes an exceptional foundation plant or specimen.

ABOVE: *Yellowish leaf margins of 'Variegata' brighten the otherwise dark green shrub.*
BELOW LEFT: *Plant 'Dorothy Wyckoff' for its abundant and stunning white flowers.*
BELOW RIGHT: *The dark pink flowers of 'Flamingo' open early in the season.*

PEAK SEASON

Spectacular in spring with its colorful new growth and chains of ivory or pink flowers; buds and leaves are ornamental throughout the year.

MY FAVORITES

'Christmas Cheer' bears bicolored pale pink and rose red flowers on red stems.

'Dorothy Wyckoff' produces white flowers from buds that are dark red.

'Flamingo' is a vigorous plant that produces dark pink flowers.

'Little Heath' grows only 2 feet tall; its leaves are edged with silver.

'Prelude' grows only 2 feet tall and wide and produces bright pink buds and white flowers. New growth is also pink.

'Variegata' has leaves that are delicately edged in light yellow; new growth is blushed with pink.

'White Cascade' is an exceptionally prolific bloomer.

GARDEN COMPANIONS

Pieris is perfect in dappled shade, along with azaleas, rhododendrons, leucothoe, and mountain laurel. For a planting that combines urn-shaped flowers, plant pieris beneath a sourwood tree (Oxydendrum arboreum) and underplant it with lily-of-the-valley.

When Plant balled-and-burlapped or container-grown plants in early spring.

Where Choose a location in part shade—high, dappled shade is ideal—in a moist, well-drained, slightly acid soil with a high organic matter content. Pieris does not do well in hot, dry conditions, or where it will be exposed to wind or hot afternoon sun. Pests are more likely on plants in full sun.

How Plant in soil that has been enriched with organic matter. For balled-and-burlapped plants, remove as much of the burlap as possible without injuring the roots. Water thoroughly with a water-soluble fertilizer and mulch with a loose organic material like shredded bark or wood chips to keep soil evenly moist.

TLC Prune faded flowers immediately after bloom. To display the gnarled stems and attractive fissured bark of older specimens, prune lower branches back to the main trunk.

Korean Spice Viburnum
Viburnum carlesii

If fragrance is high on your list of important characteristics for garden shrubs, you must consider the Korean spice viburnum—it is one of the most delightfully fragrant plants you can grow. In late April or early May, the flower's scent is enough to spread throughout most gardens, and it lasts a week or more.

This deciduous shrub grows 4 to 8 feet tall and wide, with a dense, rounded habit. In spring, its snowball-shaped clusters of pink flower buds open to spicy-scented, waxy white flowers. These mature over the summer into clusters of $\frac{1}{4}$-inch red fruits that gradually darken to blue-black.

The 4-inch leaves are dark green and fuzzy enough on top to make them appear slightly dusty. The leaf undersides are a lighter gray-green and are fuzzier than the top side. Leaves usually turn a rich, wine red in the fall. (To ensure good fall color, select a showy plant at the nursery in the fall.)

This viburnum is an excellent foundation plant or a fine addition to a shrub border. Just be sure to plant it near a walkway or garden path where its scent will be appreciated.

A blooming Korean spice viburnum perfumes steps and entryway.

PEAK SEASON

Late April and early May when the flowers open; in fall when the leaves turn wine red.

MY FAVORITES

'Compactum' is a dwarf form of the Korean spice viburnum that grows only half the size but bears full-sized clusters of flowers.

RELATED SPECIES

European cranberry bush (*Viburnum opulus*) has three-lobed leaves and clusters of white flowers that are followed by red fruit.

Linden viburnum (*V. dilatatum*) grows 8 to 10 feet tall with a 6-foot spread. Its white May flowers are followed by clusters of cherry red fruit that is attractive to birds.

'Shasta' doublefile viburnum (*V. plicatum tomentosum* 'Shasta') grows 10 feet tall and 15 feet wide. In midspring, it bears white flowers in flattened clusters on the top side of the branches.

GARDEN COMPANIONS

Viburnums perform well in the dappled shade of tall trees. Plant them in a bed with azaleas, rhododendron, oakleaf hydrangea (*Hydrangea quercifolia*), and summersweet (*Clethra*) for a season-long display of flowers and colorful foliage.

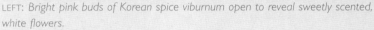

LEFT: *Bright pink buds of Korean spice viburnum open to reveal sweetly scented, white flowers.*
RIGHT: *The brilliant, wine red leaf color in fall is outstanding. To ensure similar foliage color, shop for plants during that season.*

When The best time to plant Korean spice viburnum is early spring, although it can be planted all season long if it is watered well.

Where All viburnums grow best where they receive full sun in spring and dappled shade during the heat of summer, so are ideally sited beneath tall, deciduous trees. They perform best in moist but well-drained, slightly acid soil enriched with organic matter, although they will tolerate less than ideal conditions. Plant the Korean spice viburnum near a porch or walkway where its scent can be savored.

How Plant Korean spice viburnum at the same depth that they were growing previously and water them well with a complete liquid fertilizer. Spread 2 to 4 inches of an organic mulch such as shredded hardwood bark or pine needles over the soil to maintain moisture and to prevent weeds. Keep the soil evenly moist for the first two growing seasons.

TLC Apply a complete fertilizer each spring. Prune after flowering in late spring to reduce height or to improve form.

Mountain Laurel
Kalmia latifolia

Mountain laurel ranks among the most beautiful of our native shrubs. The new leaves emerge from the tips of stems a bronzy pink, maturing to a glossy, leathery green that's dark on top and paler beneath.

In late spring, the white to pale pink flowers open from dark pink buds. Each flower is broadly bell-shaped and ¾ to 1 inch across. The blossoms are arranged in rounded, 5-inch clusters. Breeders have developed several varieties with flowers that range from pure white to bright pink, plum, maroon, and red; some are also striped or banded.

Mountain laurel is perfect for a woodland garden, mixed shrub border, or a mass planting. It can also provide an effective evergreen screen. It grows 4 to 15 feet tall and spreads 4 to 8 feet across. Flowering is best in full sun where the shrub will become more dense. In shade, growth is more open. As the shrub ages, its trunks become attractively gnarled and its shape more irregular.

When Balled-and-burlapped or container-grown plants are best planted in spring. Container-grown plants can also be planted throughout the growing season if they receive sufficient water.

Where Mountain laurel will grow in full sun or full shade, but it flowers more prolifically in sun. The shrub needs moist, well-drained, fertile soil with a high organic matter content.

How Purchase mountain laurels from local growers when possible because those plants will be best adapted to your conditions. Add organic matter such as leaf mold or compost to the planting soil and set plants at same depth that they were growing previously. Water with a complete liquid fertilizer and apply 2 to 4 inches of an organic mulch such as shredded hardwood, bark, or pine needles to maintain moisture and to reduce weeds. Keep plants well watered throughout the first two seasons; after that they are fairly drought tolerant.

TLC Apply a complete fertilizer each spring. Remove flowers after they fade to encourage more blooms the following year. Provide adequate room for growth; these plants are susceptible to leaf spots and spider mites, particularly when planted too closely.

A close-up of 'Olympic Fire' mountain laurel flower clusters in early June.

PEAK SEASON

In late spring and early summer, when flowers literally cover the plant in showy clusters. The glossy, leathery leaves are attractive year-round.

MY FAVORITES

'Carousel' bears white flowers that each have a cinnamon red starburst inside. Its leaves are very glossy, and it is resistant to several of the fungal leaf spot diseases that sometimes plague mountain laurel. It grows 10 feet tall and wide.

'Olympic Fire' has bright red buds that open to soft pink flowers.

'Pink Charm' bears dark pink buds that open to rich pink flowers. It grows 6 feet tall and wide.

Dwarf selections have leaves that are half the size of the species. 'Elf' grows only 3 feet tall and wide with pure white flowers. 'Minuet' grows to a similar size and bears white flowers that have a broad red interior band. Both are excellent understory plants for woodland gardens.

GARDEN COMPANIONS

Mountain laurel combines well with shrubs such as azaleas, rhododendron, fothergilla, Japanese pieris, and viburnums, and with perennials such as hosta, ferns, columbine, and astilbe.

OPPOSITE PAGE: *The bell-shaped flowers of mountain laurel are borne in broad clusters.*

Oakleaf Hydrangea
Hydrangea quercifolia

Although most garden hydrangeas are derived from Asian species, the oakleaf hydrangea—my favorite— is an American native. It's a big, coarse-textured plant, reaching 6 to 10 feet in height and 8 to 12 feet in width.

Oakleaf hydrangea bears white flowers that age to a dusty pink.

Each season, it displays a special beauty—beginning with the deeply lobed, leathery 8-inch-long leaves that emerge in spring and look very much like the leaves of an oak. In early summer, large, cone-shaped flower heads appear; the white blossoms age to dusty pink over the course of several weeks. In fall, the leaves turn deep burgundy with scarlet highlights, and when they drop, they expose the shredding, reddish brown bark. This shrub is a great choice for a mixed border or as a transition between lawn and woods.

PEAK SEASON

Early to midsummer for flowers, but attractive year-round.

MY FAVORITES

'Pee Wee' is a dwarf selection that grows only 3 to 4 feet tall, so it is very well suited to foundation plantings and smaller gardens. Its leaves turn wine red in fall.

'Snow Queen' produces dense, 8-inch flower clusters that are held upright on short stems. Its fall foliage turns red with a burgundy tint.

RELATED SPECIES

Bigleaf hydrangea (Hydrangea macrophylla) includes the familiar florist's hydrangea. 'Blue Wave' bears lacecap flower heads and grows 6 feet tall and wide; 'Endless Summer', a mophead type, is a bit smaller and bears flowers throughout summer.

GARDEN COMPANIONS

Plant oakleaf hydrangeas at the edge of a woodland garden beneath tall deciduous trees with perennials such as hardy geraniums, catmint (Nepeta), and astilbe. Hydrangeas also work well in mixed borders with other flowering shrubs, such as mock orange (Philadelphus), viburnums, and Virginia sweetspire (Itea virginica).

When The best time to plant oakleaf hydrangeas is in early spring, but they can be planted all season long if they are watered well.

Where Oakleaf hydrangeas will grow in full sun if the soil is sufficiently moist; otherwise they will benefit from afternoon shade. They will also grow well in dappled or light shade but will produce fewer flowers. They need a moist, well-drained, fertile soil.

How Plant oakleaf hydrangeas at the same depth that they were growing in the container, incorporating organic matter and a complete fertilizer into the planting soil. Apply a 2- to 4-inch layer of organic mulch such as shredded hardwood or bark to maintain even moisture. Water regularly throughout the first two growing seasons.

TLC Oakleaf hydrangeas rarely need pruning, although older branches can be removed to the ground to enhance shape or to rejuvenate the plant. Prune immediately after flowering. To completely renew plants, cut them back to the ground, although the next year's flowers will be sacrificed.

RIGHT: Enlongated spikes become dense with white flowers in early summer. ABOVE: In fall, oaklike leaves turn a deep ruby red.

Royal Azalea

Rhododendron schlippenbachii

Azaleas and their close cousins rhododendrons are probably the most popular flowering shrubs in the Mid-Atlantic region, and for good reason. They are relatively carefree, produce dramatic flower displays, and offer a variety of sizes, forms, flower colors, and bloom times.

My favorite among this large and lovely group of plants is the royal azalea. It grows 6 to 8 feet tall with an equal spread. Its May flowers are a delicate pink and have a sweet, light fragrance. They appear in clusters of three to six blossoms just as the leaves are expanding. The large, rounded deciduous leaves grow in distinctive whorls and turn red, orange, and yellow in fall. Royal azalea grows best in light or dappled shade, and it makes a fine specimen or an exceptional addition to a mixed border.

Both azaleas and rhododendrons are members of the *Rhododendron* genus, but distinguishing between them can be confusing. Azalea leaves are typically hairy and can be deciduous or evergreen; their flowers are small and funnel-shaped. Rhododendrons are evergreen, with larger leathery leaves; the flowers are also larger and usually bell-shaped.

Borne in clusters of three to six at branch tips, the light pink flowers of royal azalea are large and fragrant.

PEAK SEASON

Flowers are the main show in late spring, but leaves turn yellow, orange, and crimson in fall.

RELATED SPECIES

Flame azalea *(Rhododendron calendulaceum)* is a deciduous azalea native to eastern North America with an open, upright habit and brilliant orange flowers. It prefers full sun.

'Martha Hitchcock', a Glenn Dale hybrid, was developed in Maryland. It is a 4-foot-tall evergreen shrub; the lovely two-toned flowers have white centers with soft purple margins.

Plumleaf azalea *(R. prunifolium)* is native to the southeastern United States. Its red or orange flowers open in midsummer.

GARDEN COMPANIONS

Azaleas are effectively combined in mixed borders with other acid-loving shrubs like mountain laurel, pieris, skimmia, and leucothoe. One of the most delightful pairings I've ever seen was a broad drift of tiny blue-flowered forget-me-nots *(Myosotis)* covering the ground beneath the upright shrubs. Spring bulbs, ferns, hosta, heuchera, and bishop's hat *(Epimedium)* are also effective ground-level companions.

TOP RIGHT: *Long, curved stamens emerge from the center of royal azalea's pale pink flowers.*
BOTTOM RIGHT: *The flowers of plumleaf azalea open in midsummer.*

When Plant the royal azalea in early spring.

Where Choose a site in partial shade, beneath tall deciduous trees or on the north or east side of a building, for example, but avoid deep shade. The soil should be moist but well drained, and slightly acidic with a high organic matter content.

How The soil pH should be between 4.5 and 5.5; test it prior to planting and amend it if necessary. Also incorporate organic matter such as compost or leaf mold into the planting soil. Plant the azalea at the same depth that it was growing in the container; plant balled-and-burlapped plants so that the top of the root ball is right at the soil surface. Provide adequate space for the shrub's mature size. Water well and regularly for the first two seasons. Mulch around the base of the plant to maintain even soil moisture and to reduce weeds.

TLC Fertilize after flowering each year with a fertilizer specifically formulated for acid-loving plants. Prune only to remove dead or diseased branches, to cut back overly vigorous stems, or to give the plant a more open appearance. Prune immediately after flowering.

Smoke Tree
Cotinus coggygria

Dark leaves of 'Royal Purple' smoke tree contrast its pale, smokey plumes.

It's not actually the flowers of the smoke tree that are so ornamental, it's the feathery fruiting stems following the flowers that provide the unusual, billowy, pink-lavender "smoke" for which this plant is named. These showy plumes are striking from June to August. The "fire" comes in fall, when the rounded blue-green leaves turn shades of coral, orange, and red. For a colorful accent throughout the growing season, you may prefer one of the varieties with burgundy or dark purple leaves.

Some consider *Cotinus coggygria* a tree, while others think of it as a shrub (it's also referred to as smokebush). It can be grown as either. If you want a tree, purchase a young plant and, with a bit of pruning, you can train it to a single trunk. Most often, however, smoke tree is grown as a large, multistemmed shrub that reaches 10 to 15 feet tall and nearly as wide. It's a dramatic addition to a mixed shrub border—place it in the background where its "smoke" will float airily over lower-growing shrubs.

ABOVE: *Dewdrops glisten like jewels on leaves of 'Velvet Cloak'.*
BELOW: *Red leaves of 'Velvet Cloak' darken to red-purple in fall.*

PEAK SEASON

Summer to fall

MY FAVORITES

'Pink Champagne' is a compact form with green leaves.

'Royal Purple' has leaves that open maroon red, change to rich purple or nearly black in summer, and then turn red-purple in fall.

'Velvet Cloak' has rich purple leaves that tend to fade a bit in summer, but become a vibrant red-purple in fall.

RELATED SPECIES

American smoke tree (*Cotinus obovatus*) is native to parts of the southeastern United States. It may grow to 35 feet, and its fall foliage—shades of red, orange, yellow, purple, and amber—is brilliant.

'Flame', a hybrid of the common smoke tree and the American smoke tree, is prized for its bright red-orange fall foliage.

GARDEN COMPANIONS

Smoke tree adds a tall, broad presence to the shrub border, combining well with hydrangea, spirea, and Virginia sweetspire (*Itea virginica*). The purple-leaf varieties add a colorful accent to perennial beds planted with purple coneflower (*Echinacea purpurea*), black-eyed Susan (*Rudbeckia hirta*), Stokes' aster, and astilbe.

When Plant balled-and-burlapped or container-grown plants in spring or fall.

Where Plant in full sun in well-drained soil. Smoke tree adapts to nearly any soil, including rocky and infertile ones, but it does poorly in soil that remains wet. In addition, inadequate drainage will leave the plant susceptible to verticillium wilt.

How Position the plant at the same depth it grew in the container; set balled-and-burlapped plants so that the root ball flares at the soil surface. Water regularly until roots are established, after which they will tolerate some drought.

TLC Prune lightly to remove damaged or unsightly branches or to remove faded flower clusters. To limit size, restore vigor, and promote lush leaf growth prune hard by removing the oldest branches back to the ground in early spring, though this will sacrifice the "smoke" plumes for that year.

Spirea
Spiraea

Spireas are adaptable and reliable garden performers, and they are very easy to grow. The Japanese spirea *(Spiraea japonica)* is a summer bloomer, producing flat, fuzzy clusters of pink, red, or white flowers at the ends of thin stems that are flanked with serrated oval leaves. The species form of Japanese spiraea grows 4 to 6 feet tall with a similar spread, but cultivars are available in a range of sizes. Varieties are also available with gold, chartreuse, and dark green foliage, many of which develop outstanding fall color.

Vanhouette bridal wreath spirea, a traditional favorite, billows over a stone wall.

With its long-lasting summer blooms, fine texture, and dense habit, Japanese spirea makes an effective deciduous hedge. It is a welcome alternative to lawn grass, especially as a mass planting on a hillside where mowing is impractical. And it contributes summer color and a tidy growth habit to mixed borders.

Spring-flowering spireas include *Spiraea* × *vanhouttei* and *S. thunbergii*. Both are called bridal wreath spireas or just bridal wreath. In midspring, they bear white flowers on gracefully arching branches.

PEAK SEASON

In spring or midsummer according to the type. Many also display colorful fall foliage.

MY FAVORITES

Spring blooming, bridal wreath

Vanhoutte bridal wreath spirea *(Spiraea × vanhouttei)* grows 6 feet tall and 8 feet wide. In spring, delicate white flower clusters line its arching stems, creating a fountainlike appearance.

Summer blooming, Japanese spirea

'Alpina' is a dwarf form that grows 1 foot tall and bears soft pink flowers. 'Little Princess' is very similar but grows to 2½ feet.

'Anthony Waterer' grows 3 to 4 feet tall with a 4- to 5-foot spread and bears deep carmine pink flowers.

'Goldflame' bears leaves that open bronze, mature to chartreuse, and turn fiery red-orange in fall. This variety grows 2 to 3 feet tall.

'Goldmound' grows 1½ to 2 feet tall. Leaves are light yellow and flowers are pink.

GARDEN COMPANIONS

Spireas complement other summer-flowering shrubs like hydrangea and summersweet *(Clethra)*. Low-growing types, such as 'Goldflame', show well against taller dark green shrubs like 'Mohawk' viburnum.

TOP RIGHT: *'Goldmound' leaves are chartreuse yellow.*
BOTTOM RIGHT: *'Goldflame' leaves are bronze at first, chartreuse in summer, and red-orange in fall.*

When Early spring is the best time to plant spireas, although container-grown plants can be planted anytime as long as they are well watered.

Where Spireas grow best in full sun but will tolerate part shade. They are adaptable to most soils, but do not grow well where their roots are constantly wet.

How Plant spireas at the same depth that they were growing previously and space them according to their mature size. Mass plantings may look better when spaced slightly closer. Water thoroughly after planting, and continue watering regularly through the first growing season. Once established, spireas will tolerate drought.

TLC Each spring sprinkle a complete fertilizer around the base of the plant and water it in. Prune spring-flowering spireas immediately after flowering. If you remove the spent blooms, Japanese spireas will often rebloom, at least sporadically, through late summer into fall. To reduce height or to rejuvenate, cut plants back sharply in winter or early spring.

Summersweet
Clethra alnifolia

There are many shrubs with spectacular spring-flower displays. Far fewer shrubs bloom in midsummer, however, and summersweet, a native beauty, may be the best of them for Mid-Atlantic gardens. Its sweetly fragrant flowers appear at the tips of the stems in 2- to 6-inch spires that open from the bottom up starting in July. At first the blossoms are pale green, but they turn to pure white and last for a month or so, attracting numerous nectar-seeking butterflies. The leaves are bright green, turning golden yellow in fall.

The species form of summersweet grows very quickly, becoming a dense, broadly mounded shrub that ulti-

The fragrant flowers of summersweet attract a wide variety of beneficial insects.

mately reaches 8 or 9 feet in height. There are dwarf varieties better suited for smaller gardens, however. This shrub will produce suckers, and can spread if it's growing vigorously. (Control spread if you want by removing the suckers that sprout outside of the area where you want them.)

Summersweet has an informal look that works well in mixed shrub borders. Its smartly upright, sweet-scented flowers are a refreshing addition to the summer landscape.

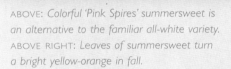

PEAK SEASON
Midsummer

MY FAVORITES

'Compacta' is a dwarf cultivar that develops a mounding form and reaches 3 to 4 feet in height.

'Hummingbird' has a dense, compact habit, growing 2½ to 3½ feet tall and wide. The variety is a particularly heavy bloomer.

'Pink Spires' has deep pink buds that open to display soft pink flowers.

'Ruby Spice' bears blossoms that retain the deep pink of the buds. The plants grow 6 to 8 feet tall.

'September Beauty' flowers nearly two weeks later than the species and has a more compact habit.

GARDEN COMPANIONS

Summersweet extends the flowering season of a mixed-shrub border through midsummer. Its relaxed form and adaptable nature allow it to fit comfortably into both sunny and shady sites. Try growing it with native viburnums, azaleas, and fothergilla for an informal, naturalized woodland garden. Dwarf forms are well suited to smaller gardens and to the foreground of mixed borders, and are especially effective planted in front of evergreens such as rhododendrons and mountain laurel.

ABOVE: *Colorful 'Pink Spires' summersweet is an alternative to the familiar all-white variety.*
ABOVE RIGHT: *Leaves of summersweet turn a bright yellow-orange in fall.*

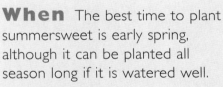

When The best time to plant summersweet is early spring, although it can be planted all season long if it is watered well.

Where Summersweet is about as adaptable as a plant can be. It will grow in shade or full sun; where summers are hot, however, afternoon shade is beneficial. Moist, slightly acidic, organic soil is optimum, but any soil is okay. Salt laden coastal air is okay too, but an extended drought is not. For planting beside a pond or at the edge of a woodland summersweet is a perfect choice..

How Add organic matter such as compost to the soil prior to planting. Keep plants well watered until they're established; mulch to retain moisture and to prevent weeds.

TLC Prune to maintain vigor by removing the oldest branches all the way to the ground in early spring. Or, prune to rejuvenate by cutting the shrub back to the ground in winter. In spring, it will grow vigorously and begin flowering on the new growth when stems are 3 or 4 feet tall.

121

Witch Hazel
Hamamelis × intermedia

Spreading branches of 'Arnold Promise' are covered in gold in late winter.

For most of the year, witch hazel is attractive enough, but come winter, it is unrivaled for its off-season blooms. Many selections also display colorful fall foliage. This species of witch hazel is a hybrid of the Japanese (*Hamamelis japonica*) and Chinese (*H. mollis*) witch hazels that includes the best aspects of both parents. It's a large, vigorous shrub, growing 10 to 20 feet tall with a slightly greater spread. It has an upright, broadly vase-shaped habit. Its leaves—medium green with wavy margins—are nothing really special; in fact, you might not even notice them until fall when they turn brilliant shades of yellow, orange, and red.

Witch hazel flowers are unusual. Each blossom has four strap-shaped yellow or red petals that unfurl along a zigzagging stem. In very cold overcast weather, the petals may curl up for protection, unfurling again when the sun shines. Depending on the variety and the location, witch hazels flower from January to mid-March.

Witch hazels are at home in a woodland garden or as a specimen in full sun. Their flowers stand out particularly well when these shrubs are grown against an evergreen background.

When Early spring is the best time to plant witch hazels, although container-grown plants can be planted anytime as long as they are well watered.

Where Witch hazels will flower most abundantly when grown in full sun, but they will require regular watering during periods of drought. They also grow well in deciduous shade. They need a moist but well-drained, slightly acidic soil that's rich in organic matter.

ABOVE: *'Jelena' flowers with snow*
BELOW LEFT: *'Jelena'*
BELOW RIGHT: *'Princeton Gold'*

How Plant witch hazel in soil that has been enriched with organic matter, spacing plants with an eye to their mature size. Water thoroughly and regularly until plants are established. Spread a 2- to 4-inch layer of an organic mulch such as shredded hardwood or bark to maintain even moisture and to prevent weeds.

TLC Apply a complete fertilizer each spring. Prune plants when young to remove poorly positioned stems and to encourage the vase shape. As they age, very little pruning is necessary other than to remove damaged branches and maintain overall shape.

PEAK SEASON
Fall for its foliage and late winter for its flowers

MY FAVORITES
'Arnold Promise' is a late bloomer, bearing fragrant bright yellow flowers in March. Its fall foliage is red and orange.

'Jelena' blooms in February, bearing large yellow flowers that are blushed with red. In fall, its leaves turn orange and scarlet.

'Princeton Gold' also blooms in February; both its flowers and fall foliage are yellow.

RELATED SPECIES
Common witch hazel *(Hamamelis virginiana)* is native to the eastern half of the United States. It blooms in late fall and is hardy throughout the Mid-Atlantic region. Witch hazel extract, which is often used as a muscle rub or skin tonic, is distilled from the bark of its young stems and roots.

GARDEN COMPANIONS
Witch hazels grow well under tall deciduous trees with other woodland shrubs like mountain laurel and viburnum. They are particularly attractive underplanted with perennials such as winter-blooming hellebore and the evergreen Italian arum.

Flowering Trees

Spring begins officially for me when I look into the woods that surround my house and see the dainty white blossoms of serviceberry (page 126) that seem to float like clouds among the bare branches of the deciduous trees. The sassy, rosy pink flowers of the eastern redbud (page 130) soon follow, providing a brilliant splash of color, along with the more substantive blooms of flowering dogwood (page 134) that pass through shades of pale green to ivory or pink as they expand on their horizontal branches.

As the trees leaf out, their bare limbs vanish, and the forest floor darkens with welcome shade. The early flowers are replaced by fruits, which feed the birds, squirrels, and chipmunks that inhabit my woods. Another growing season has begun.

Flowering trees add color and often fragrance overhead, while at the same time, they create a sense of intimacy beneath their spreading branches. Many boast multiple seasons of ornamental display: some produce colorful fruit that attracts wildlife or leaves that morph from green to red, gold, or orange in the fall. Others enhance the winter landscape with their ornamental bark.

SELECTING FLOWERING TREES

The trees you plant will be a permanent, or at least a long-term, part of the landscape, so it makes sense to select them with as much care as you can muster. And while flowers are important, they are not the only characteristic you should consider. Height, spread, form, and density will also have a significant impact on your landscape. Begin the process by identifying where you want to plant a flowering tree and analyzing the available space and conditions. This will narrow your choice significantly making it easier to select the best tree for your needs.

ABOVE: *The Mid-Atlantic is renowned for its flowering cherries.*
OPPOSITE PAGE: *These pink-tinged dogwood blooms belong to a more colorful cultivar of the native woodland dogwood.*

Most of the trees listed here are fairly small, at least compared with large forest species. Some, such as apple serviceberry, grow naturally as understory plants and are adapted to shady sites. These make great additions to woodland gardens, where they thrive alongside shade-loving shrubs. Others, such as red horsechestnut (page 138), are best in full sun and are ideal as a lawn specimen.

PLANTING

Trees are sold as bare-root, container-grown, or balled-and-burlapped. Bare-root trees are available when they are dormant and must be planted shortly after they're purchased. The roots of container-grown trees may be pot-bound, forming a circular pattern of growth. If you observe this, untangle the roots by loosening them with your fingers or, if necessary, by cutting them with a knife or pruners to encourage outward growth.

To plant a tree, dig a hole that is roughly two or three times as wide as the root ball and slightly shallower than its depth. I recommend adding organic matter and a controlled-release fertilizer to the excavated soil before backfilling around the tree roots with it. Water when the hole is half filled and again when completely filled, tamping gently to ensure good soil-to-root contact and to eliminate air pockets. Mulch around the base of the tree, but not right up to the trunk, to reduce weeds.

—RITA PELCZAR

Apple Serviceberry
Amelanchier × grandiflora

Known as serviceberry, sarviceberry, Juneberry, shadbush, and shadblow, the genus *Amelanchier* includes more than 20 species that are native to North America. They are either small trees or large shrubs, and all produce delicate white blossoms in the spring. These flowers supply nectar for an array of insects, and the edible blue, purple, or red fruits that follow feed a variety of wildlife.

A cross between two native species (*Amelanchier arborea* and *A. laevis*) produced the apple serviceberry. With its large flowers and reliably colorful autumn foliage, it is, to my mind, the best choice for home landscapes. It usually grows 25 feet tall, although it may reach 40 feet. Apple serviceberry can be grown with single or multiple trunks, and its wide-spreading crown casts moderate shade. Pendant clusters of white flowers dangle gracefully from the bare branches in late March or early April, followed by fruit that ripens to blue-black in June. In fall, the leaves turn orange and red.

The apple serviceberry is very adaptable and is at home in many garden settings. It makes a lovely lawn specimen, complements a woodland garden, or adds height and shade to a mixed bed.

One of the first trees to bloom in our region, apple serviceberry begins flowering in March.

PEAK SEASON

Early spring for flowers and fall for colorful leaves.

MY FAVORITES

'Autumn Brilliance' grows 20 to 25 feet tall and is very drought tolerant once established. Its leaves turn bright orange in fall.

'Forest Prince' bears flowers along the length of its stems rather than only at the ends.

'Princess Diana' is a slow-growing selection with red fall leaf color.

'Rubescens' has purple-pink buds that open to pale pink flowers.

RELATED SPECIES

Downy serviceberry (Amelanchier arborea) is a bit smaller with a multi-trunk growth habit. Its new leaves are covered with a soft gray down. It is spectacular in fall when the leaves turn shades of yellow, orange, and deep red.

GARDEN COMPANIONS

Grow with azaleas and rhododendrons or other early bloomers like winter honeysuckle (Lonicera fragrantissima), fragrant winter hazel (Corylopsis glabrescens), and fothergilla. Underplant with early-blooming bulbs like daffodils, crocus, and Siberian squill.

When Plant balled-and-burlapped or container-grown plants in spring as soon as they are available and the ground can be worked. Container-grown plants can also be planted in fall.

TOP: *Plant apple serviceberry against a dark background to show off the delicate flowers.*
BOTTOM: *The sweet fruits of Allegheny serviceberry (Amelanchier laevis) are sought out by birds.*

Where Plant in full sun or part shade in a slightly acid soil that's moist but well drained. Serviceberries are good additions to naturalized gardens. They grow well on stream banks and at the edge of a woodland, but will adapt to drier conditions as well.

How Plant the tree at the same depth that it was growing previously, in a hole that is wide enough to accommodate the roots without crowding. Mix organic matter such as compost or leaf mold and a controlled-release fertilizer into the excavated soil and use it to backfill, gently firming the soil around the roots and tamping to eliminate air pockets. Water thoroughly after planting and mulch with a 2- to 4-inch layer of shredded hardwood, bark, or pine needles to maintain even moisture and prevent weeds.

TLC Maintain the mulch and continue to water regularly for the first two growing seasons. Once established, serviceberry will tolerate some drought. It rarely requires pruning, other than removing suckers if they arise.

Crape Myrtle
Lagerstroemia

When spring-blooming trees have finished their annual flower displays, crape myrtles are just beginning to rev up their engines. Taking center stage from early summer to fall, the flowers, with their unusual crinkled petals, appear at the ends of the branches in clusters from 6 to 20 inches long. Blossom colors range from white and soft shades of pink and lavender to hot pinks, vibrant purples, and dazzling reds.

A tall crape myrtle, 'Natchez' blooms abundantly and is very disease resistant.

Toward fall, the flowers fade, but the leaves continue the show, turning fiery shades of yellow and orange. And in winter, the bare branches reveal an extraordinarily lovely smooth gray bark, which peels to show patches of tan, cinnamon, and copper pink.

Years ago, the National Arboretum in Washington, D.C., began a crape myrtle breeding program seeking a wider range of flower color and increased hardiness and disease resistance. All of the more than two dozen resulting cultivars are superior performers in this region, and the six at right (see My Favorites) are outstanding.

PEAK SEASON

Crape myrtle is lovely year-round.

MY FAVORITES

'Cherokee' is a selection of *Lager-stroemia indica* that grows 10 feet tall and bears medium-red flowers.

'Choctaw' is a pink-flowered hybrid. Usually grown with multiple trunks, it has a rounded form and grows 30 feet tall.

'Natchez' is a white-flowered hybrid. It has a graceful, wide, arching habit and grows about 30 feet tall.

'Osage' is a hybrid that grows 15 feet tall and has clear pink flowers and red leaves in fall. It is mildew resistant.

'Witchita' is a distinctly vase-shaped hybrid that is notably mildew resistant. It produces light magenta to lavender flowers and copper fall foliage, and it grows 25 feet tall.

'Yuma' grows 13 to 20 feet tall, developing a distinctly round crown. Flowers are lavender. Leaves are mildew resistant and turn yellow-orange in fall.

GARDEN COMPANIONS

Grow crape myrtle as a large speci-men underplanted with a ground cover such as barrenwort (*Epime-dium*), candytuft (*Iberis*), or lily turf (*Liriope*).

TOP: *Cinnamon-colored bark shows to dramatic effect as the outer layers gradually peel.*
BOTTOM: *The intense yellow-orange fall color of 'Yuma' follows lavender flowers in spring.*

When Balled-and-burlapped or container-grown crape myrtles are best planted in late fall or early spring, but container-grown plants can be planted year-round if they are well watered.

Where Plant in full sun in moist, well-drained soil. Allow for good air circulation or powdery mildew can be a problem.

How Dig a planting hole twice the width of the root ball and slightly shallower, leaving a firm center on which to set the root ball (its surface should sit slightly higher than the surrounding soil). Mix organic matter and a controlled-release fertilizer into the excavated soil and use it to backfill, tamping gently to firm. Water well and cover soil with 2 to 4 inches of organic mulch.

TLC Maintain the mulch and water during dry periods for the first two seasons. Remove lower side branches to reveal the ornamental bark. Prune in spring to remove the previous year's flowering stems and winter dieback. In interior and upper elevation regions where plants dieback in winter, you can treat them as perennials by cutting them to the ground in winter to grow back in the spring.

Eastern Redbud

Cercis canadensis

Eastern redbud with tulips makes a stunning springtime display.

When in bloom in early spring, eastern redbuds can take your breath away. Their flowers—which are usually purple-pink, not red—are tiny and are held tightly against the dark bare branches of the tree. As the flowers fade, broad, heart-shaped leaves emerge, casting significant shade beneath the tree's canopy. The flat, peapod-like fruits that follow the flowers reveal eastern redbud's membership in the pea family. They appear along the branches, and, curiously, right on the main trunk as well.

Eastern redbud grows to 15 to 25 feet tall and develops a broad, spreading crown. Native to the eastern United States, it is a frequent inhabitant of woodlands throughout our region. It is a perfect addition to shady gardens and is lovely planted at the edge of a woods, particularly one with evergreens, where the eastern redbud blossoms show up well against the dark green foliage. Eastern redbud grows fast, particularly when young, so this tree is a good choice both for quick landscape results and a dramatic announcement of spring's arrival.

PEAK SEASON

Early spring

MY FAVORITES

'Alba' lacks the red pigment in both leaves and flowers.

'Flame' is a vigorous selection with double rose pink blooms. It seldom sets fruit.

'Forest Pansy' leaves emerge bright red-purple. The color softens some-what as they mature, then turns dark purple-red in fall.

'Silver Cloud' has variegated foliage: the green leaves are marbled with creamy white. Somewhat less flower-ful than others, the colorful leaves brighten shady corners. Plant it in shade to avoid leaf scorch.

GARDEN COMPANIONS

Eastern redbuds look great when planted against a background of dark evergreens such as hemlock or yew. Their spring flowers harmonize with naturalized crocus, daffodils, or for-get-me-nots (Myosotis).

TOP: *Purple-pink flowers of eastern redbud are borne on bare twigs, branches, and even the main trunk.*
ABOVE: *'Alba' is a white form of eastern redbud.*
BELOW: *A backlit leaf of 'Forest Pansy' redbud.*

When Plant balled-and-burlapped or container-grown trees in early spring as soon as the soil can be worked.

Where Eastern redbuds grow in sun or shade, although partial shade is pre-ferred. Plant in fertile soil that is moist but well drained.

How Dig a hole twice as wide as and equal to the depth of the root ball. Remove the tree from its container carefully, keeping the root ball intact. For a balled-and-burlapped plant, roll the burlap back as far as possible and set the tree in the hole so the root flare is right at the soil surface. Amend the excavated soil with organic matter and a controlled-release fertilizer. Fill in the hole with the enriched soil, tamping gently to eliminate air pockets. Water thoroughly. Cover the soil surface with 2 to 4 inches of organic mulch.

TLC Keep the soil evenly moist from spring until the ground freezes in fall for the first 2 years and maintain the mulch. Apply a controlled-release fertilizer every other spring. Prune only to remove damaged, diseased, or crossing branches.

Flowering Cherry
Prunus 'Hally Jolivette'

Having grown up near Washington, D.C., home of the National Cherry Blossom Festival, I feel a special affinity for flowering cherries. Many are very beautiful, but my favorite is a diminutive hybrid known as 'Hally Jolivette'. It grows fast, topping out at 12 to 15 feet in about 7 years, and is great for small gardens or for growing near a patio. Its flower buds are pink, opening to semidouble white blossoms with centers tinted a deep pink. They don't open all at once, so the flowering season is longer than other cherries, lasting from late April until mid-May. And because the blossoms open later than most varieties, they are less likely to be damaged by frost. Other good choices for larger landscapes are the parents of 'Hally Jolivette': the Yoshino cherry *(Prunus × yedoensis)* and the Higan cherry *(P. × subhirtella)*. Both are outstanding trees, and are particularly attractive planted near a garden pond.

The springtime show of 'Hally Jolivette' exceeds expectations.

When Flowering cherries are sold as bare-root trees during the winter dormant period. Plant as soon as possible after purchasing. They are also sold as container-grown and balled-and-burlapped plants, which can be planted in spring or fall.

Where Plant in full sun in fertile soil that is moist but well drained. Avoid locations where the soil is compacted or waterlogged.

How Soak the roots of a bare-root tree overnight before planting. Dig the hole two to three times as wide as the roots and slightly shallower. Set the tree so that the juncture of roots and trunk is slightly above the soil line. Amend the excavated soil with organic matter and a controlled-release fertilizer. Backfill the hole with the enriched soil, tamping gently to eliminate air pockets. Water thoroughly and apply a 2- to 4-inch layer of mulch around the base.

TLC Water during dry periods for the first 2 years and maintain the mulch. Prune only to remove diseased, damaged, or crossing branches or to enhance the framework of the tree. Overpruning will reduce flowers and encourage the production of water sprouts (strong vertical suckers off the main trunk).

Upon opening, the semidouble flowers of 'Hally Jolivette' are pink in the center, but shortly fade to all white.

PEAK SEASON

Spring

RELATED SPECIES

Higan cherry (*Prunus* × *subhirtella* 'Autumnalis') has pale pink semi-double flowers that open sporadically in fall and sometimes even in winter on warm, sunny days. Its main flowering season, however, is in spring. It becomes 25 to 30 feet high and wide. The flowers of 'Autumnalis Rosea' are a deeper pink. Zones 31, 32, 34–36.

Weeping Higan cherry (*P.* × *s.* 'Pendula') has a graceful, weeping habit and bears single pink flowers in early spring. Zones 31, 32, 34–36.

Yoshino cherry (*P.* × *yedoensis*) blooms in early spring. Its flowers open a soft pink and fade to white. Growing 30 to 40 feet tall and nearly as wide, it is a good choice for planting in a lower area of a yard where it can be viewed from a distance. Zones 32, 34.

GARDEN COMPANIONS

'Hally Jolivette' combines well with dwarf azaleas and primroses. All ornamental cherries can be planted with early spring bulbs such as daffodils, crocus, grape hyacinth, or Siberian squill for a dramatic spring display.

Flowering Dogwood
Cornus florida

Basket-of-gold (Aurinia saxatilis) *and blue grape hyacinth dramatically color the ground beneath a white dogwood in full bloom.*

The flowering dogwood is one of our most beautiful native trees, and its blossom is Virginia's state flower. Dogwoods are beautiful in every season. Their wide-spreading horizontal branches turn up at the tips, creating a lovely silhouette in winter. In mid-spring, the green flowers appear, surrounded by four showy petal-like bracts (modified leaves) that are usually white, but may be pink or almost red. The tree's shiny red berries feed birds and squirrels, and in fall, the broad, green leaves turn deep red. Although some specimens reach 40 feet tall, most top out at half that height.

In recent years, a disease known as anthracnose has threatened this lovely native; keeping plants in vigorous health is the best way to avoid it. Alternatively, the Kousa dogwood *(Cornus kousa),* native to Korea and Japan, and the stellar dogwood *(C. × rutgersensis),* a hybrid between the native and kousa dogwoods, offer similar ornamental qualities and are resistant to the disease.

Dogwoods fit well into a variety of settings: as specimens, in woodland gardens, or casting their shade over mixed beds of flowering shrubs and perennials.

When Plant container-grown or balled-and-burlapped plants in early spring before growth begins.

Where Although flowering dogwoods will grow in full sun with adequate moisture, they are understory plants and prefer some protection from the hot afternoon sun. Plant in moist but well-drained soil.

How Plant a flowering dogwood at the same depth that it was growing at the nursery. Dig the planting hole twice as wide as and equal to the depth of the root ball. Amend the excavated soil with organic matter and a controlled-release fertilizer. Set the tree and backfill the hole with the enriched soil, tamping gently. Water thoroughly. To keep dogwoods vigorous and less susceptible to anthracnose and borers, cover the soil with 2 to 4 inches of organic mulch, keeping it a few inches away from the trunk.

TLC Water regularly for the first two growing seasons. Maintain the mulch to keep the soil evenly moist and to prevent damage from lawn mowers. After the first year, fertilize annually in late fall with a controlled-release fertilizer. Prune in winter to remove dead or diseased branches.

ABOVE: *Clusters of dark-eyed dogwood fruits last into winter until consumed by birds.*
BELOW: *This close-up shows unopened, green flowers surrounded by large, white bracts.*

PEAK SEASON

Flowers in spring, fruit and foliage in fall

MY FAVORITES

'Cherokee Chief' has both flowers and new growth of an attractive red.

'Cherokee Princess' is an early and heavy bloomer that bears white bracts up to 5 inches across.

'October Glory' bears pink flowers and the leaves turn a brilliant shade of red in fall.

'Rubra' has pink- to rose-colored bracts and is a long-time favorite.

RELATED SPECIES.

Stellar dogwood *(Cornus × rutgersensis)* blooms midseason, between the native and kousa dogwoods. It resists both anthracnose and dogwood borer (a type of moth whose larvae tunnel under bark, killing the branch).

GARDEN COMPANIONS

Flowering dogwood is lovely as a lawn specimen, underplanted with daffodils, grape hyacinth, and other spring-flowering bulbs or ground covers such as basket-of-gold *(Aurinia saxatilis)* or barrenwort *(Epimedium)*. They also provide height to mixed beds, combining well with bleeding heart *(Dicentra)*, astilbe, heuchera, hosta, and ferns.

Fringe Tree
Chionanthus virginicus

Although it is native to the southeastern United States, fringe tree is unfamiliar to many visitors to my garden, but they are always smitten by the sight of it in bloom. And it's no wonder—in late spring, its dark branches are cloaked in plumes of fragrant white flowers, each with four silky petals. They hang in fuzzy clusters that are 6 to 8 inches long. Fringe trees are relatively slow growers, taking 10 to 15 years to ultimately reach 15 to 25 feet in height with an equal spread. Fortunately, they bloom at a young age, beginning at about 4 or 5 years old.

Fringe trees look best when they are pruned to a single or a few (I recommend three) main trunks. In the wild, they often develop multiple trunks, giving them the appearance of a large shrub. My fringe tree anchors a large bed near the front walk, where its fragrance is appreciated by all who pass by. Fringe tree also makes an effective specimen planted alone or at the edge of a woodland. Its flowers show up well even from a distance.

A native, fringe tree is a spectacular shrub or small tree during its spring bloom time.

PEAK SEASON

Late spring

RELATED SPECIES

Chinese fringe tree *(Chionanthus retusus)* is slightly less hardy than the native species. It produces similar flowers, but they appear 2 to 3 weeks earlier. Its bark is a handsome gray-brown, and it sometimes exfoliates in attractive patterns. Zones 31, 32, 34.

GARDEN COMPANIONS

When in bloom in late spring, the fringe tree upstages all plants nearby. Its blooms, however, only last a couple of weeks, after which its medium-green, wide, oval leaves provide an attractive foil for summer-blooming perennials such as astilbe, Shasta daisy, sage, and bellflower *(Campanula)*. This is one of the last trees to leaf out in spring in this region, so you may want to plant early-blooming spring bulbs such as daffodils and crocus or the biennial forget-me-knot *(Myosotis sylvatica)* beneath its branches for early color.

TOP RIGHT: *Greenish white and lightly scented flowers of fringe tree are borne in lacy clusters.*
BOTTOM RIGHT: *Flowers of Chinese fringe tree are smaller, pure white, more numerous, and they appear about 3 weeks earlier.*

When Transplant balled-and-burlapped or container-grown plants in early spring as soon as the ground can be worked.

Where Although fringe tree is often found growing near streams in the wild, it is very adaptable. It grows best in full sun or partial shade in slightly acid soil that is moist but well drained.

How Plant a container-grown tree at the same depth that it was growing in the container. Set a balled-and-burlapped plant so that the top of the root ball is level with the soil surface. Amend the excavated soil with organic matter and a controlled-release fertilizer, then backfill and water well. Apply a 2- to 4-inch layer of mulch.

TLC Water regularly for the first 2 years and maintain the mulch. While it is young, prune it to a single trunk. Or, if you prefer a tree with a multiple trunk, select three large main branches. Remove other low branches. As the tree matures, continue to remove any new shoots that arise near the base so its attractive form is visible in winter.

Red Horsechestnut
Aesculus × carnea

If your garden needs a blast of late-spring color overhead, consider the red horsechestnut. This cross between common horsechestnut *(Aesculus hippocastanum)* and red buckeye *(A. pavia)* is intermediate in size, growing 30 to 40 feet tall with a broad, rounded crown, and it is more tolerant of drought, wind, and disease than its parents. Its flowers are a bright rosy red and are borne on 6- to 8-inch spires that rise from the tips of the leafy branches. The big, glossy, dark green leaves set the flowers off to perfection. The flowers attract hummingbirds, and the shiny brown nuts that ripen inside their bristly coats in late summer feed a variety of wildlife. Like the fruit of all horsechestnuts, however, they are poisonous to humans.

The leafy crown casts dense shade, and although the leaves don't provide fall color (they just turn brown before dropping), they do stay dark green longer than most deciduous trees. Red horsechestnut makes a bold statement in the landscape as both a specimen and a shade tree.

Hummingbirds are attracted to the red, loosely branched flower clusters of red horsechestnut.

PEAK SEASON

Late spring for flowers; all summer for dark, glossy leaves

MY FAVORITES

'Briotii' bears deeper red flowers than the species, in 10-inch-long clusters.

'Fort McNair' produces pink flowers with yellow throats.

'Plantierensis' bears flowers that are a delicate pink.

RELATED SPECIES

Red buckeye *(Aesculus pavia)* is a native of the eastern half of the United States. It is usually grown as a large, multistemmed shrub or a small tree, and is a good choice for a naturalized garden or moist woodland. The tree does not tolerate drought. Zones 31, 32, 34.

Yellow buckeye *(A. flava)* is another eastern North American native that grows 40 to 80 feet tall. It bears creamy yellow flowers with a red spot at the base of each petal. Zones 32, 34–36.

GARDEN COMPANIONS

Plant red horsechestnut alone as a specimen or combine it with shrubs such as azalea, fothergilla, viburnum, summersweet *(Clethra),* and witch hazel *(Hamamelis)* for a mixed bed with an extended flowering season.

LEFT: *'Briotii' flowers are deep red.*
RIGHT: *Flowers of red buckeye (a related species) are more tubular and narrow.*

When Transplant container and balled-and-burlapped-grown plants in spring.

Where Plant in full sun in a moderately fertile soil that is moist but well drained. The tree tolerates urban conditions, including compacted soils.

How Plant at the same depth that it was growing previously, in a hole that is wide enough to accommodate the roots without crowding. For a balled-and-burlapped plant, roll the burlap back as far as possible and set the tree in the hole so the root flare is right at the soil surface. Amend the excavated soil with organic matter and a controlled-release fertilizer. Backfill the hole with the enriched soil, tamping gently to eliminate air pockets. Water thoroughly and apply a 2- to 4-inch layer of organic mulch.

TLC Maintain the mulch and water during dry periods for at least the first two growing seasons. Fertilize annually in early spring. The trunk bark is susceptible to cracking when exposed to bright sun, so keep it shaded as much as possible by leaving the lower branches on.

Saucer Magnolia
Magnolia × soulangeana

When a deciduous magnolia blooms, everyone stops and takes notice. Large, usually white or pink flowers cover the bare branches in early spring. They're typically the largest, most dramatic flowers to appear on a tree.

The saucer magnolia is by far the most prominent and best-known deciduous magnolia. A cross between two Asian species *(Magnolia denudata* and *M. liliiflora),* its large, 6-inch-wide, saucer-shaped flowers open in late March and early April before the deciduous leaves appear. These blossoms are typically blushed reddish purple or pink on the outside and creamy white inside, and the tree has the endearing quality of producing them at a very young age. Eventually, it grows into a neat 20- to 30-foot-tall tree with single or multiple trunks.

Saucer magnolias are often called "tulip trees" because of the shape and rich colors of their flowers.

Saucer magnolia is a good choice for a moderate-sized lawn tree, or as a multi-stemmed specimen it provides a tall accent in a mixed border.

PEAK SEASON

Early spring

MY FAVORITES

'Alexandrina' flowers are purple-pink outside and white inside.

'Brozzonii' bears very large white flowers that are lightly flushed with purple on the outside.

'Rustica Rubra' bears dark reddish purple flowers.

RELATED SPECIES

Star magnolia (Magnolia stellata) grows only 15 to 20 feet tall and bears very early white flowers. In fact, they are sometimes nipped by frost because they bloom so early. Zones 31, 32, 34–36.

Sweet bay magnolia (M. virginiana) has fragrant, creamy white flowers that appear sporadically through summer. In protected areas, it is ever-green; in more exposed sites, it loses all or most of its leaves. Zones 31, 32, 34, 35.

GARDEN COMPANIONS

Underplant specimens with spring-flowering bulbs, such as tulips, daffodils, crocus, or Siberian squill, or with ground covers like pachysandra or periwinkle (Vinca). Saucer magnolia can also be included in a mixed border with flowering shrubs and perennials.

When Plant as soon as the ground can be worked in spring.

Where Choose a location in full sun, with an eastern or northern exposure. (Southern and western exposures promote earlier flowering, increasing the chance of frost damage.) Plant in rich soil that is moist but well drained.

How Dig a hole wide enough to accommodate the roots without crowding. Plant a container-grown plant at the same depth that it was growing in the container; a balled-and-burlapped tree so the root flare is right at the soil surface, rolling back or cutting and removing as much of the burlap as possible. Amend the soil with organic matter and a controlled-release fertilizer. Gently firm the enriched soil around the roots, tamping to remove air pockets. Water thoroughly and apply a 2- to 4-inch layer of organic mulch, keeping it a few inches away from the trunk.

TLC Keep soil evenly moist throughout the first two growing seasons, watering deeply to encourage deep root growth. Maintain the mulch. Fertilize annually in spring with a complete fertilizer. Prune only to remove damaged branches or to improve the overall shape.

ABOVE: 'Alexandrina' flowers are purple-pink outside but white inside.
BELOW: Saucer magnolia petals are darker on the outside.

Snowdrop Tree

Halesia carolina

Although not a common garden plant, snowdrop tree (also called Carolina silverbell) is one of our loveliest native flowering trees. In late April and early May, just before the leaves emerge, delicate white or sometimes pale pink flowers hang in clusters from the dark stems. Each flower is an inch or so long and perfectly bell-shaped. The light green, teardrop-shaped fruits that follow have four distinct "wings," and they create a show of their own in fall and early winter as they fade to brown and linger on the branches after the leaves turn yellow and drop.

The flowers and fruit both dangle below the branches, so a snowdrop tree is best viewed from below; plant it in a high spot in the yard or beside a walkway where you will pass beneath its branches. It also shows up well when planted against a background of evergreens. Snowdrop tree grows about 30 feet tall and makes a stunning specimen or a tall addition to a mixed shrub border. It is easy to transplant and to grow, as long as you provide sufficient moisture; it does not tolerate dry conditions.

White flowers of snowdrop tree open just before its leaves emerge in spring.

PEAK SEASON

Midspring for flower; late fall and early winter for fruit

MY FAVORITES

'Rosea' (also listed as *Halesia carolina rosea*) is a pale pink-flowered selection.

RELATED SPECIES

Mountain silver bell (*H. monticola*) grows to 50 feet or more and bears larger flowers than snowdrop tree. 'Arnold Pink' is a selection with rose pink flowers that fade to a very soft pink.

Two-winged silver bell (*H. diptera*) is a little smaller than *H. carolina* and can be grown as a large shrub or small tree. Its flowers are also smaller and its fruit has only two wings (rather than four).

GARDEN COMPANIONS

Snowdrop tree blooms at the same time as redbud, and planted close together, they create a wonderful show. It also adds height to mixed borders, enhancing spring-flowering shrubs, such as azaleas and rhododendron, as well as spring-flowering bulbs and perennials.

The bell-shaped and pendant snowdrop flowers show off best when you can look up at them.

When Purchase container-grown plants; balled-and-burlapped plants can be more difficult to establish. Plant in spring.

Where Plant in full sun or shade in a slightly acid, humus-rich soil that is moist but well drained. Snowdrop trees don't tolerate drought, alkaline soil, or salt spray.

How Dig a hole about two to three times as wide as and equal to the depth of the container. Mix organic matter such as compost or leaf mold and a controlled-release fertilizer into the excavated soil. Set the tree so that it is at the same depth that it was growing in the container. Backfill with the enriched soil, tamping to prevent air pockets, and water thoroughly. Finish by spreading an organic mulch over the rootball and somewhat beyond.

TLC Water regularly for the first two seasons and during dry periods. Grow snowdrop tree with either a single or multiple trunks. To grow with a single trunk, remove all but one main stem when the tree is young. To grow with multiple trunks, select three strong stems and remove the rest. Prune to enhance form if necessary immediately after flowering.

Sourwood
Oxydendrum arboreum

Sourwood leaves turn orange, scarlet, and dark purple in fall, then drop over an extended period. Fingerlike seedpods hang from branch tips.

It's difficult to decide whether the sourwood is more beautiful in summer, when its flowers open, or in fall, when its foliage turns fiery red. But it doesn't really matter—with this tree, you're guaranteed a knockout performance in both seasons.

Native to the eastern United States, the sourwood grows 20 to 25 feet tall with a narrow, oval crown, unless it is crowded by nearby trees, in which case it may reach 50 or 60 feet. The chains of white, urn-shaped flowers open in summer, standing out dramatically against the glossy pea-green leaves. The drooping 10-inch flower stems splay out from the branch tips with a sassy little upturn that is downright endearing. The flowers give way to silvery gray fruit capsules, and when the leaves turn scarlet and burgundy as the days grow short, the chains of capsules are as attractive as the flowers.

With its narrow crown, this tree is a good choice for any yard, large or small, that has appropriate growing conditions. Plant sourwood in moist but well-drained soil at the edge of a woodland, as a lawn specimen, or in a bed with flowering shrubs.

PEAK SEASON

In summer, when flowers open over a period of 3 to 4 weeks, and again in fall, when leaves turn red and fruit capsules turn yellow-green before graying. This is one of the first trees in the region to show fall color.

GARDEN COMPANIONS

The flowers of the sourwood are very similar to those of Japanese pieris and lily-of-the-valley. By growing these plants in close proximity, the garden echoes their color and form through spring and summer. Sourwood is a member of the heath family *(Ericacea)* and combines well with other plants in that family, including azalea, rhododendron, mountain laurel, dog hobble *(Leucothoe)*, and blueberry, which all share similar cultural requirements.

ABOVE: *Fragrant sourwood flowers bloom in midsummer.*
BELOW: *By fall, flowers have given way to silvery gray seedpods*

When Purchase small container-grown plants in spring; larger plants can be difficult to establish.

Where Sourwood grows well in full sun or part shade, although both flowering and fall leaf color are improved in full sun. It grows best in a slightly acidic, humus-rich soil that is moist but well drained, but occasional drought conditions are okay.

How Plant sourwood at the same depth that it was growing in the container in a hole that will accommodate its roots without crowding. Add organic matter and a controlled-release fertilizer to the excavated soil, then backfill around the roots, gently tamping to eliminate air pockets, and water thoroughly. Apply a 2- to 4-inch layer of organic mulch.

TLC Keep the soil evenly moist through the first two growing seasons; after that, water during extended dry periods. Maintain the mulch. Fertilize each spring. Low branches may bend to touch the ground. These may be pruned if desired, but otherwise, little pruning is needed.

Evergreens

We all look forward to seasonal changes in the garden, but without the contrast of the steadfast evergreens, spring- and summer-blooming flowers and colorful fall foliage would not have the same impact. Evergreens change little from one season to the next, providing continuity and definition to the landscape and creating a backdrop for the shifting colors and textures of annuals, perennials, bulbs, and deciduous trees and shrubs. Planted as a screen, evergreens provide year-round privacy, and as foundation plantings, they enhance our homes.

Many evergreens are conifers, although not all conifers are evergreen. *Conifers* are cone-bearing plants, with leaves shaped like needles or scales. Most conifers carry their seeds in woody cones, but some bear them in conelike structures that look more like berries. Junipers, for example, bear clusters of dense, pale blue

"juniper berries"; yews produce fleshy, red berrylike fruit.

While conifer foliage is usually needlelike, the leaves of other evergreens are broad and flat. Cherry laurel (page 150), boxwood (page 152), holly osmanthus (page 156), and inkberry (page 160), grown primarily for their year-

round foliage, are just a few of the broad-leafed evergreens that suit our region. Others, such as mountain laurel, Japanese pieris, and many kinds of azaleas, also bear showy flowers; see Top 10 Flowering Shrubs (page 102) for descriptions of these shrubs.

Evergreens, like deciduous trees and shrubs, do shed their leaves or needles periodically, but instead of dropping them all at once, they shed them continuously, a few at a time. Needles of many conifers serve as an attractive mulch, adding organic matter to the soil as they break down and helping to maintain the low soil pH that most conifers prefer.

RIGHT: *Narrowly upright English yew and Hinoki false cypress.*
OPPOSITE PAGE, TOP: *'Gulftide' holly osmanthus.*
OPPOSITE PAGE, CENTER: *The leaf sprays of American arborvitae.*

COLOR, TEXTURE, AND FORM

A garden of evergreens, with its contrasting hues, textures, and forms, can be the highlight of the winter landscape. Evergreens come in all shades of green, from cool blue-green to a green so dark it's almost black. Some are tinted yellow, gold, silver, or burgundy; others sport lively variegated foliage that combines shades of green with yellow or white. Textures among evergreens run the gamut as well. Most conifers, such as threadleaf Sawara false cypress (page 162), have a fine or medium feathery texture. Some broad-leafed evergreens, like boxwood and inkberry, have small, closely spaced leaves that give them a dense texture, almost like a solid object. Those with larger leaves, like cherry laurel, are coarse textured so provide visual contrast to other plants.

From creeping ground covers to towering trees, all forms of garden plants are found among evergreens. Some are upright and pyramidal—shaped like a Christmas tree; others are narrow, weeping, rounded, or wide-spreading. Even within a single plant species, such as Hollywood juniper (page 158) or white pine (page 164), varieties are available with quite different forms. Careful selection to fit your garden's style and space is critical.

PLANTING

For best results, plant evergreens in early spring, although most can also be planted in fall if you provide plenty of water. Select plants that are suited to the conditions of your site, and be sure to consider their mature size.

Evergreens are sold as balled-and-burlapped or container-grown plants. Plant them as you would a deciduous tree or shrub, digging the hole no deeper than the root ball and two to three times as wide. Space them according to the recommendations on the plant label unless you are planting a hedge, in which case you may want to set the plants a bit closer together.

—RITA PELCZAR

American Arborvitae
Thuja occidentalis

American arborvitae, a stately evergreen conifer, is native to our region. It produces feathery, flat sprays of foliage that is soft to the touch and ranges in color from yellow green to a bright medium green. Older specimens develop a shaggy trunk that can be quite attractive. There are many excellent selections that vary in shape, including spheres, cones, slender columns, and stout pyramids, all in a range of sizes. By selecting the variety with the shape and size you ultimately want, you can save yourself a lot of time pruning.

But if pruning and shaping is your cup of tea, American arborvitae can be shaped into a formal or informal hedge. Taller varieties make attractive screens, and smaller selections are useful as foundation plants or in mixed evergreen plantings. When pruning an American arborvitae hedge, be sure to keep it wider at the base than at the top so that all parts are exposed to sun; otherwise, the shaded lower branches will lose foliage and become sparse.

With its gold-tinged leaves, this arborvitae provides both a vertical accent and all-seasons color at the edge of a border.

When Plant balled-and-burlapped or container-grown plants in spring or fall.

Where Grow American arborvitae in full sun or very light shade. It is quite adaptable to most well-drained soils, whether moist or dry, or slightly acidic to slightly alkaline. Some arborvitae tend to turn yellowish brown in winter. To minimize this, choose locations where the plants will be protected from strong winter winds.

How American arborvitae is easily transplanted. Plant at the same depth that it was growing in the container, in a hole deep and wide enough to accommodate the roots without crowding. Set balled-and-burlapped plants so that the root flares are right at the soil surface, cutting and removing as much of the burlap and wire as possible without injuring the roots. Backfill and gently firm the soil around the roots to remove air pockets. Water thoroughly after planting.

TLC Water during dry spells for the first 2 years, soaking deeply to encourage root growth. Prune just after new growth has emerged in spring. Prune formal hedges again later in the season, but not after mid-August.

RIGHT: *Leaves of 'Sunkist' are bright yellow.*
BELOW: *A hedge of American arborvitae.*

PEAK SEASON

Year-round

MY FAVORITES

'Globosa' is a dwarf with a rounded form that reaches 3 feet tall and wide; it has bright green foliage.

'Golden Globe' is similar in size and shape to 'Globosa' but has yellow-gold foliage.

'Hetz Wintergreen' is a tall, narrow selection that grows to 30 feet.

'Rheingold' has bright gold foliage. It develops a conical shape and grows 3 to 6 feet tall.

'Smaragd' (or 'Emerald') grows 10 to 15 feet tall and forms a dense, narrow cone. It retains its bright green color throughout winter.

'Sunkist' grows 2 to 3 feet tall in a conical shape. Flattened sprays of foliage are orange-yellow in winter and lemon-yellow in spring.

GARDEN COMPANIONS

American arborvitae make fine backdrops for perennials like garden phlox, peony, chrysanthemum, and astilbe. Columnar arborvitaes provide a vertical accent for mixed beds, combining well with dwarf evergreens, shrub roses, and mounding perennials such as catmint *(Nepeta)* and hardy geranium. Dwarf types work well in mixed evergreen gardens or as foundation plantings.

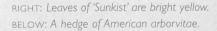

Cherry Laurel, English Laurel
Prunus laurocerasus

Cherry laurel, a native of Europe and Asia, is perfectly adapted to the Mid-Atlantic climate. It grows in sun or shade to 15 to 30 feet tall and can be pruned to the height you desire. In midspring, it produces clusters of tiny, fragrant white flowers that are followed by purple-black berries. But cherry laurel (also called English laurel) is primarily grown for its tough, glossy, dark green foliage. It makes a stunning dense hedge or privacy screen and provides a dark green background for colorful annuals or perennials planted nearby. Smaller types are well suited to foundation plantings.

Culture of cherry laurel is very simple. It needs little more than reasonably good drainage, thriving even on a stingy water budget (though regular moisture and fertilizer will speed growth). These plants are not bothered by salt-laden air, so cherry laurel is a good choice for planting near the coast.

'Otto Luyken' cherry laurel is the right size for smaller gardens.

Blooming 'Otto Luyken' grows behind a low brick wall.

PEAK SEASON

Flowers in spring; foliage year-round

MY FAVORITES

'Otto Luyken' grows 4 feet tall and nearly twice as wide. The dark green leaves are about 4 inches long. It produces abundant flowers, even in dense shade.

'Rotundifolia' grows to 15 feet tall and makes an excellent tall hedge.

'Schipkaensis', also known as the schipka laurel, tolerates colder weather than other selections. It grows 4 to 5 feet tall with a wider spread. Zones 31, 32, 34.

RELATED SPECIES

Carolina cherry laurel (Prunus caroliniana) has an upright habit and can grow to 30 feet or more. Use it as a hedge or tall screen. Zone 31.

GARDEN COMPANIONS

Cherry laurel contributes year-round greenery to woodland gardens, combining well with shade-loving perennials such as hosta, pulmonaria, and heuchera. In sunny mixed beds, it provides a dark green foil for colorful annuals or perennials. It can be planted alone as a hedge or with other evergreen shrubs as a foundation planting. Cherry laurels are vigorous plants, so don't plant anything too close to them.

When Plant balled-and-burlapped or container-grown plants in spring or fall.

Where Grow in well-drained soil, in sun or shade. In warmer areas, afternoon shade is best. Flowers and fruit can create a mess when they fall, so set cherry laurel well away from sidewalks or paved walkways.

How Plant cherry laurel at the same depth that it was growing in the container, in a hole deep and wide enough to accommodate the roots without crowding. Set balled-and-burlapped plants so that the root flares are right at the soil surface, cutting and removing as much of the burlap and wire as possible without injuring the roots. Backfill, gently firming the soil around the roots to remove air pockets. Water thoroughly.

TLC Training cherry laurel as a hedge is very popular, but maintaining it in a tight and formal shape is not advised. Its leaves are relatively large, so shearing usually results in a layer of brown-edged, ragged foliage. A better pruning technique is to reach inside the plant to make selective cuts, a method that is only suitable for maintaining an informal shape. Note: The leaves, stems, and berries of this shrub are toxic.

151

Common Boxwood
Buxus sempervirens

The natural form of 'Suffruticosa' common boxwood hedge suggests clouds.

Common boxwoods are a staple of colonial-style gardens, and where they grow well, they make beautiful foundation shrubs, edgings, or hedges for both formal and informal landscapes. They are relatively slow growing, with a dense, billowy habit and small, oval, dark green leaves that are, depending on your sense of smell, pleasantly pungent or nasty smelling. I happen to like their unmistakable scent. The species form grows 15 to 20 feet tall and wide, but dwarf varieties like 'Vadar Valley' grow only 2 to 3 feet tall and there are many intermediate-sized varieties as well.

Common boxwood thrives in loamy, well drained soil, and transplants with unusual success. Avoid planting in heavy clay soils and dry locations—plants will be weak and disease prone. They are also subject to their share of pests, including boxwood psyllid and leaf miners. But they're popular and ubiquitous for good reasons. Provide a suitable site and a bit of protection from drying winds in winter, and common boxwood will reward you with an elegance that is hard to match.

When Plant balled-and-burlapped or container-grown plants in spring or fall.

Where Plant in sun or light shade in a neutral or slightly alkaline soil that's moist but well drained. Avoid heavy clay soil. Place plants where they will be protected from drying winter winds.

How Plant common boxwood at the same depth that it was growing in the container, in a hole deep and wide enough to accommodate the roots without crowding. Set balled-and-burlapped plants so that the root flares are right at the soil surface, cutting and removing as much of the burlap and wire as possible without injuring the roots. Backfill, gently firming soil around roots to remove air pockets. Water thoroughly and apply a 2- to 4-inch layer of organic mulch. Plants in full sun may need some shading until they are established.

TLC Water regularly for the first 2 years, and during dry periods thereafter. Maintain the mulch and don't cultivate under the shrub because the shallow surface roots will be damaged. Prune in late winter; the new growth stimulated by late-summer or fall pruning is very susceptible to winter damage. To renew old plants, cut back heavily in late winter. New growth will emerge from exposed stems in spring.

LEFT: *'Graham Blandy' is a uniquely narrow and upright form of boxwood.*
RIGHT: *Common boxwood is a classic foundation shrub.*

PEAK SEASON
Year-round

MY FAVORITES
'Graham Blandy' looks like an exclamation point; after 20 years of growth it reaches 9 feet tall but only 18 inches wide.

'Handsworthiensis' is useful as a tall, dense hedge, reaching 15 to 20 feet in height.

'Newport Blue' is a low-growing selection with blue-green foliage.

'Suffruticosa' (also known as English boxwood) is an excellent choice for a low-growing hedge or edging plant. It grows very slowly, ultimately reaching about 4 to 7 feet tall and more, but it can be clipped and maintained at a much lower height.

'Vadar Valley' grows 2 to 3 feet tall and almost twice as wide.

GARDEN COMPANIONS
As a hedge, common boxwood provides a billowy green background for colorful perennials. Attractive foreground companions include campanula, columbine, astilbe, chrysanthemum, hardy geranium, and Japanese anemone. Boxwoods are also a traditional edging choice for formal rose and herb gardens.

Foster's Holly

Ilex × attenuata 'Foster's #2'

O f the many species and varieties of holly that are outstanding landscape plants in our region, the group of hybrids known as Foster's holly are some of the best. The parents of Foster's holly are the American holly *(Ilex opaca)* and the dahoon holly *(I. cassine)*, both of which are native to the eastern United States. Of the many available cultivars, 'Foster's #2' is the most cold-hardy and my favorite.

Topping out at 35 feet, 'Foster's #2' has a neat, narrow pyramidal shape that makes it very useful for tight spaces or for planting against buildings. It produces tidy, glossy green leaves that contrast dramatically with the deep red berries, which are borne in abundance and persist well into winter. 'Foster's #2' is an all-female selection, so each plant bears fruit, providing food for a variety of wildlife.

Planted near the corner of a house or between windows, 'Foster's #2' adds height to a foundation planting without occupying too much ground space. Planted in the open, it becomes a specimen with year-round appeal.

A pair of 'Foster's #2' hollies form perfect narrow pyramids that screen the view into the neighboring yard.

PEAK SEASON

Fall and winter for berries; year-round for foliage

RELATED CULTIVARS

'Longwood Gold' has dark green leaves and bright yellow-gold fruit.

'Sunny Foster' has variegated leaves with bright yellow markings. The yellow color is intense in full sun, but fades to green in shade. It adds a splash of bright color to a grouping of dark evergreens.

RELATED SPECIES

American holly (*Ilex opaca*) grows slowly to 40 to 50 feet tall with a broadly pyramidal shape. It has spiny, dull or glossy dark green leaves and bright red fruit. There are hundreds of named varieties. Zones 31, 32, 34, 35.

GARDEN COMPANIONS

Foster's holly adds a tall accent to foundation plantings, providing a pleasing contrast to shorter plants with mounding, rounded, or irregular forms. It combines well in mixed evergreen plantings with boxwood, spreading English yew (*Taxus baccata* 'Repandens'), arborvitae (*Thuja occidentalis* 'Smaragd'), dwarf selections of false cypress (*Chamaecyparis*), and Japanese pieris.

Shiny evergreen leaves of Foster's holly are accented in fall and into winter by red berries.

When Plant balled-and-burlapped or container-grown plants in early spring.

Where Plant in rich, slightly acid soil that is moist but well drained. Although Foster's holly adapts to partial shade, plants will be denser and berry production greater in full sun. Choose a site that's protected from drying winter winds.

How Plant at the same depth that the plant was growing in the container or at the nursery in a hole that is twice as wide as the root ball and equal to its depth. Backfill, tamping gently to eliminate air pockets. Water thoroughly. Apply a 2- to 4-inch layer of organic mulch to prevent weeds and to keep the soil cool and moist.

TLC Maintain the mulch and keep the soil evenly moist from spring through fall for the first two growing seasons. Fertilize each spring with a complete fertilizer for acid-loving plants. Prune in winter to remove dead or damaged branches or any overly exuberant growth. Shearing can mangle the leaves, so selective pruning is best to enhance desired shape.

Holly Osmanthus, False Holly
Osmanthus heterophyllus

The trick to determining whether a plant is a true holly or a holly look-alike is to observe the arrangement of its leaves. On true hollies, leaves occur alternately along the stems, whereas the leaves of most holly look-alikes, such as holly osmanthus, occur directly opposite each other along the stem. That said, this shrub sure resembles a holly! It usually grows about 8 feet tall, with a rounded or oval form, although taller and shorter varieties are also available. Its spiny leaves are usually dark green on the upper surface and yellow-green on the undersides. As the plants age, they begin to produce leaves with a single terminal spine. In fall, holly osmanthus bears clusters of tiny white flowers hidden beneath the foliage; you could easily miss them if it weren't for their heady fragrance.

Holly osmanthus makes a dense, year-round hedge or screen. Grow it near a walkway so that its sweet fragrance will be appreciated by all who pass by. Individual plants, particularly variegated selections such as 'Aureomarginatus' and 'Goshiki', make effective formal specimens.

This variety, 'Gulftide', is somewhat more cold hardy than the species.

PEAK SEASON

Fall for fragrant blooms; year-round for foliage

MY FAVORITES

'Aureomarginatus' has leaves with dark green centers and bright yellow margins.

'Goshiki' is a compact form that grows 3 to 4 feet tall with a spread of 3 to 5 feet. Its new leaves emerge pink in spring, maturing to green with creamy yellow splotches.

'Gulftide' grows 10 to 15 feet tall and has very glossy green leaves.

'Ogon' has spiny, green-gold leaves and grows 3½ feet tall.

'Purpureus' has leaves that emerge a dark purple-black and mature to green with a purple tint.

'Rotundifolius' grows 10 feet tall and wide and bears spineless leaves.

GARDEN COMPANIONS

A solid planting of holly osmanthus makes a stunning hedge or screen. Add individual plants to a mixed evergreen garden or foundation planting for textural interest; variegated selections add a dramatic accent.

When Plant balled-and-burlapped or container-grown plants in early spring or fall.

Where Plant in rich soil that is moist but well drained. Choose a site in full sun or partial shade where plants are protected from drying winter winds.

How Plant at the same depth that the plant was growing in the container or at the nursery in a hole that accommodates the root ball without crowding. Backfill, tamping gently to eliminate air pockets. Water thoroughly, and apply a 2- to 4-inch layer of organic mulch to prevent weeds and to keep the soil cool and moist.

TOP: *Dark green leaves of 'Rotundifolius' lack the spines typical of most varieties.* CENTER: *Leaves of 'Ogon' are bright gold in spring but gradually fade to green-gold.* BOTTOM: *'Goshiki' leaves emerge all pink in spring but become green with cream splotches by midsummer.*

TLC Keep soil evenly moist from spring through fall for the first two growing seasons. Once established, holly osmanthus is fairly drought tolerant. Fertilize each spring with a complete fertilizer. Prune in winter to remove dead or damaged branches. Holly osmanthus can be sheared for a more formal look, but stop by mid-August to avoid winter damage to new growth, which may not have time to harden before cold weather sets in.

Hollywood Juniper
Juniperus chinensis 'Kaizuka' ('Torulosa')

Branches of Hollywood juniper naturally develop the twisted, open form typical of a bonsai tree.

The slight twist to its branches gives the Hollywood juniper an exotic, Asian look, which makes sense because it is a variety of Chinese juniper, native to China, Mongolia, and Japan. It has an asymmetrical upright growth habit and can be grown as a large shrub or small tree (it can reach 30 feet tall but is usually half that), so is generally used as a specimen or an accent. I have Hollywood junipers on both sides of my garage, where they add architectural interest and provide tall accents for two different beds. By removing the lower branches and selectively thinning upper ones, I have exposed the attractively gnarled trunks, with their shaggy reddish brown bark. The scalelike needles are bright green. An all-female variety, Hollywood juniper bears rounded, blue-green cones.

There are many other varieties of Chinese juniper worth growing, from low-spreading ground covers to tall, upright, pyramidal trees, and some of my favorites among these are also listed at right.

PEAK SEASON
Year-round

MY FAVORITES
Variegated Hollywood juniper (*Juniperus chinensis* 'Kaizuka Variegata') has the same spiraling branches but the vivid green foliage is variegated with gold. Height and width is the same as for the all green form, about 15 feet high and about 10 feet wide.

RELATED CULTIVARS
'Blue Point' juniper (*Juniperus chinensis* 'Blue Point') has a broadly columnar shape and grows to 8 feet tall. Its needles are blue-green.

'Gold Coast juniper (*J. c.* 'Gold Coast') has rich golden yellow foliage. It is compact, growing 4 feet tall with a slightly greater spread.

Pfitzer juniper (*J. c.* 'Pfitzeriana') is a wide-spreading shrub (5 to 6 feet tall and up to 20 feet wide). 'Pfitzeriana Compacta' grows 2 feet tall and 4 to 6 feet wide.

GARDEN COMPANIONS
Hollywood juniper provides a tall accent to beds of mixed perennials and other shrubs. It can be under-planted with ground covers like barrenwort (*Epimedium*) or creeping thyme, or with low-growing perennials like hardy geranium, catmint (*Nepeta*), or lamb's ears (*Stachys byzantina*).

When Plant balled-and-burlapped or container-grown plants as early as you can work the ground in spring. Hollywood juniper can also be planted in fall if you provide ample water.

Where Like most junipers, the Hollywood juniper grows best in full sun in a light, sandy soil, but it is adaptable to light shade and most soils as long as they are not constantly wet. Once established, junipers tolerate drought fairly well. Give the tree plenty of space to develop to its full size.

How Plant at the same depth that the plant was growing in the container or at the nursery in a hole deep and wide enough to accommodate its roots without crowding. Backfill the hole, gently firming the soil around the roots to eliminate air pockets, and water thoroughly. Provide a 2- to 4-inch layer of organic mulch to help prevent weeds.

ABOVE: *A close-up of a Hollywood juniper branch shows its green leaves and berries.*
BELOW: *'Gold Coast' juniper is a compact, low-growing shrub with arching branches.*

TLC Maintain the mulch, and water the plants well until they are established, then keep them on the dry side. Apply a complete fertilizer each spring. Selectively prune in spring to enhance the twisted, asymmetrical shape and to expose the gnarled branches and shaggy bark.

Inkberry

Ilex glabra

Some plants assume center stage in the landscape; others are better suited to the no-less-critical supporting roles. Inkberry, a shrub native to the eastern United States, is a real garden workhorse that excels in a supporting role. Adaptable and trouble free, it provides definition to garden spaces, and when planted as either a hedge or foundation plant, it creates a dense, dark green backdrop for colorful annuals and perennials.

Actually a type of holly, inkberry serves much the same function as boxwood, but is easier to grow. Use it for a mass planting; it requires no pruning and holds soil against erosion. Given room, it will produce suckers, spreading to form colonies. The species grows 6 feet tall and slightly wider, but several smaller and more compact selections are available. All produce small, oblong leaves that are quite tidy; they are dark green on top with lighter undersides and in winter, they usually develop a bronze cast. Female plants usually produce shiny black fruit, although white-fruited varieties are available.

Hardy and versatile inkberry is an ideal shrub to use for a low- to medium-height hedge.

PEAK SEASON
Year-round

MY FAVORITES

'Compacta' is a dwarf female variety that grows 4 to 6 feet tall with a compact, oval shape.

'Nordic' grows only 3 to 4 feet tall and wide; it has a compact, rounded habit.

'Shamrock' is a slow-growing variety that tops out at 5 feet tall with a similar spread. In spring, its new growth is bright green, which stands out attractively against the older dark green foliage.

'Viridis' has a distinctly pyramidal shape and grows 3 to 6 feet tall.

GARDEN COMPANIONS

Inkberry provides a dark green foil for colorful annuals and perennials in mixed beds, either in sun or shade. Compact selections are good choices for foundation plantings, where they combine well with other evergreens that have contrasting textures, such as the mugho pine, dwarf false cypress (Chamaecyparis), and low-growing junipers. The foliage of these conifers varies in color from yellow-green to blue-green, providing a subtle yet lovely contrast to the dark foliage of inkberry.

This close-up of inkberry leaves also shows the tiny white-petaled flowers.

When Plant balled-and-burlapped or container-grown plants in early spring.

Where Although inkberry will adapt to most soils, it grows best in soil that is moist but well drained. Inkberry thrives in full sun or moderate shade.

How Plant at the same depth that the plant was growing in the container or at the nursery in a hole that is twice as wide as the root ball and equal to its depth. Backfill, tamping gently to eliminate air pockets. Water thoroughly. Apply a 2- to 4-inch layer of organic mulch to prevent weeds and to keep soil cool and moist.

TLC Inkberry is very easy to grow, and once established, requires minimal care. Maintain the mulch and keep soil evenly moist from spring through fall for the first two growing seasons. Prune in winter to remove dead or damaged branches. Inkberry can be sheared for a more formal look, but stop pruning by mid-August to avoid winter damage to new growth, which may not have time to harden before cold weather sets in.

Sawara False Cypress

Chamaecyparis pisifera 'Filifera'

The needles of the Sawara false cypress, are held tightly along stringy "threadleaf" branchlets that seem to erupt from the center of the plant and droop downward, giving the entire plant the look of an upside-down mop. This shrub provides great textural contrast in almost any sunny garden, where its shaggy, almost weeping habit is sure to attract notice. The bark is also ornamental; it is reddish brown and peels off in strips.

In most gardens, this shrub, which is native to Japan, grows to about 8 feet tall and nearly as wide, although it is capable of becoming a much larger tree, given time and adequate space. It is a good choice for a specimen or an accent plant. Pruning is rarely necessary.

When Plant balled-and-burlapped or container-grown plants in early spring as soon as the soil can be worked.

Where Plant in slightly acid soil that is moist but well drained. Threadleaf Sawara false cypress grows best in full sun but will tolerate some shade, although yellow selections may not be as colorful. Protect from drying winds.

How Plant at the same depth that the plant was growing in the container or at the nursery in a hole that is twice as wide as the root ball and equal to its depth. Backfill, tamping gently to eliminate air pockets. Water thoroughly. Maintain a 2- to 4-inch layer of organic mulch while plants are young to prevent weeds and to keep soil cool and moist.

TLC Keep soil evenly moist from spring through fall for the first two growing seasons. Fertilize each spring with a complete fertilizer. As this shrub matures, some of its wide-spreading branches reach the ground, effectively providing their own mulch. Other than removing dead or damaged branches, pruning is rarely necessary.

ABOVE: 'Boulevard' has silvery blue needles and grows to 10 feet tall. BELOW: 'Filifera Aurea' is a yellow-needled form of Sawara false cypress.

PEAK SEASON

Year-round. False cypress looks particularly attractive with a dusting of snow on its weeping branches.

RELATED CULTIVARS

'Boulevard' (or 'Cyano-Viridis') has silvery blue-green needles. It grows to 10 feet high and wide.

'Filifera Aurea' (or 'Gold Thread') is a large fine-textured shrub with needles and threadlike branchlets.

'Mops' has threadlike branchlets. It typically grows to 2 feet tall, but will reach 4 feet in good soil with regular moisture. 'Golden Mops' is similar but with more yellow color.

RELATED SPECIES

Dwarf Hinoki false cypress (*Chamaecyparis obtusa* 'Nana Gracilis') has very dark green foliage arranged in graceful fans. A very slow grower, it ultimately reaches 6 feet tall and 3 to 4 feet wide. Zones 32, 34, 36.

GARDEN COMPANIONS

Sawara false cypress makes an outstanding specimen or accent in a bed of mixed evergreens.

OPPOSITE PAGE: 'Mops' threadleaf Sawara false cypress grows into a golden mound of drooping branches from which long, threadlike leaves dangle.

White Pine

Pinus strobus

'Pendula', a weeping form of the normally tall white pine, serves well as a border specimen.

The white pine is the tallest conifer that is native to the eastern United States, with the potential of growing a whopping 220 feet tall. Mature specimens were harvested in great quantities during the eighteenth century—largely to become masts for ships of the British Navy—so you will rarely find one today that exceeds 90 feet. But even at that height, a white pine is a spectacular sight. These are straight-trunked trees with layered whorls of horizontal branches. Their needles are long, soft, and gray-green. Young trees have a symmetrical, pyramidal shape, which may become more irregular with age.

Given its potential size, the white pine is a good choice for growing in a woodland, or in a very large garden or park. But in home gardens of typical dimensions varieties, such as those listed on the next page, with compact, weeping, or columnar habits make lovely specimens.

PEAK SEASON

Year-round

MY FAVORITES

'Fastigiata' has a narrow, upright habit with sharply ascending branches. It grows 40 to 70 feet tall and only 15 to 20 feet wide.

'Pendula' has a distinctly weeping habit. A young plant needs support and looks awkward, but it will mature into a dramatic garden specimen with long branches that reach to the ground. Mature height is about 12 feet, but width is nearly 30 feet.

RELATED SPECIES

Japanese black pine (Pinus thunbergii) develops an irregular, appealingly gnarled habit that can be enhanced with judicious pruning. It is useful as a specimen or an anchor for a mixed bed or rock garden. All zones.

Mugho pine (P. mugho) usually grows 4 to 10 feet tall, although its size is variable, and has an irregularly rounded shape. The variety 'Mops' grows about 3 feet tall with a slightly greater spread. Zones 32, 34, 35.

GARDEN COMPANIONS

In a woodland garden, the needles of white pines provide an ideal mulch for acid-loving understory plants like azalea, Japanese pieris, and mountain laurel.

When Plant balled-and-burlapped or container-grown plants in early spring as soon as the ground can be worked. Fall planting can also be successful if you provide plenty of water.

Where Pines grow best in full sun in well-drained, slightly acidic soil. Most are sensitive to salt damage from roadways. White pine can be used as a windbreak or a background planting. Dwarf and weeping varieties are useful as accents or specimens.

How Plant at the same depth that the plant was growing in the container, in a hole deep and wide enough to accommodate the roots without crowding. Plant a balled-and-burlapped tree so that the root flare is right at the soil surface, rolling back, cutting, and removing as much of the burlap and wire as possible without injuring the roots. Firm soil around the roots and water thoroughly, making sure to eliminate air pockets. Apply a starter fertilizer solution around the base of the plant, diluted according to the product's instructions. Water deeply and thoroughly.

TLC Keep the soil evenly moist from spring until the ground freezes in fall for the first 2 years, watering deeply to encourage deep root growth. To encourage dense top growth, train the trees when they are young. Prune them annually in early summer while they're small and still accessible, cutting back the upward-growing new growth (called "candles") by half.

An white pine covered with fresh snow becomes a delicate winter sculpture.

Yew

Taxus

Yews are survivors. Unlike many conifers, they grow equally well in sun or shade, and they don't seem the least bit bothered by air pollution. Their dense foliage, made up of tightly packed needles that are dark green above and lighter beneath, gives them a solid, formal look. They're often sheared as hedges and are among the very best plants for that purpose, but left to grow into their natural shape, they make handsome trees or shrubs. Attractive red berry-like fruits appear on female trees in late summer and fall. (Except for the fleshy cups that surround the hard seeds, all parts of a yew plant are poisonous.)

To my mind, there is no more elegant foundation shrub than the spreading English yew (*Taxus baccata* 'Repandens'), and it makes a stunning year-round specimen. It grows well in shade, so it also can be a lovely addition to a woodland garden. New growth emerges apple green, contrasting boldly with the older black-green needles. The fleshy, scarlet fruit, borne on female plants, provides an additional color-ful contrast. Although slow grow-ing, it ultimately reaches 4 feet tall and spreads 12 to 15 feet wide.

Yews work well as screening plants, individual specimens, or as sentinels flanking a driveway. But be sure to give them plenty of room to reach their mature height and spread.

English yew is available in many cultivars, including this 4-foot-tall wide-spreading form with golden leaves, 'Repandens Aurea'.

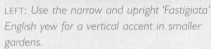

PEAK SEASON

Year-round

MY FAVORITES

English yew *(Taxus baccata)* grows to 25 feet tall and 15 feet wide, with dark needles. 'Aurea' has new foliage that is golden yellow from spring to fall, then turns green. 'Fastigiata', or 'Stricta' grows 20 to 30 feet tall. 'Repandens' and 'Repandens Aurea' spread to 12 to 15 feet, but are only 4 feet tall. Zone 32.

The Japanese yew *(T. cuspidata)* is a large shrub or small tree with an irregular, upright habit. The variety 'Capitata' grows 25 to 40 feet tall with a pyramidal form. 'Densa' is a slow-growing variety that reaches 4 feet in height. Zones 32, 34, 35, 36.

T. × media is often grown as a hedge. The variety 'Hicksii' forms a tall shrub or small multistemmed tree that is narrow toward the bottom and arches outward at the top. 'Wardii' is an all-female selection with a flat-topped, wide-spreading habit. Zones 32, 34, 35, 36.

GARDEN COMPANIONS

The spreading English yew's black-green needles provide a pleasing contrast to other evergreens with light green, blue-green, yellow-green, or variegated foliage. It also provides a lovely background for colorful perennials or bulbs.

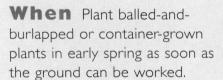

LEFT: *Use the narrow and upright 'Fastigiata' English yew for a vertical accent in smaller gardens.*
RIGHT: *Hardier Japanese yew is a good evergreen in colder regions.*

When Plant balled-and-burlapped or container-grown plants in early spring as soon as the ground can be worked.

Where Plant in full sun to moderate shade in moist soil. Good drainage is essential: poor drainage is lethal to any yew. Choose a site where the plant will be protected from drying winter winds. Provide plenty of room for their mature height and spread.

How Plant at the same depth that the plant was growing in the container or at the nursery, in a hole that is twice as wide as the root ball and equal to its depth. Backfill, tamping gently to eliminate air pockets. Water thoroughly. Maintain a 2- to 4-inch layer of organic mulch to prevent weeds and to keep the soil cool and moist.

TLC Keep soil evenly moist from spring through fall for the first two growing seasons. Fertilize each spring with a complete fertilizer. Little pruning is necessary, other than to remove dead or damaged branches. Yews are a favorite food of foraging deer, so plants may need protection.

Shade Trees

Nothing adds as much dignity and grace to a home landscape as a shade tree. Without one, a house looks naked and exposed. Every yard needs at least one tall, leafy tree growing in the spot where it can do the most good—casting cooling shade over the patio or in through the windows in a part of the house that would otherwise bake in the hot summer sun. If you don't already have such a tree, you can plant one to improve the microclimate around your home and beautify your yard at the same time.

Shade trees are the largest and longest-lived elements of a home landscape. When you plant a shade tree, you plant for future generations as well as for yourself—all the more reason to choose carefully and select a tree that will have enduring appeal.

Trees are miracles of nature that grow to gigantic proportions, though it doesn't seem that way when you first plant them. When you look at the small whip you have placed in the ground, you may think that having a lofty shade tree is decades away.

But trees grow faster than children. Soon the tree you plant will add distinction to your yard.

In addition to their grace and beauty, there are practical reasons for planting a shade tree. As trees grow taller, they cast more shade, something that can significantly alter the temperature in and around your home. Planting a shade tree is a "simple and effective way" to cool the interior of a home or building, thus reducing the amount of air conditioning needed, according to the Environmental Protection Agency.

A tree-shaded wall can be significantly cooler than an unshaded surface at peak surface temperature. Trees also cool the air around them by absorbing water through their roots, drawing it up into and through the leaves where it evaporates. Called *evapotranspiration*, this process can reduce air temperature by as much as nine degrees. Shade trees also improve air quality and absorb atmospheric carbon dioxide, while their roots help decrease storm-water runoff.

To receive the most benefit from your shade tree, place it strategically. Plant a deciduous shade tree far enough away from a house wall, sidewalk, foundation, or driveway to avoid crowding later on, and be sure to keep it at least 10 feet away from underground utilities and safely distant from overhead wires.

Equally important, for protection from the summer sun, make sure the tree is on the west, southwest, southeast, or east side of the building. Trees planted directly to the south will not provide as much protection because the summer sun stays high in the sky at midday.

—CAROLE OTTESEN

Beech
Fagus

B eech trees are true aristocrats of the tree world. They grow slowly and gracefully to majestic proportions, maturing at 50 to 80 feet in height and up to 50 feet in width. The native American beech *(Fagus grandiflora),* a familiar resident of Mid-Atlantic woodlands, is instantly identifiable in winter by its lacy branching pattern, pointed buds, and smooth, gray buttressed trunk. In summer, the neatly serrated leaves are an attractive green. In fall, the foliage turns shades that vary from golden orange to caramel. On young trees, burnt-orange leaves remain on the branches throughout the winter.

Where there's space, purple-leaved copper beech makes a stunning specimen tree.

Like its American relative, the European copper beech *(F. sylvatica)* grows tall and broad, reaching 50 feet tall by about 40 feet in width at maturity. It has dark, toothed, elliptical leaves that range from dark copper to purple. The copper beech has a rounded spreading crown and smooth gray bark, and it often branches close to the ground. It is one of many attractive forms that have been developed from the common green European beech.

When Plant beeches in early spring as soon as they are available and before they are in leaf.

Where A beech is a large tree, so give careful consideration to the place where it will grow. Avoid sites that are under overhead wires or too close to sidewalks. Choose a place in full sun with acidic soil that is moist but well drained.

How Dig a hole that is roughly twice as wide and as deep as the tree's root ball. Mound some soil in the center so the top of the root ball is even with or slightly above the soil around it. Carefully loosen roots of container-grown plants so they do not strangle the root ball; cut off any roots that appear to encircle the root ball. The idea is to encourage the roots to grow outward into the surrounding soil where they will find nourishment and anchor the tree.

TLC Water during dry or hot spells until the beech is very well established, after which time you can wean it and water only during extreme droughts. Most plants struggle under a big beech, so mulch beneath the tree instead to provide a neat look and to conserve moisture. Avoid, however, a mulch "volcano"—a mound of too much mulch that touches the trunk. Prune away crossing, dead, or damaged branches to establish an attractive shape and growth habit.

The frosted leaves of European copper beech persist long after most leaves fall.

PEAK SEASON

In summer, when the beeches are in full leaf, they cast deep, cooling shade. Spring, when the leaves emerge a coppery purple, is another lovely time for the copper beech, and fall is a third peak season for the American beech, when its green leaves turn to shades of gold and burnt orange.

MY FAVORITES

American beech, *Fagus grandiflora,* is an absolutely splendid, elegant tree that gets better and better as it ages. A well-grown specimen is riveting both for people and for the wildlife that visit it for its nuts. 'Purple Fountain' is a weeping form with dark purple leaves that are green on the undersides. It remains narrow in overall shape while reaching 30 to 50 feet in height.

European copper beech, *F. sylvatica* 'Riversii', is a classic. First selected and propagated in 1880, it is still the most outstanding form for the rich, dark, purple-maroon color of its leaves and the wine red of its new shoots.

GARDEN COMPANIONS

Beeches' great size make them the perfect backdrop for smaller trees such as eastern redbud (*Cercis canadensis*) and dogwood (*Cornus*).

Honey Locust

Gleditsia triacanthos inermis

Honey locust is a North American native tree that is found in the wild from southern Ontario south to Florida. It grows to about 75 feet tall and 30 feet wide. But the wild form of honey locust has two drawbacks: it has long thorns on the branches and bark that make it tough to handle and to be around, and it produces long seedpods that are messy. Fortunately, many cultivated forms have been developed that are splendid additions to a home landscape. Not only are these forms thornless and virtually podless, but their leaves often sport unusual colors as well.

For gardens, choose one of the refined honey locusts (they often have the term "inermis" or "thornless" in their names), and you'll have a fine-looking, fast-growing, spreading tree with a delicate, fernlike texture that is perfect over a patio. Honey locust's airy branches and small leaves cast dappled shade. In autumn when the leaves fall, their small size makes cleanup an easy chore.

This tree is the perfect choice to shade a wall or window on the southwestern side of a house in summer and, with its open branching structure, it will allow the winter sun to warm the house.

The chartreuse leaves of 'Sunburst' honey locust contrast with magenta azaleas.

PEAK SEASON
Spring and fall

MY FAVORITES
'Rubylace' is virtually podless, with new leaves that emerge a burgundy color before deepening to bronze-green, a display of color that makes this tree a spectacle in spring. All summer long, new burgundy leaves appear, contrasting attractively with older green foliage.

'Sunburst' grows 30 to 40 feet tall and has small, elegant leaves and few, if any, seedpods. New leaves emerge a bright chartreuse, making the tree a standout in spring. Later, the bright new leaves contrast with older foliage that has darkened to this tree's summer green.

GARDEN COMPANIONS
Honey locusts cast light shade, so a lawn or ground cover will grow beneath them. A circle of dark green, grasslike dwarf mondo grass (*Ophiopogon japonicus* 'Nana' or 'Kyoto') as a ground cover around the tree is spectacular and can be underplanted with crocuses or miniature daffodils. Japanese spurge (*Pachysandra terminalis*) or Japanese forest grass (*Hakonechloa*) are other good choices for ground covers.

Just before dropping in fall, the leaves of honey locust turn golden.

When Plant honey locusts in late winter or early spring so that they can take root during the cool, moist days of spring.

Where Plant honey locusts in sun and well-drained soil. Once well established, honey locust will stand up to the stresses of urban sites such as parking strips. It is tolerant of poor and alkaline soils, heat, drought, and salt spray. It is also resistant to gypsy moths.

How Dig a hole that is roughly twice as wide and as deep as the tree's root ball. Loosen and mound some of the soil in the center to support the tree so that it rises slightly above the depth that it was growing in its container or as a balled-and-burlapped tree. Fill in the hole, firming the soil and watering well. Make sure the trunk is standing straight; stake it if necessary.

TLC Water during dry spells for the first year, during extended droughts, and renew mulch each spring. Prune only to remove crossing or ill-placed branches or dead wood. With just a little care at the outset, a honey locust will grow swiftly into a graceful and beautiful shade tree.

Japanese Pagoda Tree
Sophora japonica

In midsummer a Japanese pagoda tree offers both shade and showy blossoms.

Actually from China, not Japan, Japanese pagoda tree was first imported to Europe nearly three centuries ago. It has been cherished there and on several continents ever since.

This is hardly surprising because the pagoda tree is the perfect image of what a tree should be. It is utterly symmetrical, with a graceful rounded crown and wide-spreading branches that grow fairly quickly to be as wide as the tree is tall—about 50 feet. In midsummer, showy, fragrant, cream-colored to pale yellow flowers bloom, followed by long-lasting cream-colored seedpods. The fine-textured leaves throw light shade and have a delicate look that belies this tree's tough constitution. It is a good street tree that withstands heat, drought, and air pollution.

PEAK SEASON

Summer, when the showy flowers scent the air

MY FAVORITES

'Pendula' is a weeping form, suitable as a specimen or an accent. It reaches only about 15 to 25 feet tall and rarely flowers.

'Princeton Upright', also known as 'Fastigiata' or 'Columnaris', is a narrow form that grows to about 50 feet in height but only about 35 feet wide and produces dense foliage.

'Regent' is a superb cultivar of Japanese pagoda tree that grows very quickly and begins to flower earlier—at about 6 to 8 years of age—than the species. It has glossy foliage and thrives in urban areas.

GARDEN COMPANIONS

Japanese pagoda tree casts rather light shade, so lawn and other ground covers can grow beneath it. A mixture of shade-tolerant perennials, such as hostas, ferns, hellebores, and sweet William phlox (Phlox divaricata), makes a lovely shade garden under this tree.

ABOVE: *All Japanese pagoda trees develop a uniform and attractive shape. This cultivar, 'Regent', grows fast.*
BELOW: *Summer's flowers are followed in fall by improbably large clusters of seedpods.*

When Plant a pagoda tree in late winter to early spring.

Where The Japanese pagoda tree will grow in full sun to part shade, but it flowers best in sun. To promote rapid growth, plant it where the soil is reasonably moist but very well drained. The pagoda tree is adaptable, however, and it tolerates urban sites and salt spray.

How Dig a hole that is roughly twice as wide and as deep as the tree's root ball. Mound some soil in the center so that the top of the root ball is at the same depth as or slightly above the soil around it. Gently loosen the roots of container-grown trees so that they will grow outward into the surrounding soil. Backfill the hole and carefully firm the soil around the tree. Water thoroughly to eliminate air pockets.

TLC Water deeply during hot or dry weather for the first 2 years to encourage deep rooting. Prune to encourage a single central leader on the tree for a strong structure. After a single trunk develops, prune side branches to encourage the natural strong and balanced shape. An organic mulch will help to keep the roots evenly moist, but avoid overmulching (more than 4 inches) and don't let the mulch touch the trunk.

175

Kentucky Coffee Tree
Gymnocladus dioica

The Kentucky coffee tree was named by the pioneers who roasted the seeds as a coffee substitute. Frequently found shading old homesteads throughout the Mid-Atlantic region, Kentucky coffee tree eventually grows 50 feet tall, thriving in a wide range of soils and even in urban conditions.

Despite its sturdy constitution, Kentucky coffee tree produces graceful, fernlike foliage that is a delicate pink in spring. Fragrant greenish white spring flowers accompany the foliage, which deepens to bronze before taking on an appealing bright green in summer. In fall, the small leaves turn a clear yellow before dropping to reveal a silhouette that, on female trees, is studded with hundreds of bean-shaped seedpods.

PEAK SEASON

The tree is lovely in spring, and the shade cast by the graceful, spreading crown is especially welcome during the hot days of summer.

MY FAVORITES

'Espresso' is a male Kentucky coffee tree that eliminates cleanup by not producing seedpods.

'JC McDaniel' (also sold as 'Prairie Titan') is a male tree (no seedpods) with a pronounced upright, elmlike branching habit.

GARDEN COMPANIONS

Kentucky coffee tree is slow to leaf out in spring, so it is the perfect companion for Virginia bluebells (*Mertensia virginica*) and spring-blooming bulbs, such as grape hyacinths, winter aconites, and daffodils. These plants bloom and complete their growth cycles in spring before the tree's crown is fully leafed out.

OPPOSITE PAGE: *A Kentucky coffee tree is growing into its role as principal shade tree.*
TOP, LEFT: *Last year's seedpods persist as new leaves emerge in spring.*
TOP, RIGHT: *Deeply fissured bark attests to the age of this Kentucky coffee tree.*

When Plant in late winter to early spring so that the roots can get established during the long, cool days of spring.

Where Plant Kentucky coffee tree in sun in a place where it has plenty of room to spread. It does best in a well-drained, rich soil with adequate moisture. Once established, it can tolerate normal periods of drought as well as urban situations where it will be exposed to air pollution as well as salt and heat.

How Dig a hole that is twice as deep and wide as the tree's root ball. Loosen the soil and create a mound in the center of the hole on which to set the root ball so that the root ball sits at or above the level of surrounding soil. Cut away any circling roots so they will grow out into the surrounding soil and anchor the tree firmly in the ground. Backfill and firm the soil. Water thoroughly to eliminate air pockets.

TLC Keep the tree watered during hot or dry periods for the first year or two. A location in full sun will maximize Kentucky coffee tree's moderately swift growth rate. Although this tree's shade, cast by ferny foliage, is light enough to support lawn beneath it, a mulch for the first few years will keep the roots evenly moist. In suburban areas populated by deer, a tree guard (a commercially available plastic cylinder) will protect the young trunk from their browsing.

Maple

Acer

There is nothing as brilliant in fall as the high color of a well-grown maple. And, of the hundreds of maples in cultivation, the red, or scarlet, maple *(Acer rubrum)* is one that truly turns its name into an understatement every autumn.

Actually, the "red" in red maple is present throughout the year, but it shows itself in different ways. The growing season begins when red maple's small red-orange flowers confidently declare that spring has arrived, often while gardeners are still wondering when, if ever, it will come. In summer, the papery helicopter seeds are a reddish tan and in fall, the red maple passes into dormancy with a spectacular show of fiery red-oranges. Even in winter, the reddish twigs remind us that this tree is well named.

The paperbark maple *(A. griseum)* is another colorful maple with wonderful, cinnamon-colored bark and leaves that flame in the autumn. A smaller tree, it grows to about 25 feet high and wide, and its up and out angled branches create a striking silhouette in winter.

PEAK SEASON

Summer and fall

MY FAVORITES

'October Glory' red maple (*Acer rubrum* 'October Glory') has a moderate to fast growth rate and reaches about 40 feet tall with a rounded crown. It has smooth silvery gray bark and very dense foliage. One of the last maples to color in fall, it makes up for its tardiness with an exceptionally long display of outstanding color.

Paperbark maple *(A. griseum)* is smaller than red maple, slowly reaching an upright, oval shape that is only about 25 feet tall by about 20 feet wide. Its amazing papery cinnamon-colored bark makes it a real standout in winter. Leaves are in three-parts, and are green on top and green-gray underneath. In fall they turn glorious shades of red and orange.

GARDEN COMPANIONS

Plant ferns, such as the striking evergreen tassel fern *(Polystichum polyblepharum),* or hostas under a red maple. Combine paper bark maple with autumn fern *(Dryopteris erythrosora).* The orange color of its emerging fronds blends beautifully with paper bark maple's cinnamon bark.

OPPOSITE PAGE: *Few trees can match the brilliant fall color of 'October Glory' red maple.*

A small tree, paperbark maple is a good choice for planting adjacent to patios and decks, and in city gardens.

When Transplant in early spring.

Where Red maple grows quickest in full sun; the paperbark maple tolerates light shade. All maples prefer soil that is consistently moist, but the red maple, also called "swamp maple," will tolerate wet soil. All maples require slightly acidic soil.

How Dig a hole that is roughly twice as wide and as deep as the tree's root ball. Carefully tease out any roots that encircle the root ball so they will grow outward into the surrounding soil. Mound some soil in the center so that the tree is at the same depth that it was growing in the container. If the tree is balled and burlapped, position it so that the root flare is right at the soil surface. Cut away any burlap aboveground to prevent moisture wicking. Backfill, firming the soil around the tree, and water thoroughly to eliminate air pockets.

TLC These maples are not drought tolerant. Keep them deeply watered during their first 2 years and afterwards during any periods of drought. Apply an organic mulch up to 4 inches deep around, but not touching, the trunk. Remove branches that grow upright through the crown. Prune branches so they form wide angles with the trunk to promote a strong branching structure.

Oak
Quercus

Once held by the Druids to be sacred, oaks are the kings of the forest. In ancient times, they symbolized strength, solidity, and protection. To this day, something of the age-old reverence for these trees lingers. Despite this high regard, however, they are not planted as often as they could be. There is the notion that because they are long-lived, oaks are very slow growing. Actually, oaks respond to the conditions of their sites. When they are young and if their needs are met, they grow relatively fast.

A mature white oak provides shade, shelter, and sustenance to myriad creatures.

Oaks native to the Mid-Atlantic area occupy a variety of environmental niches. In nature, some grow in bottomlands where the soil is moist and fertile. Others may inhabit sandy ridges where water drains very quickly and the soil dries out fast. It is important, therefore, to choose a species that suits your planting site.

PEAK SEASON

Summer, when oaks cast cooling shade

MY FAVORITES

Pin oak *(Quercus palustris)* will tolerate a poorly drained site and even occasional flooding. One of the fastest-growing oaks, it shoots up straight and tall to more than 70 feet. Autumn color is an orangey brown.

Scarlet oak *(Q. coccinea)* has brighter autumn color than most other oaks. Scarlet oak grows quickly to more than 25 feet in 10 years, eventually reaching more than 75 feet tall. In the wild, it grows in poor soil and is often found on sandy hillsides or in mixed forests. The cultivar 'Splendens' has exceptionally colorful foliage.

White oak *(Q. alba)* is a tree you plant for posterity. It is long-lived and only gets better over time. This tree grows to about 70 feet tall by nearly as wide if given room. Even lacking the Spanish moss, a well-grown white oak still comes fairly close in habit and grandeur to the live oaks of the South and the Pacific Coast. Autumn color of the round, lobed leaves is a rusty brown.

GARDEN COMPANIONS

Acid-loving shrubs such as lily-of-the-valley *(Pieris)*, azaleas, and holly *(Ilex)* make good companions to oaks.

LEFT: *Pin oaks grow straight, tall, and strong, eventually assuming a pyramidal shape.*
RIGHT: *Leaves of scarlet oak grow 4 to 6 inches long and change to bright red in fall.*

When Plant oak trees in late winter to early spring.

Where All oaks thrive with sun and moist, fertile, well-drained soil, although the pin oak tolerates wet soil. Allow plenty of room for the trees to develop a broad crown.

How Carefully remove the oak tree from its container and gently loosen the roots so they do not encircle the root ball. Dig a hole that is roughly twice as wide and as deep as the tree's root ball. Set the root ball into the hole on a mound in the center of the hole so that the roots aren't crowded and so final level is at or slightly above ground level. Backfill and tamp the soil, and finish by watering deeply.

TLC Keep the soil moist throughout the growing season and water during droughts for at least the first 2 years. A mulch of wood chips or shredded bark will help to conserve moisture and to prevent competition from lawn. Prune only to remove dead or crossing limbs.

River Birch
Betula nigra

River birches are the Mid-Atlantic's answer to the white-barked birches that thrive in the North, such as the canoe birch *(Betula papyrifera)* and the European white birch *(B. pendula).* These northern trees fare poorly in the hot summers of the Mid-Atlantic region and often fall prey to bronze birch borers. Not so the river birch. This is its home territory, where it can be seen growing alongside streams. It grows swiftly to 70 feet by as much as 50 feet wide, with shaggy, flaking bark that curls off the tree in cinnamon-colored sheets. River birches tolerate moist soils and even places that may flood occasionally.

In early spring, 'Heritage' river birch sprouts fresh green leaves that complement its attractive white bark.

When Plant river birch in late winter or early spring.

Where Plant in moist soil and sun. Trees growing in light shade grow much more slowly and will reach toward the light instead of growing straight up. Those planted in heavy shade remain stunted and may eventually die.

How Remove the river birch from its container and gently tease out any roots that encircle the root ball. Dig a hole that is roughly twice as wide and as deep as the tree's root ball, so that the roots aren't crowded. Mound soil in the center so the plant is at the same depth that it was growing in the container. Backfill the hole, gently firm the soil, and water thoroughly.

PEAK SEASON

Year-round. In spring, dainty leaves appear. In summer, birches cast light shade. In fall, their small, bright yellow leaves dance in the sun and in winter, the textured trunks are beautiful.

MY FAVORITES

'Heritage' river birch is a cultivar with very white bark, the closest in color to the canoe and European white birches, but with the river birch's strong constitution. 'Heritage' retains the growth habit and shaggy, exfoliating bark of the species.

'Little King' is a very round, compact river birch that grows to only about 12 feet tall by 12 feet wide. The dense growth of dark cinnamon-colored twigs against the white bark with its peeling pink and salmon colors creates a sculptural effect.

GARDEN COMPANIONS

In a moist place, a ground cover of cinnamon ferns is lovely under a grove of river birches. Cardinal flower (Lobelia cardinalis) is another good companion that thrives in light shade and moist soil.

TLC The best care for river birch is to plant it in the right site: a place that is consistently moist and where the tree will get plenty of sun. Water for the first year or two until the tree is established, and renew mulch every spring.

LEFT: *The peeling, cinnamon-colored inner bark of 'Heritage' river birch stands out in winter.*
BELOW: *Multiple clumps of 'Heritage' river birch lend a naturalistic look to a landscape.*

Southern Magnolia
Magnolia grandiflora

Southern magnolia with its large leaves and flowers is an iconic Mid-Atlantic tree.

One of the perks of gardening in the Mid-Atlantic region is the possibility of growing "southern" plants such as the evergreen southern magnolia. This magnificent tree grows at a moderate rate to 80 feet tall by 30 to 40 feet wide. The big leaves are leathery and shiny. Throughout the summer, a mature southern magnolia produces big, fragrant, waxy white flowers that are followed by striking cones of seeds that turn from salmon to bright red and are quickly taken by birds.

Some of the best forms have leaves that reverse to an underside that is coated with a rust-colored down. In addition to being more ornamental, these trees tend to bloom sooner.

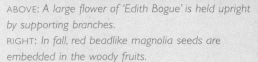

ABOVE: *A large flower of 'Edith Bogue' is held upright by supporting branches.*
RIGHT: *In fall, red beadlike magnolia seeds are embedded in the woody fruits.*

PEAK SEASON

Summer, when the fragrant flowers bloom

MY FAVORITES

'Bracken's Brown Beauty' is a more compact form of southern magnolia growing to about 30 feet tall and 18 feet wide, lending this tree a narrower, pyramid-shaped crown. The flowers are also smaller, measuring about 5 inches across. The very dense foliage is shiny above and very markedly downy and rusty brown beneath, resulting in a bicolor appearance.

'Edith Bogue' is a small, broad-spreading tree, reaching to about 25 feet in height and width. Vigorous and very cold hardy, it withstands heavy snow loads. The flowers, which measure 8 to 10 inches across, are outstanding.

GARDEN COMPANIONS

Southern magnolias cast dense shade and drop their old leaves, which makes growing anything beneath them a challenge. For these reasons as well as purely aesthetic ones, it is best to allow the lower branches to remain on the tree. This evergreen tree serves as a beautiful backdrop to small flowering trees such as dogwood (*Cornus*) or silver bell (*Halesia*).

When Plant southern magnolia in late winter to early spring.

Where Choose a place that receives at least a half day of sun, is out of the path of strong winds, and has soil that is moist but well drained. In colder regions, southern magnolia grows well as an espalier against a south-facing wall.

How The roots of southern magnolias have a tendency to girdle. Be very careful to tease them out from the root ball and prune away any that threaten to choke it. Plant the tree in a hole roomy enough to accommodate the roots at the same depth that the tree was growing in the container.

TLC Keep the soil evenly moist from spring through fall, until there is usually plenty of natural precipitation. Mulch to conserve moisture, being careful not to let the mulch mound up against the trunk. Do any pruning to shape the tree in the winter so you can use the cut branches for decoration.

Sycamore, Plane Tree
Platanus

Sycamores, or plane trees, are a familiar sight in the Mid-Atlantic region. They can often be spotted along riverbanks, where in winter, their pale, mottled limbs stand out against the grays and browns of other trees. The mottling occurs when pieces of bark are shed, exposing the lighter-colored trunk beneath. Some horticulturists think that this shedding allows the tree to rid itself of impurities, making it an ideal tree for urban use. If given plenty of room, sycamores develop wide, spreading limbs and grow tall quickly. In the wild, a few have reached as much as 150 feet tall. They also live a long time—there are sycamores estimated to be 400 years old.

Sycamores are a part of history. It is said that Menelaus, the husband of Helen of Troy, planted a sycamore tree before he left for the Trojan War. The Mogul emperors of India had sycamore trees brought from Persia to plant in the gardens they made in Kashmir, in northern India. And George Washington planted them at Mount Vernon.

The most popular sycamore tree in the world today is the London plane *(Platanus × acerifolia)*, a cross between the American sycamore, *P. occidentalis,* and the Persian sycamore, *P. orientalis.* It's the tree you see lining the Champs Elysées in Paris and along Lake Constance in central Europe, as well as here in the Mid-Atlantic.

ABOVE: *Very tolerant of urban conditions, London plane tree can also be pruned to fit almost any space.*
RIGHT: *In winter, the creamy gray bark of 'Bloodgood' remains attractive, especially on sunny, clear days.*

PEAK SEASON

Sycamores are at their best when their light-colored, exfoliating bark brightens the days of the Mid-Atlantic winter.

MY FAVORITES

'Bloodgood' London plane (*Platanus* × *acerifolia* 'Bloodgood') grows to about 85 feet tall, has beautifully exfoliating bark, and needs little, if any, pruning.

'Columbia' London plane (*P.* × *acerifolia* 'Columbia') was developed at the U.S. National Arboretum in Washington, D.C. It is highly resistant to sycamore anthracnose, a fungal disease that attacks young trees. It grows to about 50 feet tall and bears fruits that sometimes appear as two or three dangling balls.

GARDEN COMPANIONS

Winterberries and sycamore trees combine wonderfully in winter, and both thrive in a moist spot. Hostas, ferns, and wildflowers such as Jack-in-the-pulpit and Dutchman's breeches are other good companions.

OPPOSITE PAGE: *An American sycamore shelters beds of blooming narcissus. Redbud trees bloom in the background.*

When Plant sycamore trees very early in spring.

Where London plane tree is a great and well-tested choice for urban landscapes. It tolerates poor drainage, parking lot islands, and compacted soil.

How Sycamore trees are usually sold balled-and-burlapped. Set it into the hole so that the top of the root ball is even with the surrounding soil, and then remove any wrapping. If the tree comes in a container, carefully remove it and gently tease out any roots that encircle the root ball. Set the plant in a hole that is wide enough to accommodate the roots without crowding. Make sure it is at the same depth that it was growing in the container. Backfill the hole, gently firm the soil, and water thoroughly.

TLC If a sycamore receives plenty of sun, water, and mulch, and has adequate room, it will grow swiftly.

Yellow Wood
Cladrastis kentukea

Although yellow wood has been known to take as long as 10 years before flowering, it's well worth the wait. Foot-long, white, wisteria-like blooms hang from the tree in early summer. The flowers, which may only bloom in alternate years, have a fragrance that is sweetly reminiscent of vanilla. Flat pods follow the blossoms. But even without flowers, yellow wood is a handsome medium-sized shade tree. It looks neat and presentable through the year, with smooth gray bark and an attractive rounded shape.

Growth is usually slow to moderate, and a mature tree is typically 35 feet in height by about 25 feet in width, but it can reach 50 feet tall. Yellow wood's attractive, bright green leaves contain between seven and 11 oval leaflets, which turn a bright banana yellow in fall.

Draping clusters of wisteria-like flowers are a summertime bonus of yellow wood.

PEAK SEASON

Yellow wood is handsome year-round, but the flowers put on a splendid show in early summer.

MY FAVORITES

'Rosea' is a form of yellow wood that has pink flowers. These are especially attractive against the bright green leaves.

GARDEN COMPANIONS

Yellow wood is deep-rooted, so shade-tolerant shrubs can be planted beneath it. Azaleas, drooping leucothoe (Leucothoe walteri), Skimmia japonica, and daphnes are all good companions. Yellow wood is also attractive rising out of a ground cover of autumn ferns (Dryopteris erythrosora). Like other members of the pea family, yellow wood has a symbiotic relationship with some soil bacteria and can "fix" atmospheric nitrogen, converting it to a plant-usable form. This is not only good for the tree, but can benefit the plants growing around it as well.

ABOVE: *Many shrubs and perennials will thrive beneath the deep-rooted yellow wood.*
BELOW: *Spring leaves and long strings of flower buds are backlit on a sunny day.*

When Plant yellow wood in the early spring.

Where Yellow wood thrives in most acidic to alkaline soils, whether sandy, loamy, or clay, as long as they stay moist. Sun and good drainage are essential.

How Dig a hole that is roughly twice as wide and as deep as the tree's root ball. Mound some soil in the center so that the top of the root ball is at the same depth as or slightly above the soil around it. Gently loosen the roots of container-grown trees so that they will grow outward into the surrounding soil. Backfill the hole and carefully firm the soil around the tree. Water thoroughly to eliminate air pockets.

TLC Siting yellow wood in sun and rich, moist soil is the best way to care for it. Don't prune it in winter or spring; it will bleed sap profusely at those times. Wait until late summer to remove poorly angled limbs and do so when they are small.

189

Vines

Vines are some of the most useful plants in a landscape, but they need to be selected and placed with discretion—and you need to keep the upper hand. Left to grow on their own, vines wander along until they find something—anything—to climb on, then they take off. The results can be chaotic. By planting a vine alongside an appropriately sturdy and attractive support, you direct its growth, and the results can be spectacular.

At their best, vines tie together different parts of the landscape. They can extend a bed up a wall or over a fence, camouflage an eyesore, provide a dense privacy screen or flowering backdrop, or create an overhead canopy that con-nects adjacent garden areas.

SUPPORTS AND STRATEGIES

To make the most of a vine, you need to provide a support that suits its growth habit as well as the style of your landscape. Supports for vines range from the simple (an old stump, a section of fence, or a vertical post encircled with chicken wire) to the ornate (a Victorian pergola, a wrought-iron trellis, or an arching wooden arbor). Other plants can provide support for vines, although careful pairing is important; some vines will overtake a living support and may cause injury. Many vines are quite at home in containers, particularly hanging baskets, where their wandering stems can climb support wires or cascade over the edge and grow vertically, often a distance of several feet.

Knowing just how vines manage their gravity-defying feats can help when it comes to designing a support. Some vines, like passion vine (page 210), have tendrils that curl around any nearby, suitably sized brace—suitably sized

RIGHT: *Boston ivy offers a cool dark green covering for a stone wall.*
OPPOSITE PAGE: *A fast-growing annual vine, like this 'Heavenly Blue' morning glory, covers a railing in one season.*

being the operative term. Too broad a brace will frustrate the vine's attempt to clasp it. The tendrils of Boston ivy (page 196) are equipped with tiny suction cup–like tips that adhere very well to stone and brick walls. Climbing hydrangea (page 200) produces aerial roots that attach to rough surfaces like brick. Clematis (page 198) wraps its twining *petiole* (leaf stem) around a trellis or another plant. Here again, the supports cannot be too broad. On the other hand, entire stems of wisteria (page 192) and honeysuckle (page 202) twine around and embrace their support systems, so these vines require sturdy structures.

VINE DIVERSITY

As their climbing strategies indicate, vines are an incredibly diverse group of plants. Some are grown for their magnificent flowers, others for their dense foliage. Some vines are annuals and need to be replanted each year; others are long-lived plants with woody stems. Vines such as mandevilla (page 206) and most passion vines

are indigenous to far warmer climates than ours, but their exotic flowers and luxuriant growth add such tropical flavor to our summer gardens that we willingly grow them as annuals.

With all this variety, you'd think that garden centers would offer more choices in vines than they do. To find a really good selection, you will probably have to do a bit of searching. Seed catalogs will help, as will mail-order nurseries. It's worth the effort to look.

Vines soften harsh lines, hide ugly structures, provide screens, cast shade, contribute seasonal color, and literally weave together parts of a garden. They do all this while requiring so very little planting space in the garden. Their growth follows your direction—by providing an appropriate framework on which they can grow and some initial coaxing, you can use vines to dramatically extend your garden area. Few plants give you such bang for the buck.

—RITA PELCZAR

American Wisteria
Wisteria frutescens

When someone says "wisteria,'" you probably think of Chinese *(Wisteria sinensis)* or Japanese wisteria *(W. floribunda)*—they are by far the most common types grown. Gorgeous they are, with their long clusters of fragrant spring flowers, but I don't recommend you plant either one here in the Mid-Atlantic. Both of those wisterias are extremely aggressive, and unless carefully and continuously monitored, they can smother and strangle any tree or shrub that gets in their way. In fact, both species make the invasive plant lists of several regional native plant societies.

But there is a delightful alternative. The American wisteria, an eastern North American native, is much better behaved in the garden than its exotic cousins. Granted, its 4- to 6-inch flower clusters are not as long as those of the Asian species, but they last considerably longer. They are typically violet-blue and appear on the current season's growth, perched above the dark gray-green leaves.

American wisteria usually grows to a comfortable 10 to 25 feet in height and requires minimal care, although it does need a sturdy support. It's a great choice for an arbor or for training on a trellis against the wall of a garage or garden shed.

LEFT: *The blue of 'Amethyst Falls' flowers is darker than most forms of American wisteria.*
RIGHT: *'Nivea' is the white-flowered variety of American wisteria.*

PEAK SEASON

Flowers open over a 2- to 4-week period from the late spring to the early summer.

MY FAVORITES

'Amethyst Falls' is a vigorous, blue-flowered selection that also bears flowers on very young plants.

'Nivea' produces tight clusters of pure white flowers in late spring; blooming often repeats sporadically throughout summer.

RELATED SPECIES

Kentucky wisteria (*Wisteria macro-stachya*, also listed as *W. frutescens macrostachya*) tolerates colder temperatures, so would be the best choice for colder pockets of zones 32 and 34. It bears violet flowers in clusters up to a foot long. 'Abbeville Blue' bears soft blue-violet flowers. 'Clara Mack' is a late-flowering selection with white blooms.

GARDEN COMPANIONS

Plant near other moisture-loving plants such as summersweet (*Clethra*), Virginia sweetspire (*Itea virginica*), bee balm (*Monarda*), or cardinal flower (*Lobelia cardinalis*).

OPPOSITE PAGE: *American wisteria is better adapted to Mid-Atlantic gardens than the species native to Asia.*

When Plant container-grown plants in early spring.

Where Plant in full sun in moist to wet soil. American wisteria will grow in light shade, but it will produce fewer flowers. Position the support so that the vine's attractive gray bark is visible in winter.

How Transplant container-grown plants into soil that has been improved with organic matter and a complete slow-release fertilizer. Set the plant at the same depth that it was growing in the pot. Water well and apply an organic mulch to prevent drying out and to discourage weeds.

TLC This is a twining vine, so guide young stems toward a sturdy support that they can coil around. Remove unwanted suckers that rise from the base of the plant. Flowering occurs on the current season's growth, so prune to maintain the size in late winter or very early spring.

Black-eyed Susan Vine
Thunbergia alata

The center of each flower of the black-eyed Susan vine is so dark, it might be better named the "black-hole vine." I can easily imagine wandering insects getting lost in its depths. The dark center contrasts with the flower's dazzling yellow or orange petals. Varieties with shades of pink, red, and ivory flowers have also been developed. Some lack the dark eye—a serious loss, I think.

Here in the Mid-Atlantic, we grow this tropical perennial as an annual. The thin twining stems support a steady parade of flowers all summer, which are offset by the dark green triangular leaves. Black-eyed Susan vine is quite vigorous and if you plant it in the ground and allow it to wander, it will grow 5 to 8 feet in all directions, twining through and over nearby plants, covering stumps and whatever else is in its path. With a bit of encouragement, it will cover a freestanding trellis to become a tower of flowers. I prefer containing its enthusiastic growth in a pot. It's a terrific subject for a hanging basket, where it will twine its way up the wires that support the pot and hang over the edge to trail well below. Combine it with other plants at your own risk, however—it can take over a mixed planting.

Fast-growing black-eyed Susan vine covers a wooden lattice trellis.

PEAK SEASON

Early summer through early fall

MY FAVORITES

'Alba' produces white flowers with deep purple-brown eyes.

'Blushing Susie' bears blossoms in shades of pink, ivory, apricot, red, and a few white, all on one plant.

'Lemon Star' has clear yellow flowers with dark eyes.

'Spanish Eyes' bears flowers in the colors of a sunset: pink, yellow, apricot, and orange, all with a dark eye.

'Sunny Orange Wonder' is a slightly brighter, larger version of the species.

'Sunrise Surprise' is similar to 'Spanish Eyes', with dark-eyed rose, apricot, and ivory blooms.

RELATED SPECIES

Blue trumpet vine (Thunbergia grandiflora) has large oval leaves that give this vine a lush, tropical appearance. Its 3-inch lavender flowers are borne in clusters.

GARDEN COMPANIONS

Given its vigorous nature, I prefer growing black-eyed Susan vine by itself in containers. For an interesting vertical accent, grow it on a tall free-standing bamboo trellis in a bed with other brightly colored annuals.

TOP: 'Sunny Orange Wonder'
BOTTOM: 'Blushing Susie'

When To grow from seed, start plants indoors 2 months prior to the last expected frost. Transplant young plants outdoors after the weather has warmed in late spring.

Where Although plants will grow in full sun, their colors can fade. Dappled or afternoon shade is best. Plant in a moist, well-drained soil where there is some protection from wind.

How Sow seeds in peat pots or directly into the containers where the plants will grow. Acclimate indoor-grown seedlings to the outdoors by placing them in a protected, shady location for a few days before transplanting.

TLC Keep plants well watered and apply a complete liquid fertilizer at 2-week intervals throughout the growing season. Trim plants or guide stems to prevent them from growing into unwanted areas. You can bring a pot or basket of black-eyed Susan vine indoors for winter and, if properly acclimated, return it outdoors the following spring.

*Grown as an annual.

Boston Ivy

Parthenocissus tricuspidata

By late spring, Boston ivy covers itself in shiny green new leaves.

Boston ivy lends a well-established, traditional look to a landscape. Buildings on many college campuses, as well as brick homes and public buildings, are often elegantly adorned with this vine that can reach 60 feet in height. Its neat, three-lobed deciduous leaves are dark glossy green. No vine can match its fiery autumn leaf colors of red, orange, and yellow, except perhaps its close relative Virginia creeper *(Parthenocissus quinquefolia).*

Boston ivy is a fast-growing vine. The tendrils along its stems are equipped with tiny adhesive disks, perfect for clinging to brick or stone. It needs no support other than a vertical wall. But be sure you want it growing where you plant it. If you should later change your mind, those adhesive disks can leave dark marks that are particularly noticeable on light-colored siding or wood, and they are difficult to remove.

Despite its misleading common name, Boston ivy is an Asian native. Nevertheless, it is well adapted to our climate. It grows in sun or shade and withstands air pollution, drought, and seaside conditions.

PEAK SEASON

Leaves emerge in spring and blanket walls in shiny green throughout summer. In fall, leaves turn bright shades of red, yellow, and orange.

MY FAVORITES

'Lowii' produces small leaves that have as many as seven deeply cut lobes.

'Purpurea' is a selection with leaves that remain reddish purple throughout the growing season.

'Veitchii' develops small green leaves that turn dark purple in fall.

RELATED SPECIES

Virginia creeper (Parthenocissus quinquefolia), a North American native climber, is commonly found rambling up tree trunks in the woods and along fencerows. It is useful for covering up stumps and bare walls and dressing up chain-link fences, or as a ground cover. The attractive 6-inch leaves, each with 5 leaflets, turn bright red to deep crimson in fall. It bears purple-blue fruit that attracts birds.

GARDEN COMPANIONS

Boston ivy works well in formal, traditional landscapes with boxwood, yew, and holly (Ilex). It complements other plants that have colorful autumn foliage.

When Plant in early spring or fall near a supporting wall. Cuttings for new plants can be taken in spring.

Where Boston ivy is very adaptable and will grow in sun or shade in most soils. It will perform best, however, in a fertile, well-drained soil.

How Prepare the soil by incorporating about 3 inches of organic matter to a depth of 12 inches. Space new plants 3 to 4 feet apart along the support wall. Water well until plants are established. Mulching the planting bed will help retain moisture and reduce weeds.

TLC Prune to restrain or direct growth in early spring.

TOP: *In fall, the crimson leaves of Boston ivy contrast sharply with evergreen English ivy on a stucco wall.*
BOTTOM: *Red leaves of Virginia creeper grow on a trellis intertwined with clematis.*

197

Clematis
Clematis

Clematis adds romance to a front porch, drama to a trellis or an arbor, and a touch of class to a mailbox or lamppost. Best of all, with the proper selection of variety, and the right site and support, it is easy to grow. These perennial vines produce very showy flowers in a range of colors that, depending on the variety, bloom in spring, summer, or fall. Some, like the sweet autumn clematis *(Clematis terniflora),* bear flowers that are only an inch wide, while those of hybrid types are often 8 inches across.

Clematis grow best with their roots in the shade and their leaves in the sun, so finding the right spot can be a little tricky. They work well planted in the shade of a shrub that they can use as support. Provide extra shade to the roots with a layer of organic mulch. Clematis vines climb by twining their leaf stalks, or *petioles*, around thin props, so be sure the braces of your trellis, fence, or other support are not too broad.

Sweet autumn clematis produces billowing masses of 1-inch-wide flowers in fall.

PEAK SEASON

Depending on the species and variety, clematis bloom in spring, summer, or fall. Some bloom during two seasons.

MY FAVORITES

Anemone clematis *(Clematis montana)* bears abundant 2-inch, white or pink scented flowers from late spring to early summer on vines that can grow 20 to 30 feet or more. Flowers are produced on growth from the previous year and are followed by attractive, feathery seed heads.

Jackman clematis *(C. × jackmanii)* produces large violet-purple flowers in summer on the current season's growth. The plants grow 12 feet tall. Other varieties with a similar bloom-ing habit include *C. ×* 'Hagley Hybrid', which bears large mauve pink flowers with red anthers, *C. ×* 'Niobe', with rich crimson flowers, and *C. ×* 'Henryi', which has creamy white flowers.

Sweet autumn clematis *(C. terniflora)* flowers in late summer and fall, pro-ducing masses of small, star-shaped white blossoms that cover the 15- to 20-foot vine. The feathery seed heads are very showy.

GARDEN COMPANIONS

Clematis complement roses, peonies, hydrangeas and many other flowering perennials and shrubs.

ABOVE: *Anemone clematis produces white flowers in early spring.*
RIGHT: *Jackman clematis, with its 4- to 5-inch-wide blossoms, is the classic clematis.*

When Plant in fall or early spring.

Where Plant in fertile, well-drained soil in full sun or light shade where its roots will be shaded by nearby perennials or a shrub. Sweet autumn clematis is more shade tolerant.

How Once planted, you can leave clematis in the same place indefinitely, so prepare the soil well, incorporating organic matter and a slow-release fertilizer into the planting hole. Provide a trellis or other support. Once the clematis is in place, don't set other plants within 5 or 6 feet of it because clematis roots are shallow and delicate.

TLC Water as needed to keep the soil moist and mulch to keep it cool. Clematis stems are brittle, so take care when handling them. Prune spring flowering varieties a month after flowering; prune summer- and fall-bloomers in early spring before buds swell.

Climbing Hydrangea

Hydrangea anomala petiolaris

If you're looking for a sturdy vine that produces billowy masses of attractive foliage and will bloom in sun or shade, the climbing hydrangea is just the ticket. It's a big old thing—clinging with its aerial roots, it can climb 70 or 80 feet to the top of tall structures, if you let it. Or, with the proper support, cover wide expanses of walls, creating a dense, green screen.

The dainty white flowers of this Asian import are borne in large, flat clusters. The tiny fertile blooms in the center are surrounded by larger sterile flowers in what is called a "lacecap" arrangement. Glossy, dark green leaves provide the perfect foil for the summer flowers. When the leaves drop in the fall, they expose the shredding cinnamon-colored bark, which adds interest to the winter garden.

Although climbing hydrangeas are slow growers the first couple of years after planting, they are quite vigorous once established.

Climbing hydrangea is a shade-tolerant vine that's nearly indestructible once established.

PEAK SEASON

This vine has year-round appeal: its leaves are attractive from spring through fall, flowers appear in midsummer, and the colorful bark provides subtle winter interest.

RELATED PLANT

A closely related vine known as wood vamp or wild hydrangea (*Decumaria barbara*) is a native of damp woodlands of the southeastern United States. Like its Asian relative, it will grow in considerable shade, although it blooms best in light shade or morning sun. Wood vamp and climbing hydrangea (both deciduous species) have similar leaves and rough reddish bark, and both climb by way of aerial roots. The flowers of wood vamp, however, lack the showiness of climbing hydrangea blossoms. The clusters are smaller (about 2 or 3 inches across), and they lack the showy sterile bracts around the cluster's edge. Wood vamp is useful as a ground cover or climber in woodland gardens.

GARDEN COMPANIONS

Climbing hydrangea is ideal for the edge of a woodland garden where it can light up a shady wall. Planting hosta, lily-of-the-valley, wild ginger (*Asarum*), pachysandra, or ferns in its shade adds interest at the ground level.

ABOVE: *Plant climbing hydrangea where it can climb with abandon: its aerial roots cling tenaciously.* RIGHT: *"Lacecap" hydrangea flowers ornament the vine in summer.*

When Plant potted nursery-grown plants from spring through fall.

Where Grow climbing hydrangea in full sun or light shade in a rich, moist, well-drained soil. Avoid very dry sites. Plant near a sturdy support such as a brick or stone wall. Keep the vine off your house, unless it's made of brick or stone. Choose a spot where this hydrangea's attractive shredding bark can be seen at close range in winter.

How Plant in well-drained soil that has been supplemented with organic matter such as compost or leaf mold.

TLC Water regularly for the first 2 to 3 seasons; after plants are established, they are fairly drought tolerant. Mulch with shredded hardwood, wood chips, or leaf mold to maintain even soil moisture, provide winter protection, and reduce weeds. Fertilize each spring with a complete fertilizer. Prune in winter or early spring to direct growth and maintain shape.

Goldflame Honeysuckle
Lonicera × heckrottii

Goldflame honeysuckle at peak bloom spills over a garden wall.

To my way of thinking, nothing decks out a fence like honeysuckle, and although there are many fine selections, goldflame honeysuckle is my favorite. All honeysuckles are fast growing, to the point that some can become a nuisance. For example, despite its sweet-smelling blooms, the Japanese honeysuckle *(Lonicera japonica)* is an invasive vine of the first order.

Not so with goldflame honeysuckle—its growth is vigorous but restrained. Round, blue-green leaves occur in pairs along the twining stems that can extend 15 feet or so. The leaves provide a pleasing backdrop for the clusters of carmine red buds, which open to reveal fragrant, two-lipped flowers. Their color is stunning; each is rosy coral on the outside and yellow within. Even as they age to a more subdued pink, the flowers are lovely. Rivaling flower color as this vine's best trait is its lengthy flowering season—it erupts in a burst of blooms in late spring or early summer, but new flowers continue to appear through late fall. Not surprisingly, another common name for this species is everblooming honeysuckle.

PEAK SEASON

The vine blooms most profusely in early summer; it remains attractive throughout summer and fall with a steady stream of colorful flowers. Red berries often provide additional color in fall.

RELATED SPECIES

Scarlet trumpet honeysuckle (*Lonicera* × *brownii* 'Dropmore Scarlet') is hardier than most vining honeysuckles. It bears clusters of orange to red flowers from early summer into fall.

Trumpet honeysuckle (*L. sempervirens*) is native to the eastern United States. Throughout summer, it bears clusters of large, unscented reddish orange flowers with yellow-orange interiors, which are very attractive to hummingbirds. It typically grows to a manageable 10 to 20 feet long or high, depending on the support you supply. The variety 'Manifich' bears light orange flowers with yellow centers. 'Sulphurea' (also sold as 'Flava') bears clear yellow flowers.

GARDEN COMPANIONS

Goldflame honeysuckle looks great scrambling along a wooden fence or scaling a trellis. It makes a pleasing background for blue- and purple-flowered perennials such as catmint (*Nepeta*), campanula, veronica, salvia, and stokesia.

When Plant goldflame honeysuckle in spring or fall.

Where Goldflame honeysuckle grows best in a rich, well-drained garden loam in full sun or light shade near a supporting trellis or fence. Honeysuckle can also be used effectively as a trailing ground cover to prevent erosion on a steep bank.

How Before planting, enrich soil with organic matter such as compost or leaf mold. Goldflame honeysuckle rarely needs additional fertilization unless it is planted in poor soil.

TLC Water plants regularly for the first 2 or 3 seasons until they are well established. Provide a support for the stems to twine around; young stems may need to be tied on at first. Prune plants after flowering to maintain size and direct growth. To encourage new growth from the base, remove some of the oldest stems each year.

TOP: *Goldflame honeysuckle blooms here with beauty bush (Kolkwitzia amabilis).*
BOTTOM: *Trumpet honeysuckle flowers come in clusters and are nearly 2 inches long.*

Hyacinth Bean

Lablab purpureus (also listed as *Dolichos lablab*)

Hyacinth bean has it all—appealing flowers, colorful leaves, attractive colorful pods—plus it's easy to grow. This tropical perennial, which we grow as an annual, puts on a fabulous summer show. It is the fastest-growing flowering vine I know. Easily started from seed, its twining stems with their purple-tinged green leaves will quickly cover a trellis or fence with lush vegetation.

Leaves, flowers, and pods of hyacinth bean quickly make a colorful, purplish screen.

Sprays of flowers held on purple stems appear in July or August and continue until frost. The pealike blooms are fragrant and usually rosy purple, although white and reddish purple selections are available. The flowers are followed by shiny, 4-inch, magenta-purple pods that contrast well with the leaves and with the continuing parade of blossoms. Cut stems of the colorful pods make attractive and unusual additions to indoor arrangements.

This vine is a good candidate for a bean teepee. Simply set three to five 10-foot bamboo poles in the ground and lash their tops together with twine to form the frame. Plant seeds at the base of each pole, then step back and watch this vine grow!

ABOVE: *Plant hyacinth bean where you can easily admire the delicate flowers close up.*
BELOW: *Purple hyacinth bean pods are growing here with tomato plants.*

PEAK SEASON

Flowers, followed by pods, begin in midsummer and continue until frost.

MY FAVORITES

'Darkness' and 'Moon Shadow' bear deep purple flowers.

'Ruby Moon' produces pink and purple flowers and deep purple-brown leaves and stems.

GARDEN COMPANIONS

Grow hyacinth bean on a fence or trellis to provide a lush background for an annual flower bed; brightly colored flowers like zinnias, marigolds, cosmos, and petunias stand out well against its deeply hued leaves. It can also be grown on a large obelisk or other freestanding support to create a vertical accent in the landscape. Its purple flowers and magenta pods contrast well with yellow and orange flowers and harmonize attractively with pink flowers.

When Plant seeds in the garden after the soil has warmed in the spring. To get a head start, sow seeds indoors in peat pots 4 weeks before the last expected frost. Handle seedlings carefully, and transplant them in the peat pots to avoid disturbing the roots.

Where Plant in full sun in moist, well-drained average to fertile soil, and near a free-standing support or trellis.

How Plant in soil that has been enriched with organic matter such as compost or leaf mold. Space plants 9 to 12 inches apart. Water with a dilute complete fertilizer after planting and at 2- to 3-week intervals throughout the summer.

TLC Provide a sturdy support—these vines produce significant vegetation that can become heavy. Mulch to retain soil moisture and reduce weeds. Hyacinth bean will quickly twine its way up strings suspended from a horizontal brace or porch roof to create a fast and effective summer screen. The beans are edible, but only if boiled in three changes of water first. They contain cyanogenetic glycosides, which can be toxic if eaten in large quantities.

Grown as an annual.

Mandevilla

Mandevilla

With its glossy leaves and 2- to 4-inch, funnel-shaped flowers that are hot pink with yellow or white throats, mandevilla is an elegant climber. This vine is native to the American tropics, where its thick, leathery leaves are evergreen.

Here in the Mid-Atlantic, we must be content to grow mandevilla as an annual or to bring it indoors over winter. I've successfully overwintered plants, but find myself frustrated because, lacking a greenhouse, my plants begin flowering several weeks later than those I see at the nursery, so I usually end up buying a new plant anyway.

Whether you keep the same plant from year to year, or purchase a new one each spring, mandevilla repays your investment with nonstop flowers from late spring until fall. Its stems gracefully twine around their support and will climb a lamppost, mailbox, trellis, or arbor, easily reaching 10 to 20 feet. By growing mandevilla in a planter or hanging basket—a very good idea if you plan to overwinter it indoors—you will restrict its growth somewhat, and it will still flower freely.

'Alice du Pont' mandevilla and ivy geranium combine to form a flowering garland around a bench.

PEAK SEASON

Flowers appear continuously from late spring into fall.

MY FAVORITES

Mandevilla × *amoena* 'Alice du Pont' is a vigorous selection with leathery leaves and clusters of up to 20 flowers. Each bloom is pink with a darker pink throat and yellow center. 'Summer Snow' has white blossoms.

M. boliviensis is a slender vine that grows 10 to 12 feet. It bears 2-inch white flowers with yellow throats.

M. sanderi 'Red Riding Hood' bears deep red flowers that have a distinct yellow throat.

M. splendens 'Rosacea' has rose pink blossoms that gradually deepen to purple-pink at the margins with a bright pink ring near the throat.

GARDEN COMPANIONS

Mandevilla can be adapted to both formal and informal garden styles. It is particularly well suited to growing in containers on the patio or porch. It combines well with Madagascar periwinkle (*Catharanthus roseus*), floss flower (*Ageratum houstonianum*), and pink, purple, or white petunias. Dark red varieties of coleus or 'Blackie' sweet potato vine provide a pleasing contrast to the bright pink flowers and glossy green leaves.

When Purchase plants when they become available in spring, and plant in the garden after all danger of frost has passed. Cuttings can be taken from plants in February. Don't move overwintered plants outside until weather has warmed up.

Where Plant in full sun in moist, well-drained fertile soil.

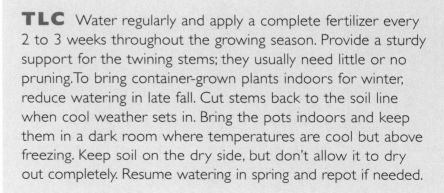

TOP: *A close-up of the quilted leaves and 4-inch flowers of 'Alice du Pont'.* BOTTOM: M. splendens *flowers are small and the leaves are smooth.*

How For inground planting, prepare soil by incorporating organic matter such as compost or aged manure to a depth of 10 to 12 inches. To grow in a container, use a commercial potting soil.

TLC Water regularly and apply a complete fertilizer every 2 to 3 weeks throughout the growing season. Provide a sturdy support for the twining stems; they usually need little or no pruning. To bring container-grown plants indoors for winter, reduce watering in late fall. Cut stems back to the soil line when cool weather sets in. Bring the pots indoors and keep them in a dark room where temperatures are cool but above freezing. Keep soil on the dry side, but don't allow it to dry out completely. Resume watering in spring and repot if needed.

Grown as an annual.

Moonflower

Ipomoea alba

Moonflower, bearing its audacious 6-inch-wide fragrant white flowers, climbs wire supports to reach the roof.

If you asked me to choose one vine to grow in my garden, I wouldn't hesitate: Moonflower is, hands-down, my favorite climber. An annual, its heart-shaped leaves are deep green—the perfect foil for the pure white flowers that are 6 inches across. Ah, those flowers! Watching one of the long, spiraled buds unfurl is one of summer's great pleasures. Children are fascinated by the flowers. The sweetly fragrant blooms open around dusk and last only until the next morning, but there will be new flowers come evening. Pick a newly opened flower and bring it indoors, and it will perfume an entire room.

I plant the vine along my front porch so I can enjoy it both from the porch swing and from the front rooms of my house as its fragrance wafts through the open windows. Also use moonflower as a living screen, to cover a fence or trellis, or to create a charming, scented enclosure around an arbor or pergola.

PEAK SEASON

Flowering begins in midsummer and continues until frost. Flowers only last one night, but new flowers open each evening.

RELATED SPECIES

Cardinal climber *(Ipomoea × multifida)* is a slender climber with small scarlet flowers that show up well against the dark green, deeply lobed leaves.

Morning glory *(I. tricolor)* is a fast-growing, 20- to 30-foot climber. It blankets its foliage with 3- to 6-inch blooms that open in the morning and last only a day. Among the many colorful selections are 'Heavenly Blue' (sky blue flowers with white throats); 'Flying Saucers' (marbled white and purple-blue); and 'Crimson Rambler' (red with white throats).

Spanish flag or mina *(I. lobata)* has small tubular scarlet flowers that open along one side of their crimson stalks in late summer. As the flowers age, they turn from red to orange to yellow to white.

Sweet potato vine *(I. batatas)* is grown for its attractive foliage. Leaves of 'Marguerite' are chartreuse; deep purple leaves of 'Blackie' are nearly black.

GARDEN COMPANIONS

Plant moonflowers on the same support as morning glories for flowers both night and day.

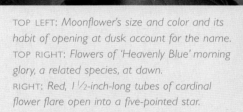

TOP LEFT: *Moonflower's size and color and its habit of opening at dusk account for the name.* TOP RIGHT: *Flowers of 'Heavenly Blue' morning glory, a related species, at dawn.* RIGHT: *Red, 1½-inch-long tubes of cardinal flower flare open into a five-pointed star.*

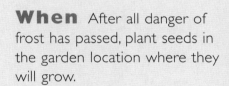

When After all danger of frost has passed, plant seeds in the garden location where they will grow.

Where Plant in full sun, in a moist, well-drained soil next to a sturdy support.

How Prepare soil by incorporating organic matter into the upper 10 to 12 inches. To aid germination, nick the seeds with a file and soak them overnight before sowing them in the garden.

TLC Water regularly but fertilize sparingly. Too much fertilizer will encourage leafy growth and reduce the number of blooms. Moonflowers and their relatives grow rapidly. If they climb beyond the area where you want them, unwind their stems and redirect their growth. Pruning is rarely necessary.

Grown as an annual.

Passion Vine
Passiflora caerulea

To add an exotic touch to your garden, grow a passion vine. The complex and exquisite structure of its flowers is guaranteed to elicit notice. Each blossom is composed of a wide ring of 10 petals and sepals surrounding a fringe of filaments with a prominent stamen and pistils—the flower's reproductive parts—at the center. The fragrant, 4-inch flowers appear from early summer to fall, just a few at a time, which seems enough given their individual beauty. They are predominantly white with blue and purple markings and are favorites of several species of butterflies. The deeply lobed, bright green, glossy leaves are attractive in themselves and provide a lush background for the flowers. Yellow-orange fruit may develop after the vine flowers.

Plant passion vines in the ground or in containers. They climb by tendrils, and the stems can grow as long as 30 feet. In zone 31 they may come back after winter from roots, but otherwise treat them as annuals. Plant your passion vine in a patio planter, near a walkway, so you can enjoy the flowers close-up.

The intricate flowers of passion vine have long inspired gardeners. Edible, egg-shaped fruits often follow flowers later in the season.

LEFT: *Flowers of maypop are slightly smaller than hybrids, but plants are hardier.*
TOP RIGHT: *Alternating petals of 'Jeanette' have white streaks down their centers.*
BOTTOM RIGHT: *Red flowers of 'Coral Seas' are 4 inches in diameter.*

PEAK SEASON

Flowers appear from early summer through fall.

MY FAVORITES

'Amethyst' (also listed as 'Lavender Lady') produces purple-blue flowers with darker filaments.

'Constance Elliott' bears very fragrant flowers with pure white petals, sepals, and filaments.

'Grandiflora' blossoms reach 5 to 6 inches in width with mauve petals and sepals and purple filaments.

'Jeanette' produces purple, lavender, and white flowers with purple-black filaments.

RELATED SPECIES

Maypop *(Passiflora incarnata)* is native to the southeastern U.S. and can survive temperatures of −10°F/−23°C. It produces 3-inch pale lavender flowers and edible fruits.

Passiflora jamesonii 'Coral Seas' has showy, 4-inch-wide red flowers.

GARDEN COMPANIONS

Passion vines will cover a freestanding support to add a dramatic vertical element to a flower bed. Balance the vertical growth with a lush planting of annuals, such as Madagascar periwinkle *(Catharanthus roseus)*, petunia, floss flower *(Ageratum houstonianum)*, and dusty miller, at the vine's base.

When Purchase potted plants when they become available in spring. Move plants that have been overwintered indoors to the garden after all danger of frost has passed. Cuttings can be rooted in summer.

Where Plant in full sun in a rich, moist, well-drained soil. The vines will grow in partial shade, but won't bloom as prolifically there.

How Plant passion vine in soil that has been enriched with organic matter or in a large container using commercial potting soil. Apply a dilute complete liquid fertilizer at planting time.

TLC Fertilize at 2- to 3-week intervals throughout the summer. Water when soil becomes dry. To overwinter a potted plant, cut it back to a manageable size and bring it indoors. Place it in a sunny window in a warm room with a freestanding trellis or teepee in the pot to support the stems. Although passion vine is native to the American tropics and subtropics, its roots will sometimes survive a mild winter in parts of the Mid-Atlantic if protected by a heavy layer of mulch. To optimize the chances of winter survival outdoors, plant the vine against a south-facing wall.

Grown as an annual.

Ground Covers

Ground covers are the garden's unsung heroes. They are the background plants that work hard so you don't have to. They cover bare ground attractively and in doing so, crowd out weeds and keep flower beds and shrub plantings looking neat. When ground covers are planted around trees, they protect the trunks from damage by lawn mowers and string trimmers. When they are interplanted with spring bulbs, they not only provide a handsome backdrop for the blooming bulbs, they also camouflage the unattractive, sprawling after-bloom foliage.

Ground covers are far more than just substitutes for lawn. In fact, their only feature in common with the familiar greensward is the ability to create a fairly uniform living blanket over bare earth. With these spreading plants, you can get infinite foliage variety, flowers, decorative fruits—and, yes, just plain green if you wish.

serve the purely practical purpose of growing where lawn is ill adapted. The less-thirsty ground covers are fine conservation alternatives wherever you want a low-growing surface in an area that's unlikely to get any foot traffic. And in outlying areas of the garden, where keeping a lawn is awkward, you can plant tough ground covers to beautify areas that otherwise would generate weeds and dust. Ground covers make attractive, leafy carpets on sloping ground too steep for easy lawn maintenance, and some have dense root systems that will bind the soil and reduce erosion.

USING GROUND COVERS

Lawn (page 226) is the classic ground cover, and it is still preferred in some situations. At the most mundane level, other ground covers

RIGHT: *Here phlox combines with ferns, tulips, and other annuals and perennials to create a naturalistic garden around a birdbath.* OPPOSITE PAGE: *A close-up view of diminutive* Mazus reptans *'Albus' growing here alongside a walk.*

Ground covers also shine in a number of less utilitarian roles. Planted en masse, they can define spaces in the garden—separating areas or uniting them, depending on the garden design. They function readily as transition zones between other garden plantings and paving or lawn. A base of ground cover can immeasurably enhance the trees, shrubs, and even the garden ornaments, stone walls, and rock outcrops rising above it. With a bit of ingenuity, you can create dynamic tapestry plantings by combining two or more ground covers within a given area.

While a shag-carpet lawn invites walking, most ground covers emphatically suggest "keep off." That traffic-control function can let you determine access patterns within a garden while maintaining a feeling of openness.

ESTABLISHING GROUND COVERS

Among my Top 10 ground covers, you'll find plants that need regular watering and those that need less—even to the extent of subsisting on rainfall alone. But regardless of a mature plant's water needs, young plants establish more quickly if soil is kept moist. Wide swings between wet and dry soil prolong the march to maturity, so you should pay close attention to watering during the first year or two. In addition, mulch the soil in between plants until they fill in. This prevents rapid evaporation of soil moisture, fosters good root growth by keeping the soil more evenly moist and cool, and suppresses weeds. In time, the ground-cover growth will fill in to become the plant's own living mulch.

—CAROLE OTTESEN

Barrenwort

Epimedium

Barrenwort suffers from more than one unfortunate name. When it is referred to as an herb, the name "horny goat's weed" points to its use as an aphrodisiac. At least "barrenwort," its other common name, though not attractive, is accurate. "Barren" describes the poor, dry places where this plant will grow and "wort" is Middle English for "plant." Barrenwort, then, is a plant that normally grows in poor soil. In the garden, it will not only survive in dry shade, it will thrive there, eventually forming an attractive, weed-defying mat about 10 inches tall.

'Sulphureum' barrenwort and daffodils flower in the dappled shade of a crabapple.

The typically heart-shaped leaves form a beautifully textured ground cover. In some varieties, they emerge a pale copper color before turning green. Some mature leaves are tinted red, creating a contrasting pattern with the green veins, a trait that makes this ground cover even more appealing. It flowers in spring, bearing delicate, spurred, down-ward-facing blossoms held above the clumps of leaves on fine, wiry stems. Here in the Mid-Atlantic region, barrenwort takes on a beautiful caramel color after frost that is handsome in winter.

ABOVE: 'Roseum' barrenwort bears lavender flowers in spring.
BELOW: New leaves of 'Sulphureum' brighten a shaded bed.

PEAK SEASON

Spring through midwinter

MY FAVORITES

'Frohnleiten' (*Epimedium × perralchicum* 'Frohnleiten') is a very vigorous grower. Stems hold the yellow flowers above the red-tinted leaves.

'Roseum' (*E. × youngianum* 'Roseum') is a more compact, clumping plant with light green leaves and long-lasting pale lavender flowers that bloom early.

'Sulphureum' (*E. × versicolor* 'Sulphureum') bears large, two-toned flowers of white and yellow.

GARDEN COMPANIONS

Barrenwort is great at the foot of shrubs of any kind, but those that are leggy, such as chokeberry (*Aronia*), benefit more than most.

When Plant in spring or fall. Divide in fall.

Where While barrenworts will grow in dry, inauspicious places, they grow faster, thicker, and better where the soil is moist and rich. If possible, give them a location that gets morning sun followed by afternoon shade. They spread slowly but steadily, even in the shade of a maple tree.

How Before planting barrenwort, remove weeds from the bed and work in a plentiful amount of compost. Space barrenworts 12 inches apart. Mulch and water regularly until the plants establish. Once established, they are exceptionally drought tolerant.

TLC When the barrenwort has spread, it will choke out most weeds, but when plants are small, be sure to remove weeds such as onion grass. Later on, it will be impossible to dig them out through barrenwort's thick roots. Cut back the old foliage in late February or early March; new leaves and flowers will follow shortly thereafter.

Black-eyed Susan
Rudbeckia fulgida 'Goldsturm'

Gradually spreading into a dense clump, 'Goldsturm' black-eyed Susan serves well as a ground cover.

True, black-eyed Susans are most often thought of as candidates for the perennial border. And, while 'Goldsturm' black-eyed Susan is wonderful in flower gardens, it has a number of attributes that make it superb as a ground cover as well. 'Goldsturm' plants are different from many other forms of black-eyed Susan. For starters, they were bred to be especially uniform in size and habit. They are extremely flowerful, producing big crops of golden flowers that all bloom at the same height. When a mass of these plants comes into bloom, the effect is like a golden flower carpet, studded with black "eyes."

There are also practical reasons to choose this black-eyed Susan for use as a ground cover. It spreads quickly and densely, forming a green mat that prevents weeds from sprouting. It is effective throughout the year, bringing something to enjoy each season. In winter, the dark green leaves cling tightly to the ground. In spring, they stretch outward and upward, forming a dark green mass that is eventually seamless. In midsummer, the flowers provide a month-long show. After the petals fall, dark chocolate–colored seed heads form. These are attractive in the fall and winter and always draw birdlife into the garden.

PEAK SEASON

Summer, when the plants are in full bloom

GARDEN COMPANIONS

'Goldsturm' black-eyed Susan is especially lovely in combination with fountain grass (*Pennisetum alopecuroides*).

Golden 2½-inch flowers of 'Goldsturm' have a black or dark brown central cone.

A bed of 'Goldsturm' is accented by upright 'Karl Foerster' feather reed grass.

When Fall planted black-eyed Susans establish fastest, but you can also plant them in early spring.

Where Plant in full to partial sun.

How Prepare the bed by removing weeds and incorporating plentiful amounts of compost into the soil. Space the plants about 18 inches apart. Water well and mulch. Keep the plants watered until they are established.

TLC 'Goldsturm' black-eyed Susan loves sun and water. The displays of it in public places throughout the Mid-Atlantic are invariably irrigated. But in lieu of an irrigation system, consider planting it in a moist place, enriching the soil with plenty of compost and covering the soil between the plants with a deep mulch. After blooms fade, leave the seed heads on the plants for as long as they are attractive—they are bird magnets. When they cease to please, cut them back.

Green and Gold

Chrysogonum virginianum

Green and gold spreads via underground runners, thereby forming dense green carpet dotted with yellow, daisy flowers.

Green and gold is an outstanding ground-cover plant that is, despite its many charms, too little known and, unfortunately, not always easy to find at the average garden center. It may take a little surfing the web or attending native plant sales to find it, but it's worth the trouble.

The dark green, 6-inch-tall plants have attractively lobed, semievergreen to evergreen leaves. Cheerful, golden yellow flowers bloom in May, sporadically throughout the summer, and again in fall. Green and gold spreads rapidly in sun to partial shade to form a weed-suppressing mat that will even tolerate a little foot traffic. It isn't fussy about soil types, requiring only good drainage. Green and gold would be an excellent choice for the lawn area of a townhouse whose owners prefer not to mow. In addition to a mostly evergreen carpet of dark green foliage, a green and gold "lawn" provides a bonus crop of golden daisy flowers.

ABOVE: *Yellow starlike flowers are offset by the bright green, 2-inch-long leaves.*
BELOW: *White tulips and blue violas are color foils for a patch of green and gold.*

PEAK SEASON

Spring, when green and gold blooms most abundantly

MY FAVORITES

'Allen Bush' is a robust form that grows to 10 inches tall with a long, prolific bloom time.

'Lacquered Spider' is a strongly spreading plant that covers the ground quickly. It has gray-green leaves with red veins and grows just 7 inches tall.

'Pierre' is a vigorous spreader that grows 6 inches tall and bears large flowers.

GARDEN COMPANIONS

Interplant with small, early-flowering bulbs such as glory-of-the-snow, winter aconite, or snowdrops.

When Plant in fall or spring.

Where Choose a site in sun to partial shade that is reasonably moist and well drained.

How Prepare a bed by removing weeds or turf and incorporating liberal amounts of compost. Space green and gold plants 12 inches apart. Mulch and water until the plants are established.

TLC Green and gold is fairly self-supporting once it is established. Water the plants during dry periods for the first year or two. Top-dress with compost in early spring.

Japanese Spurge
Pachysandra terminalis

Japanese spurge is one of the most popular ground covers in the Mid-Atlantic region, or, for that matter, most everywhere else. There are good reasons for this. It is evergreen and the leaves are lustrous and interestingly whorled, giving a textured effect to a bed. It spreads quickly by underground runners to form a uniform mass. It isn't fussy about soil and can even adapt to dry, shady spaces, and compete successfully with trees and large shrubs. It is one of the best plants for preventing erosion on a shady bank. The spreading roots anchor the soil and the dense foliage will prevent most weeds from seeding, or, if they do, from penetrating the 6-inch-tall, thick, green mat of lustrous leaves. Japanese spurge does all of this with few maintenance demands. The small flower spikes that appear in early summer are modestly showy, but the real reason to grow this plant is for the way its uniform foliage keeps beds looking neat all year.

Japanese spurge spreads quickly to create a uniform, glossy green mat.

PEAK SEASON
Year-round

RELATED SPECIES
Allegheny spurge *(Pachysandra procumbens)* is the native alternative to Japanese spurge. While there are some similarities between the two plants, there are many differences. Allegheny spurge also produces whorled leaves on short stems, but the leaves are bigger and longer, and the stems are taller, growing about 12 inches high. It doesn't spread rapidly by underground runners, but fans out slowly. The evergreen foliage emerges a bright grass green in spring, sends up 6-inch, white, fragrant flowers, and then turns a very dark green color that is mottled silver in winter.

GARDEN COMPANIONS
Japanese spurge is an ideal ground cover under large trees such as oaks or beeches or around azaleas. Interplant with spring-flowering bulbs such as daffodils or grape hyacinths.

ABOVE: *Toothed leaves of Japanese spurge mix here with low-growing azalea flowers.*
BELOW LEFT: *'Silver Edge' Japanese spurge brightens shady locations.*
BELOW RIGHT: *'Halcyon' hostas are surrounded by Japanese spurge.*

When Plant in September or in early spring.

Where Plant Japanese spurge in slightly acid, fertile soil in full to partial shade.

How Japanese spurge is frequently sold in flats of rooted cuttings. Space these about 6 to 10 inches apart in a bed that has been cultivated and amended with plenty of compost. Water well and mulch to conserve moisture.

TLC Japanese spurge is relatively carefree. Top-dress newly established beds with compost and water regularly during the first season and during periods of drought. Don't be afraid to pull up plants that creep over the edges of the bed.

Lady's-Mantle
Alchemilla

One of the most attractive traits of lady's-mantle is the way droplets of dew sparkle in the morning sun on this plant's neatly pleated, fanlike leaves. This trait gave rise to its botanical name, *Alchemilla:* In the Middle Ages, these droplets were considered to be magical and were collected for use in alchemy. The common name, "lady's-mantle," refers to the leaf's shape, thought to be similar to the mantle or cloak of the Virgin Mary. With its handsome evergreen foliage that forms a soft gray-green, ruffled

clump, lady's-mantle is usually considered a foliage plant. It is charming in June, however, when the billowing yellow flowers appear. The bloom is especially showy when lady's-mantle plants are massed as a ground cover. The small, chartreuse flowers are held on slender stalks above clumping plants that are about 15 inches tall by 20 inches wide.

With its ruffled foliage, lady's-mantle is a handsome addition anywhere in the garden. Grow it as ground cover in shade or beneath roses. It is very drought tolerant and will self-seed even in gravel or in cracks between paving. It can be invasive if left to go to seed, so cut the flowers—they make lovely fresh or dried bouquets.

The deep blue flowers of 'Six Hills Giant' catmint makes a classic color combination with the chartreuse flowers of lady's-mantle.

ABOVE: *Clusters of flowers spill generously from a clump of lady's-mantle in late spring.*
BELOW: *Water drops sparkle on the fuzzy leaves of lady's-mantle.*

PEAK SEASON

June, when it blooms

MY FAVORITES

Alchemilla erythropoda is a diminutive plant, growing only about 5 inches high. In autumn, its flower heads turn a beautiful orange red.

A. mollis 'Auslese' is a selection with bigger leaves that form a beautifully upright clump.

A. mollis 'Thriller' produces large, billowing heads of star-shaped flowers that grow to 18 inches tall. They are excellent for cutting or drying.

GARDEN COMPANIONS

Lady's-mantle and roses are a classic combination.

When Plant in the early spring.

Where In the Mid-Atlantic, lady's-mantle needs a bit of shade. A location that gets morning sun is perfect. Adequate drainage is also a key consideration. Lady's-mantle is a good plant to cover a bank.

How Incorporate a plentiful amount of compost into a bed that has been cleared of weeds or lawn grasses. Space plants 12 inches apart. Mulch and water well until the plants are established.

TLC Top-dress lady's-mantle with compost in early spring. If the foliage looks a bit shabby in the heat of summer, cut it back. Fresh new leaves will sprout. Lady's-mantle self-sows readily. Transplant seedlings in early spring; they will take 2 years to flower. Divide established plants in March or April.

Lamb's Ear
Stachys byzantina

Flower spikes only rarely interrupt the mat of velvety soft, silver leaves of 'Silver Carpet' lamb's ear.

With its sprawling, gray-green, semievergreen foliage clumps, lamb's ear is the perfect ground cover for a dry, sun-baked slope where other plants only wither. The dense leaves cast their own shade to keep roots cool and the fuzz on the leaves keeps them from desiccating. Lamb's ear sends out new growth that roots as it goes, quickly spreading into a low, dense mat. In early summer, tall flower stalks with tiny purple flowers rise about 15 inches above the plants. Some gardeners cut them off, either because lamb's ear self-sows or because they don't like them. The flower stalks are very effective en masse, however, especially on a slope. Gardeners who would rather not have them can choose selections that flower rarely, if at all.

Lamb's ear is one of the easiest ground covers you can grow. And they are great plants for deer-infested gardens because they are usually not eaten.

When Plant in fall or spring.

Where Choose a place in full sun to light shade that is well drained with good air circulation. Lamb's ears will rot in dank places.

How Plant containers or divisions of lamb's ears in a bed that is free of weeds. Mulch lightly and water well.

TLC Lamb's ears are fairly trouble free when given sun, good drainage, and good air circulation. If foliage rots in wet weather, simply remove it. New leaves will sprout when the plant dries out.

PEAK SEASON

The only time lamb's ear doesn't look good is in late winter when the leaves have been skeletonized by rain and snow.

MY FAVORITES

'Big Ears' (also called 'Countess Helene von Stein') is similar to the species and tolerant of heat and humidity.

'Silver Carpet' has large woolly leaves and rarely flowers.

GARDEN COMPANION

A bed of lamb's ear combines nicely with a mass of anise hyssop (Agastache foeniculum).

RIGHT: *Leaves of 'Big Ears' are both larger and greener compared with standard varieties.*
BELOW: *Silvery lamb's ear is combined here with chives, mint, and thyme. Its upright spikes are shown just prior to flowering.*

Lawn Grasses

There is no question that nothing sets off the trees, shrubs, and flowers of a home landscape like a fine stretch of velvety green grass. For that reason, lawn has long been the most popular home-landscape feature. There are concerns over the amount of water and fertilizer needed to support typical lawn grasses, however. Research has shown that not only do lawn grasses require more irrigation than any other garden plant, but fertilizing them with high-nitrogen fertilizer produces runoff that has a negative impact on the plants and animals that live in our waterways and wetlands.

There are ways to be responsible about lawn care and still enjoy a beautiful greensward. One easy and attractive way is to minimize the lawn area by expanding beds of shrubs and ground covers. Reducing lawn just a little bit can make a big difference, and save you maintenance time, too. Another effective step is to choose the type of turf grass you plant according to its adaptability. Even within the Mid-Atlantic region, conditions vary widely; a good source of local information is the county cooperative extension agent.

No other ground cover can unify the different parts of a landscape like a lawn.

PEAK SEASON

Spring through fall

MY FAVORITES

'Midnight' Kentucky bluegrass (*Poa pratensis* 'Midnight') is suitable only for the inland and higher elevation Mid-Atlantic zones, where it serves as a fine-textured blue-green turfgrass that is naturally dwarf.

Perennial ryegrass (*Lolium perenne*) germinates and grows fast and is usually included in seed mixes. 'Applaud' is a disease-resistant perennial rye.

Tall fescue (*Festuca arundinacea*) is a better choice than Kentucky bluegrass for the hotter parts of the Mid-Atlantic. 'Rebel Supreme' and 'Rebel III' are two good tall fescues. They are both fine-textured with dense, dark green foliage.

LAWN LOOK-ALIKE

Pennsylvania sedge (*Carex pensylvanica*) is a grasslike, native lawn look-alike that tolerates shade and grows to just under 10 inches. It is perfect for hard-to-mow places, especially around the roots of very large trees.

GARDEN COMPANIONS

Lawn sets off everything beautifully. Encircling it with a low-growing perennial such as lady's-mantle or lily turf makes the transition from grass to shrubs gradual and attractive.

When The best time to seed lawn grasses is in mid-September to capitalize on the cool, mild fall days that are optimal for growth.

Where Plant in full sun to very light shade in soil that is slightly acid and well drained.

How New lawns require proper site preparation. This includes removing the existing sod, soil testing, amending the existing soil with compost, and tilling to about 6 to 8 inches deep. If your soil is too acid, add limestone to raise the pH. Before sowing seed, rake the area smooth, remove rocks and stones, and fill low spots. Water to settle the soil 2 to 3 days before planting.

TOP: *A small, circular lawn unifies this formal landscape.*
BOTTOM: *This lawn of tall fescue has attractive color and texture.*

TLC Allow a newly planted lawn to grow at least 3 inches high before mowing. Leave the grass clippings on the lawn to replace lost nitrogen rather than gathering them. To avoid disease problems, irrigate before noon to give the grass time to dry before nightfall. Water thoroughly and regularly using only a fine spray.

Lily Turf

Liriope muscari

Lily turf is a popular ground cover in the Mid-Atlantic states. A shade-loving member of the lily family, it does eventually form a tough "turf." It grows into 15-inch-tall clumps of flat, narrow, dark evergreen leaves that spread steadily outward and look a lot like giant clumps of grass. Unlike grass, however, lily turf is allowed to bloom. In summer, it sends up flower spikes that look like giant grape hyacinths. A crop of lustrous, blue-black berries follows the flowers.

Lily turf is a true survivor. In fact, it is actually hard to kill it. Clumps that have been tossed into the compost heap or those that you have somehow forgotten to plant all winter often surface the following spring in perfect health. For this reason, lily turf is an ideal choice for the difficult spaces under large trees. It tolerates dry shade and isn't fussy about soil.

One reason for lily turf's strong constitution is what happens underground. It is firmly anchored by a dense root system that a weed would find nearly impossible to penetrate.

PEAK SEASON

Showiest when it blooms in summer

MY FAVORITES

'Big Blue' is a vigorous plant with broad leaf blades and big, lavender blue flowers.

'Monroe's White' produces white flowers.

'Variegata' is a yellow and green form that can take some sun.

RELATED PLANT

Mondo grass (Ophiopogon japonicus), another member of the lily family, looks like a miniature liriope. It is an absolutely splendid creeping grasslike plant that can be used in place of lawn. Planted at 9-inch intervals, it will cover an area in moist shade in two seasons. It is glossy and dark green, and it never needs mowing. 'Kyoto Dwarf' and 'Nana' are two good cultivars.

GARDEN COMPANIONS

Plant lily turf as a ground cover in a bed that surrounds trees such as flowering dogwood and honey locust. Plant daffodils between the clumps of lily turf.

OPPPOSITE PAGE: Cutting back 'Variegata' lily turf in early spring will rejuvenate it, and cause it to produce more yellow-edged leaves.

When The best times to plant lily turf are fall and spring, but this tough plant will survive summer planting if watered well until established.

Where Plant in light to full shade in average garden soil.

How Space lily turf that has been growing in quart containers 18 inches apart in a prepared bed. Use a sharp knife to divide large clumps for replanting. Space these smaller pieces about 10 inches apart. Mulch and water well until established. Check to make sure deer don't pull newly planted lily turf plants out of the ground.

TLC Once established, lily turf is a tough customer that needs only a little grooming. By February, the foliage will be tattered, windblown, and possibly deer eaten. Cut it back to 4 or 5 inches with hedge clippers or the lawn mower. New growth will quickly cover the cut foliage.

TOP: Spikes holding violet flowers rise well above leaves of 'Variegata'.
BOTTOM: Lawnlike mondo grass never needs mowing and takes shade.

Mazus
Mazus reptans

This pretty, evergreen, 1–inch–tall creeper grows fastest when supplied with both sun and abundant moisture. If you have that unusual combination of moist but sunny ground, mazus will cover it like greased lightning. If not, plant mazus in light shade where it won't dry out, and you'll have quick coverage anyway. A one-quart plant in moist, rich, high shade will spread to cover about 3 to 4 square feet in a single season.

Purplish blue flowers of mazus bloom just above the diminutive, inch-high leaves.

If you are fed up with weekly lawn mowing, consider mazus. In a small area, it is a perfect substitute for lawn. It stays very low, tolerates light foot traffic, and never, ever requires that you haul out that sputtering mower.

The bright green, round leaves are smaller than a dime, but they grow densely, creating their own shade. In spring, mazus produces a big flush of small, orchidlike, purple flowers that are extremely showy.

PEAK SEASON

May, when mazus is covered with flowers

MY FAVORITES

'Albus' is a white-flowered form.

GARDEN COMPANIONS

Mazus will cover bare ground under deciduous shrubs such as azaleas and winterberries. The small early *Crocus tommasinianus* are also good companions.

When Plant in fall or spring.

Where Mazus requires moist soil and will grow in sun or partial shade if you provide adequate moisture. Once the plants are established, however, the densely layered leaves actually create their own moist shade.

How Plant mazus 24 inches apart in a prepared bed of moist soil. Mulch, water, and stand back!

TLC Water a newly planted bed of mazus until it is established. Remove weeds as soon as they appear. Clip off errant growth.

ABOVE: *'Albus' mazus adds to the show by flowering at the same time as these azaleas.*
LEFT: *Mazus is well suited to filling in between stepping-stones because of its tolerance for occasional footsteps. This is white-flowered 'Albus'.*

Moss Pink
Phlox subulata

The phlox family is a big one, with a member to occupy each and every environmental niche, but evergreen moss pink is my favorite. The one for sun-baked, exposed places, moss pink is beloved for the bright flowers that cover the plant in spring. When the plants bloom, a slope planted with them looks as if it has been strewn with brightly colored clothes. There are white, pink, lavender, blue, and bright coral forms, as well as a pink and white, candy-striped moss pink. All provide dependable spring color for two weeks or more. This 1-inch-tall creeper is a classic ground cover for sunny slopes and rock gardens, where it spreads quickly in moderately dry, well-drained soil.

Like a lavender wave, moss pink spills over a stone wall.

PEAK SEASON

Spring, when in flower

RELATED SPECIES

Creeping phlox *(Phlox stolonifera)* is a very low creeper (less than 1 inch tall) when not in bloom. It prefers the moist, rich soil and high shade of open woodland. It is a good choice for the hot parts of the Mid-Atlantic region where its small, round leaves are evergreen.

Wood phlox *(P. divaricata)* also prefers woodland conditions. It is more fragrant, showier, and larger—a foot tall in bloom—than creeping phlox. The long, pointed leaves of wood phlox are not truly evergreen and, in hotter parts of the region, may suffer more insect damage.

GARDEN COMPANIONS

A perfect companion for moss pink is the low-growing Missouri evening primrose *(Oenothera macrocarpa)*, known for having the largest lemon yellow flowers on the smallest plant of any evening primrose. Its stems are 8 to 12 inches long, but are lax and sprawl on the ground in sunny, well-drained soil.

ABOVE: *The white, blue, and lavender flowers of creeping phlox rise 6 inches above the leaves.*
RIGHT: *With its larger, fragrant flowers, wood phlox is moss pink's showiest relative.*

When Moss pink is best planted in fall so the plants can get established before blooming in spring, but often, plants are only available in spring.

Where Moss pink needs sun, good drainage, and good air circulation. It is extremely cold hardy and will endure a location in the teeth of the wind with grace.

How Prepare the bed for moss pink by removing all weeds. While it will acclimate to less-than-fertile soil, weeds growing in and over this low-growing plant can shade it out. Sodlike flats or containers of moss pink are often available in spring. Set both into a bed so that the roots are covered with soil. Space container plants about 12 inches apart. Water well and mulch to conserve moisture while the plants establish.

TLC Moss pink is a tough plant and will require little maintenance if weeds are controlled at the outset. Prune away dead or errant branches.

Edibles

Growing edible plants is satisfying to both body and soul. When you grow plants for food, your garden activities extend beyond the backyard to many other parts of your life. Meals are planned around harvest dates; bumper crops will have you flipping through magazines and cookbooks for new recipes; you may even find yourself planning social gatherings to celebrate an abundant strawberry harvest or the first ripe tomatoes.

And if you find that your family cannot eat all the zucchinis, tomatoes, and cucumbers produced during the high season, you can share your bounty with neighbors or the local food kitchen.

There are many reasons to include edibles in your landscape. You can grow your favorite varieties, try out the latest hybrids, and experience old-fashioned, heirloom varieties. And rather than buying produce that was picked green last week so that it's still presentable when it reaches the supermarket shelves, you can harvest your crops at the peak of maturity and use them literally minutes later! There is no way to beat the flavor and texture of a freshly picked, fully matured tomato (page 254), or the sweet-tartness of homegrown blackberries (page 252), ripened to perfection. Fresh herbs (page 242) pinched from plants and sprinkled in a sauce or omelet transform ordinary fare into gourmet cuisine.

Most edible plants grow best in well-drained soil, with a minimum of 6 hours of sun each day. Vegetables and fruits prefer rich soil and benefit from a regular supply of water. Many herbs, on the other hand, often thrive and produce their best flavor in lean soils, and most are fairly drought tolerant once they are established.

LEFT: *Make vegetable gardening more convenient and more successful by building permanent raised beds.*
OPPOSITE PAGE: *Grow your own vegetables to enjoy those that are rare, exotic, or otherwise unavailable at the local supermarket. These are dangerously hot habanero peppers.*

DOUBLE-DUTY PLANTS

Included in this chapter are vegetables, herbs, and small fruits that can be grown in a relatively small space. Most edible plants have traditionally been grown in rows. This arrangement is great if you have the room, but there are alternatives for smaller landscapes. Many edibles are also very ornamental; they have attractive flowers, fruit, fragrance, or foliage. Lettuce, Swiss chard, mustard (see Salad Greens, page 246), and dill, for example, make pleasing companions for annual flowers when grown in large containers or window boxes. Many other vegetables and herbs also add texture, fragrance, and color to annual flower beds, and a planter filled with herbs placed by the back door is both beautiful and handy for cooking. Blueberries are perfectly suited to a sunny shrub border; in addition to their delectable summer fruit, they bear delicate spring flowers and their green leaves turn deep red, orange, and yellow in fall.

THE KITCHEN GARDEN

An old-fashioned garden style that has regained popularity in recent years is the kitchen garden. This style combines vegetables, fruit, herbs, flowers, and even clipped shrubs, laid out in orderly, often geometric arrangements. Trellises and fences lend a sense of order to the garden and support the vigorous, vining plants. A variety of garden art, limited only by the gardener's imagination, further enhances this garden style. Regardless of the size or style of your garden, however, consider including a few edibles and enjoy the fruits—and vegetables—of your labor.

—RITA PELCZAR

Beans

'Royal Burgundy' snap beans have attractive red-pink flowers and dark purple pods that change to dark green after cooking.

Beans generally fall into three categories—snap, shell (or shelling), or dried—signifying the growth stage at which they taste best. Bush and pole varieties of each type are available. Bush beans don't need support and usually mature relatively quickly. Pole beans require a fence, trellis, or other support upon which to climb. They mature more slowly, but produce two to three times the harvest in the same amount of garden space.

Snap beans (also called green beans or string beans) are harvested for their edible pods and are best picked when young and tender, before the seeds are fully mature. *Wax beans* are similar but their pods are yellow. *Filet beans*—my favorites—are long and thin, harvested when their pods are no thicker than the width of a small pencil. *Romano beans* have flattened pods.

Shell and *dried beans* are grown for the seeds that develop inside the pods. Shell beans (and lima beans) are at their best when their seeds have just matured. Allow the seeds of dried beans to mature fully and dry on the vine before harvesting.

PEAK SEASON

Midsummer to first frost

MY FAVORITES

Snap beans

'Kentucky Blue' and 'Kentucky Wonder' are very similar pole beans that produce abundant 7- to 8-inch dark green, straight pods on vines that grow 6 feet tall. Both can be harvested over a long season, but 'Kentucky Blue' matures earlier.

'Maxibel' is a delicious and tender filet bush bean.

'Rocdor' is a bush bean that produces slim, yellow, 6-inch pods.

'Tendercrop' is a bush bean that produces heavy crops of 6-inch pods.

Bush lima beans

'Fordhook 242' and 'Dixie Butterpea' can be harvested for fresh use (as shelling beans) or left to dry on the vine and harvested for storage.

GARDEN COMPANIONS

Plant beans with other vegetables and herbs. Pole beans can be grown on a fence, trellis, or tepee, adding height and definition along the back row of a bed of vegetables.

TOP: *Pole beans twine up stakes.*
BOTTOM: *The classic 'Kentucky Wonder'.*

When Sow seeds outdoors after all danger of frost has passed and the soil has warmed. Seeds will rot if planted in a cold, wet soil. For a continuous harvest of bush beans, sow successive plantings at 2- to 3-week intervals until midsummer.

Where Plant beans where they will receive a minimum of 6 hours of direct sun. They grow best in rich, well-drained soil, supplemented by organic matter such as well-rotted compost or leaf mold. Place pole beans along the north side of the garden so they will not shade other crops.

How Sow seeds 1 inch deep and 2 to 3 inches apart. Pole beans need some support such as a trellis or tepee (see TLC), which should be set in place prior to planting seeds. Space rows of bush beans 2 to 3 feet apart and rows of pole beans 3 to 4 feet apart. After seeds have germinated, thin the seedlings so that bush types are 5 to 6 inches apart and pole beans are 6 to 8 inches apart. Keep plants well watered.

TLC To avoid spreading disease, never handle bean plants when they are wet. To make a trellis for pole beans, string wires between two stout poles and weave string between them. To construct a tepee for pole beans, lash 5 or 6 8-foot-long bamboo poles together at the top with twine and settle the bottoms in the soil to secure them.

Blueberries

lueberries are native to eastern North America. In addition to producing delicious and healthful fruit, blueberry plants are very ornamental. Planted among other acid-loving shrubs in a border or alone as a hedge, they fit easily into most landscape designs. They bear small, white, urn-shaped flowers in spring, and in fall, their dark green or blue green leaves turn shades of deep red, orange, or yellow.

At peak flower highbush blueberries prove their ornamental value.

There are several types of blueberries, and you can select varieties that will provide your table with fruit over a long season. The type sold in grocery stores is the highbush blueberry *(Vaccinium corymbosum),* which grows 5 to 15 feet tall. Lowbush blueberries *(V. angustifolium)* grow wild in some areas. They are usually less than 2 feet tall and spread by underground roots. Highbush and lowbush types have been crossed to produce "half-high" blueberries that grow 3 to 5 feet tall.

Two blueberry plants per person will usually produce all the fresh blueberries the average gardener can enjoy, with enough left over for cobblers, pies, muffins, and pancakes.

PEAK SEASON

Depending on the variety, fruit ripens from July through August. Small white flowers are borne in spring; leaves turn intense shades of red, orange, and yellow in fall.

MY FAVORITES

Highbush blueberries

'Bluecrop' is a midseason variety with large fruit; it is drought tolerant.

'Bluejay', another midseason selection, produces medium-sized fruit and is resistant to mummy berry, a common fungal disease.

'Duke' produces medium-sized fruit early in the season.

'Elliott' is a late-season producer; it is also resistant to mummy berry.

Half-high hybrids

'Northland' produces small fruit with great wild flavor. The plants have a spreading habit.

GARDEN COMPANIONS

In a shrub border, combine blueberries with other acid-loving shrubs such as azalea, rhododendron, Japanese pieris, and fothergilla.

When Plant rooted cuttings as early as possible in spring. Plant container-grown plants in spring or fall.

Where Blueberries need well-drained acid soil with a pH between 4.0 and 5.2. If it is not sufficiently acid, add peat moss, pine needles, or rotted sawdust into the soil a year in advance of planting.

How Plant at least two different varieties to ensure good fruit production. Maintain the appropriate soil pH by mulching plants with a 4-inch layer of composted sawdust or bark. The pH can also be lowered with sulfur, but have a soil test done to determine the recommended amount.

TLC For an extended harvest, select several varieties that ripen at different times. Cover plants with plastic netting to protect fruit from foraging birds. Avoid cultivating, because blueberries produce lots of shallow roots that are easily damaged. Fruit is produced on the previous year's growth, and best fruiting occurs on stems that are about the thickness of a pencil. While plants are dormant, remove the oldest stems that have become unproductive back to the soil line.

ABOVE: A standard variety because of its hardiness and versatility, 'Bluecrop' grows 4 to 6 feet high and bears generously.
LEFT: The number of flowers predicts the number of fruits that will follow. This variety is 'Northland'.

239

Cucumbers

A vining cucumber with mature fruits climbs a tepee of bamboo poles.

There are two main types of cucumbers: slicers and picklers. Slicers are grown for eating fresh; the fruit is straight, with medium to dark green skin that's waxy. Pickling cucumbers, grown mainly for pickles and relishes, are usually smaller and often curved, and their skins are lighter and thinner. If you have room for only one variety, choose a pickling cucumber—they are great for fresh eating too, and they don't need peeling. If space allows, grow some of both, and if you find yourself enjoying a bumper crop, enjoy cold cucumber soup for a delicious and refreshing summer lunch.

Both types come in either vining or bush varieties. Vining plants can grow to 9 feet long and perform best on a trellis or climbing a wire cage. Bush cucumbers require less garden space and no support; they will even grow quite happily in a large container.

Cucumbers are susceptible to several diseases, such as powdery and downy mildews, wilt, and scab, but there are many good disease-resistant varieties.

PEAK SEASON

Midsummer to frost

MY FAVORITES

Slicers

'Salad Bush' produces lots of 8-inch, smooth-skinned cukes in a small space, and it has excellent disease resistance.

'Straight Eight' is a popular vining heirloom variety that produces 8-inch, white-spined fruit.

'Sweet Success' is a vining, burpless (nonbitter), disease-resistant, all-female variety (see TLC) that bears an abundance of dark green–skinned fruit, each up to 12 inches long.

Picklers

'County Fair' is a vining, disease-resistant plant that produces plump, thin-skinned, 3-inch fruits that are just the right size for pickles.

'Pickalot' is a bush type pickler that bears only female flowers (see TLC). The fruit grows to 5½ inches long.

GARDEN COMPANIONS

Grow dill nearby for convenience. Bush types make lush container plantings that will complement annuals and other ornamentals on the patio or deck. Vining types can be trained on strings or wires to provide vertical interest.

When Sow seeds directly in the garden after all danger of frost has passed, or start indoors 4 weeks before the last frost and transplant after the last frost and after the first true leaves appear.

Where Grow cucumbers in a sunny spot where the soil is rich, moist, and well-drained. Add compost or leaf mold to the soil prior to planting. Grow vining cucumbers on a trellis at the back of a bed or the north side of a vegetable garden.

How You can let vining cucumbers sprawl on the ground, but they will produce longer, straighter fruit and take up less garden space if they are grown on a trellis or in a cage. Grow bush types in rows or hills in the garden or in containers. Water well during dry weather and keep the soil mulched to retain moisture and reduce weeds.

TOP: *Identify female cucumber flowers by the immature fruits between the flower and stem.*
BOTTOM: *'Salad Bush' plants require much less space than vining cucumber varieties.*

TLC Once your cukes start producing, check them every day and pick the fruit before it reaches its maximum size. If you let mature fruit stay on the plant, production will slow. Don't worry if the first few flowers don't set fruit. Those are the male flowers, and they're followed about a week later by the female flowers that have baby cucumbers at their bases. Exceptions to this pattern are all-female hybrids.

Herbs
Basil, dill, parsley, sage, and thyme

Herbs add considerable charm to a garden and a world of flavor to food. Hardy in all zones, plant them liberally throughout your gardens, so you're sure to have plenty for fresh use.

BASIL

Basil *(Ocimum basilicum)*, a tender perennial grown as an annual, loves hot, sunny weather. Plants grow 6 inches to 2 feet tall, with flavorful bright green or burgundy leaves.

MY FAVORITES The purple leaves of 'Dark Opal' make a beautiful flavored vinegar. 'Genovese' grows to 2 feet tall and makes terrific pesto. 'Minimum' is a dwarf with tiny, flavor-packed leaves. 'Siam Queen' has great flavor, and the plants are lovely, with deep burgundy stems and flowers.

GROWING AND HARVESTING TIPS Sow seeds indoors about 6 weeks before the last frost or directly in the garden after all danger of frost has passed and soil has warmed. Water regularly, and pinch frequently to encourage branching and discourage flower development. Plant seed at monthly intervals for continuous harvests.

DILL

Dill *(Anethum graveolens)* is an annual herb grown for both its flavorful leaves and seeds. Additionally, flower heads are great for summer arrangements. Fresh dill leaves add flavor to salads, vegetables, fish, and poultry. Seeds are used for pickles.

MY FAVORITES 'Dukat' produces an abundance of sweetly flavored leaves on 2-foot plants that are slow to develop flowers and seeds. 'Fernleaf' is a dwarf with a delicate appearance but a rugged constitution. It can be grown in containers.

LEFT: *Green and purple leaves of sweet basil.*
RIGHT: *Tiny yellow dill flowers are pollen rich.*

GROWING AND HARVESTING TIPS Sow seed directly in the garden in early spring and make successive plantings at 3- to 4-week intervals. Dill does not transplant easily. Thin plants to stand 6 to 8 inches apart. To preserve, leaves can be frozen or used to make flavored vinegar. To harvest seed, cut flower heads when they have turned brown and hang them upside down in paper bags to catch the seed. Dill will self-sow if you leave a few seed heads in the garden.

PARSLEY

Parsley *(Petroselinum crispum)* is a biennial grown as an annual. It makes an attractive edging or addition to a container garden or flower bed. It is useful as a garnish and for flavoring soups, sauces, vegetables, meats, and salads. Fresh parsley sweetens your breath.

MY FAVORITES The tightly curled leaves of 'Extra Curled Dwarf' hold their shape for hours, so they are great for garnishing. The flat leaves of 'Italian Plain Leaf'

have a stronger flavor and a more relaxed habit; I prefer it for cooking.

GROWING AND HARVESTING TIPS Soak seed in warm water overnight before sowing indoors 8 to 10 weeks before the last frost date. Seed can also be directly sown in the garden or plants can be purchased in early spring. Water regularly. Harvest leaves from the outside of the clump; more leaves will grow from the center.

SAGE

Sage *(Salvia officinalis)* is a short-lived perennial herb; in my garden it usually survives for 3 or 4 years. It is grown for its leaves, which are typically soft gray-green, but varieties with purple as well as variegated leaves are available. Whatever the color, sage leaves make great foils for colorful perennial flowers. In the kitchen, sage is used to flavor fish, meat, poultry (it's a must for turkey dressing), sauces, cheese, and salad dressings.

MY FAVORITES 'Berggarten' produces an abundance of flavorful, rounded gray leaves; it rarely flowers. 'Aurea' has variegated green and yellow leaves. Leaves of 'Purpurascens' are flushed with purple. All grow 1 to 2 feet tall.

GROWING AND HARVESTING TIPS Purchase plants in spring and transplant to the garden after the last frost. Sage prefers a lean soil and is drought tolerant. Cut established plants back by a third in early spring. Pinch leaves as needed but stop harvesting in early fall to harden plants for winter. Preserve leaves by drying in a single layer on racks placed out of sunlight, or by freezing.

THYME

Common thyme *(Thymus vulgaris)* is both a perennial herb and an effective evergreen ground cover that grows to a height of 12 inches. Densely held along trailing stems, its tiny leaves form a neat mound that, when brushed against or walked upon, emits a heady fragrance. In the kitchen, thyme flavors meat and vegetable dishes, sauces, and stews.

TOP: *'Italian Plain Leaf' parsley is noted for its strong flavor.*
BOTTOM LEFT: *Yellow-edged leaves of 'Aurea' golden sage.*
BOTTOM RIGHT: *Diminutive lemon thyme spills out of its container.*

MY FAVORITES Creeping thyme *(T. serpyllum)* grows only an inch or two tall, spreading to make a dense evergreen mat. The fragrance of lemon thyme *(T. × citriodorus)* has decidedly lemony overtones. The variety of common thyme 'Aureus' (also called golden thyme) has gold and green foliage. Caraway-scented thyme *(T. herba-barona)* is a resilient creeper, good for the toughest places.

GROWING AND HARVESTING TIPS Thyme grows best in lean soil and a warm, sunny site. To keep plants neat, cut back after flowering. Thymes don't mind a bit of foot traffic, so they are great choices for growing between pavers and along paths.

GARDEN COMPANIONS FOR HERBS

Grow herbs in a formal garden, or mix them with flowering annuals and perennials, vegetables, and fruit in a casual kitchen garden.

Peppers
Sweet, spicy, and hot

Peppers come in such a variety of interesting shapes and vibrant colors, they are almost as ornamental as they are delicious. Tuck at least one plant into an annual flower bed; its glossy green leaves and colorful fruit will fit right in.

Peppers can generally be divided into those that are sweet and those that are hot. Sweet peppers include the familiar bell peppers, which have a blocky, square shape. They can be picked green or allowed to mature to red, orange, yellow, or purple (depending on the variety), which will give them a sweeter flavor. Other sweet peppers include pimientos,

Italian frying peppers, and sweet Hungarian peppers.

Hot peppers run the flavor gamut from the relatively mild 'Anaheim Chili' to the intensely hot 'Habanero'. Their shapes range from long and thin to fat and round (and everything between).

Peppers are great sources of vitamin C and fiber. They are easy to grow and prepare—either fresh or cooked—and they adapt to a wide range of dishes. The challenge of peppers is deciding which varieties to grow.

PEAK SEASON

Summer to fall

MY FAVORITES

'Anaheim Chili' is a mildly hot roasting pepper with long slender fruits that mature to bright red.

'Big Dipper' is a bell pepper with 4½-inch green fruits on robust plants.

'Giant Marconi' is a large, sweet-flavored Italian frying pepper that matures quickly to bright red.

'Habanero' is a pepper for those who really like it hot.

'Hungarian Wax' fruits are similar to sweet Hungarian peppers except they pack some heat. They mature to red and are great for pickling or for hot pepper relish.

'Sweet Banana' bears tapered, sweet yellow peppers that mature to orange and red. All colors of fruit are often on the same plant simultaneously.

GARDEN COMPANIONS

In a vegetable garden, interplant with lettuce or mesclun. After the fast-growing greens are harvested, the peppers will fill the space.

OPPOSITE PAGE, TOP: *'Sweet Banana' is a slender Italian frying pepper.*
OPPOSITE PAGE, BOTTOM: *The tangy flavor of 'Anaheim Chili' is released by roasting.*

ABOVE: *Immature and still green 'Habanero' peppers pack more pepper heat than others.* RIGHT: *This bell pepper was left to mature to red, sweetening its flavor.*

When Sow seed indoors 8 to 10 weeks before the last frost or purchase seedlings in spring. Set out plants after the last frost and once the soil has warmed.

Where Grow in full sun, in rich, well-drained soil that has been enriched with compost or leaf mold. Peppers are related to tomatoes, eggplant, and potatoes and are susceptible to many of the same diseases and pests, so don't plant peppers in the same space that any of those crops occupied the previous year.

How Space plants 18 to 24 inches apart in rows 2 to 3 feet apart. Water well after planting and apply a water-soluble balanced fertilizer.

TLC Water regularly, supplying the equivalent of approximately 1½ inches of rain per week, and fertilize again as the fruits begin to mature. Keep plants productive by harvesting fruit regularly as it matures. Harvest by cutting fruit from the plant with hand shears or a knife to avoid breaking the stems.

Salad Greens
Lettuce, mustard, Swiss chard

Salads become much more interesting when you grow your own greens, although the moniker "greens" is a bit deceiving. Many fit the bill; others, however, are red, purple, or bronze, shaded, speckled, or blotched. By growing several different types of greens, your options for color, texture, and flavor go way beyond the standard iceberg lettuce salad of old. If limited by space, try growing one of the mesclun mixes—combinations of several greens that you harvest when leaves are young and tender. Or let greens do double duty in the flower bed: use a frilly leaf lettuce as an edging, for example, and mix upright-leafed Swiss chard or purple mustard among the flowers.

Interplanting 'Red Sails' with green 'Buttercrunch' makes for a colorful garden bed.

Most salad greens grow best in cool weather, which means you must get them growing in early spring. As temperatures rise in summer, leaves turn bitter and plants "bolt" (begin to flower and produce seed). Remove them to make room for your summer tomatoes and peppers. But fall provides a second season for salad greens; sow seed in late summer and you may still have fresh greens for your Thanksgiving table.

PEAK SEASON

Spring and fall (Swiss chard persists through summer)

MY FAVORITES

'Bright Lights' Swiss chard has dark green or purple-green leaves with yellow, orange, pink, red, or purple midribs. Harvest young, 2-inch shoots for salad. Cook the larger leaves like spinach.

'Buttercrunch' lettuce develops a small, compact head with a sweet flavor and a buttery texture.

'Osaka Purple' mustard has sharply flavored crinkled purple leaves that are great for salads when they're about 2 inches long, and for stir-fries once more mature. It lasts through the fall.

'Red Sails' lettuce is a slow-to-bolt variety. The leaves are bronze red at the tips, fading to green at the base.

'Simpson Elite' lettuce is a heat-tolerant loose-leaf variety with crinkled, light green leaves.

GARDEN COMPANIONS

Use leaf lettuce to edge flower beds or in a kitchen garden. Plant fast-maturing greens between summer crops that will fill in the space after the lettuce is harvested. The colored foliage of purple mustard provides a wonderful foil for brightly colored annuals like marigolds and zinnias.

When Sow seeds directly in the garden as soon as the soil can be worked in the spring. Sow again in late summer for a fall crop.

Where Although lettuce prefers a sunny site, it is one of the few vegetables that can be grown in part shade. Plant it in rich, well-drained soil that has been amended with organic matter.

How Rake the planting bed smooth before sowing seed. Sprinkle seed on the soil surface and press lightly. Do not cover lettuce seeds—many varieties need light to germinate. Keep bed moist until seeds germinate, then water regularly (but avoid splashing the leaves with wet soil). Mulching with straw or well-rotted compost or leaf mold will help keep soil moist and reduce weeds.

TLC Pick outer leaves of mature loose-leaf lettuce, mustard, and Swiss chard individually; plants will continue to grow from the center. Cut entire heads of romaine and butterhead lettuce types when mature.

ABOVE RIGHT: *Purple mustard and frilly green mizuna look different but share a peppery flavor.* RIGHT: *Mesclun mixes include many kinds of flavorful salad greens.* BELOW RIGHT: *Stems and leaves of colorful 'Bright Lights' Swiss chard taste as good as they look.*

Squash

The sprawling vine of this butternut squash continues to flower, even late in the season as a fruit nears ripeness.

Although squashes come in an amazing array of shapes, colors, sizes, and flavors, they can be divided into two main types: summer and winter. Summer squash includes fast-maturing types like zucchini and pattypan. Plants have either a bush-type or vining growth habit, and fruits should be harvested when young for best flavor and texture. Acorn, butternut, hubbard, and pumpkin are among the many types of winter squash. These develop more slowly, and most have a vining habit. The fruit has a tough outer skin you remove before eating and a meatier flesh; winter squashes usually mature in fall, sometimes after frost.

All squashes are easy to grow and adaptable to a wide range of uses—for bumper crop years, it is a good idea to keep lots of different recipes handy. Squash can be stuffed, sautéed, and stir-fried, or used to make delicious breads, pies, quiches, soups, stews, soufflés, relishes, and pickles. Pumpkins, the largest winter squash, are grown as much for decoration as for culinary uses.

LEFT: *'Table King' is an acorn-type squash that's produced on a compact vine.*
RIGHT: *The heirloom winter squash 'Delicata' has creamy, sweet orange flesh.*

PEAK SEASON

Summer squash can be harvested from summer to fall. Winter squash is harvested in fall, and can be stored for winter use.

MY FAVORITES

Summer squash

'Peter Pan Hybrid' is a pattypan type with light green or white skin, meaty flesh, and a flattened, scalloped shape.

'Roly Poly' is a round zucchini, perfect for stuffing.

'Sunray' is a straight-necked squash with butter yellow fruit. It has good keeping quality.

'Sweet Zuke' is a very productive, nutty-flavored zucchini with medium green skin.

Winter squash

'Delicata' is an heirloom variety with sweet orange flesh; use it like acorn or butternut squash.

'Small Sugar' is an heirloom pumpkin that makes great pie.

'Table King' is a large-fruited acorn squash with a small center cavity.

GARDEN COMPANIONS

Train vining squashes to a fence or trellis to save space. Plant squash in hills with beans and corn for a traditional Native American planting.

When Plant seedlings or sow seed directly in the garden after all danger of frost has passed and the soil has warmed.

Where Grow in a sunny site in moist, well-drained soil that has been enriched with organic matter and a slow-release fertilizer. Vining winter squash requires space—ideally an 8 foot diameter circle—with minimal competition for sun or water.

How Space plants 3 to 5 feet apart in rows 4 to 6 feet apart. Water regularly and mulch young plants with straw, grass clippings, or chopped leaves to help maintain moisture and prevent weeds. Black plastic can also be used as a mulch. Sow successive plantings of summer squash at 3-week intervals for an extended harvest.

TLC Harvest squash with a sharp knife or hand shears. For summer squash, check vines daily—the fruit matures quickly. For winter squash, allow fruits to remain on the vines until they die back, then cut off the fruits, leaving an inch of stem, remove dirt, and cure in a dry, well-ventilated location. Store them in a cool, dry place for winter use.

Strawberries

Strawberries are worth every bit of the extra effort required to grow them. The flavor of perfectly ripe fruits, freshly plucked from the plant is exquisite, and most store-bought berries pale by comparison. And they are well suited to small gardens. If you don't have room for a patch of strawberries, grow them in raised beds, patio tubs, or decorative strawberry pots. If you have a controlling hand and are willing to keep their wanderings in check, grow strawberries along the edge of your vegetable garden or as a ground cover for a sunny bed.

Strawberries at peak bloom in early spring promise an abundant harvest to come.

There are two kinds of strawberries grown in our region, those that fruit primarily in June ("June bearers"), and those that bear intermittently all season ("everbearers"). The former are by far superior in flavor, so are the type I recommend here. But the latter have their merits, particularly as container plants.

You will probably find no shortage of "helpers" to harvest the fruit when the berries are in season. The hard part of growing strawberries is tending them long after the berries have been consumed. Weeding the patch in summer can be a chore. But just keep in mind the promise of next season's crop.

PEAK SEASON

June

MY FAVORITES

'Allstar' is a very productive mid- to late-season variety with elongated orange-red fruit.

'Cavendish', a midseason variety, is a heavy producer of firm, large fruit over several weeks. It's very cold tolerant.

'Earliglow' is the standard for early-bearing strawberries with glossy, sweet, medium-sized fruit. The berries are excellent for freezing.

'Lateglow' produces large berries late in the season, followed by those of 'Latestar'.

GARDEN COMPANIONS

If growing strawberries in the ground, consider planting them near other perennial edible crops such as rhubarb and asparagus. Locate tubs or raised beds in a sunny spot near the patio.

ABOVE: *Remind yourself what real strawberry flavor is by growing your own.*
BELOW: *The best strawberries are handpicked at their peak of succulent ripeness.*

When Plant in early spring as soon as plants are available and the ground can be worked.

Where June-bearing types grow well in rows, as ground covers, or in raised beds. Plants need full sun and rich, fast-draining, slightly acid soil.

How Before planting, soak roots in water to rehydrate. Dig a hole for each plant that will accommodate roots without crowding, and set plants so the crown (where the stems and roots join) is slightly above ground level. Space the plants 14 to 18 inches apart, in rows 3 to 4 feet apart.

TLC Removing runners will result in large plants with fewer but larger berries. For a larger harvest (but smaller berries), allow some runners to develop new plants, maintaining a spacing of 7 to 10 inches between them. Remove blossoms the first year and keep plants well weeded. In late fall, mulch with a 4-inch layer of straw to protect plants over the winter. Rake straw from plants in March, placing it between the rows to help reduce weeds and keep fruit clean. After harvest season, renovate the planting by mowing over the plants using your lawn mower's highest setting. If your planting is too dense, remove mother plants to allow new plants room to develop. Water thoroughly and apply a complete fertilizer.

Thornless Blackberries

I've always loved blackberries, but as a child, I paid a high price for them in scrapes and scratches as my berry-seeking fingers battled the thorny stems. Today's thornless varieties have taken the pain out of blackberry production; they are the easiest and most productive backyard fruit that I've ever grown. Blackberries thrive with little care, produce abundant crops over several weeks in summer, and are absolutely delicious eaten fresh, baked into cobblers or pies, or put up as preserves or jam.

Blackberry roots are perennial, but their canes are biennial—each cane grows leaves the first year, flowers and fruits the following year, and then dies. It's a straightforward growth pattern that makes for easy pruning: after harvest, remove the old fruiting canes, leaving the new canes to bear next year. Trailing and semierect types can be grown on a fence or trellis, or on wires stretched between sturdy posts. Erect types don't really need support, although they are often trained to wires to make picking more convenient.

ABOVE: *A close-up of ripening 'Arapaho' blackberry fruits.*
RIGHT: *'Chester' is a semierect, heavy-bearing blackberry.*

PEAK SEASON
Summer

MY FAVORITES

'Arapaho' is an early-bearing erect variety.

'Chester' is a productive semierect type that begins to ripen about a week later than 'Hull' (see below). It is exceptionally cold tolerant.

'Hull' is a late-season, vigorous, semierect variety. It produces heavy crops of medium-sized fruit with excellent flavor over a long season (almost a month).

'Navaho' has an erect growth habit and does not need support. It bears small fruit with excellent flavor over a long season.

'Triple Crown' has a semierect habit and bears large, midseason berries.

GARDEN COMPANIONS

Grown on a fence, blackberries make an effective background planting for a cutting garden of fresh flowers or a vegetable garden.

When Plant in spring as soon as plants are available.

Where Plant in full sun in rich, well-drained soil in an area with good air circulation. Do not plant where soil is constantly wet.

How Space plants 4 feet apart in rows 8 to 10 feet apart. Cut back new plants to about 6 inches. Grow semierect varieties on a fence or trellis, or on two horizontal wires placed at 3 feet and 5 feet above the ground, supported by stout posts. Erect types can be grown without support but should be cut back during summer to maintain plant height at 3 feet. Mulch plants to reduce weeds and maintain even moisture.

TLC After harvest, cut to the ground the canes that produced fruit and any that are weak. Shorten the first-year canes of erect types to encourage branching. Remove and burn or discard pruned canes to prevent disease. In spring, apply a complete fertilizer and shorten lateral shoots to about 12 inches to increase fruit production.

OPPOSITE PAGE: *'Arapaho', an erect type, trains easily along wires strung between posts.*

Tomatoes

Summer just wouldn't be the same without juicy, vine-ripened tomatoes. They are such a rewarding crop that it's easy to understand why they are the most popular backyard vegetable grown in this country.

There are hundreds of varieties, from old-fashioned heirlooms to the newest hybrids. They offer choices in color, flavor, shape, and disease resistance. Sizes vary from bite-sized cherries you can pop in your mouth to gigantic beef-steaks perfect for slicing on sandwiches and burgers. But all varieties, regardless of their size, color, or shape, can be divided into two main camps. *Determinate tomatoes* are bushy plants that grow to a certain size and then stop, producing a concentrated crop over a relatively short period—great if you're into canning. These can be grown with or without support. *Indeterminate tomatoes* have a more vinelike habit and will need to be caged or staked. They grow continuously, and once they start producing tomatoes, they just keep flowering and fruiting until frost kills the plants.

The cherry tomato 'Sungold' is noted for its excellent flavor. This one is twining up a spiral support.

When Start seed indoors 8 weeks before you expect to plant seedlings outdoors, or purchase young plants in spring. Plant outdoors after all danger of frost has passed and the soil has warmed.

Where Grow in full sun in moist, well-drained soil that has been enriched with organic matter, such as well-rotted compost or leaf mold, and a slow-release complete fertilizer.

How Transplant seedlings on a still, overcast day if possible. Don't plant where tomatoes, peppers, eggplant, or potatoes grew the previous year. Space determinate plants 2 feet apart, indeterminate plants 3 feet apart. Remove bottom leaves and set plants deeply; water thoroughly. Determinate plants do not require support, but are easier to manage when grown in cages. Indeterminate plants require support. Water regularly and mulch.

TLC For best flavor, allow tomatoes to ripen on the vine. Fruit that is harvested before it is fully ripe can be set on the windowsill to ripen. Refrigeration diminishes flavor.

RIGHT: *'Early Girl' is one of the top-performing tomatoes in the Mid-Atlantic region.*
BELOW: *Tomatoes come in many shapes, colors, sizes, and flavors.*

PEAK SEASON
Midsummer to frost

MY FAVORITES
Determinate
'Early Girl' bears early, heavy yields on compact plants.

'Celebrity' bears uniform, medium tomatoes that resist cracking. They're great for canning or fresh eating.

'Fresh Salsa' bears meaty, 4- to 5-ounce fruits that don't turn soupy when chopped—perfect for salsa.

'Viva Italia' produces blocky, meaty, oblong fruit that is good for sauce. The plants are disease resistant and heat tolerant.

Indeterminate
'Brandywine' is a purple-red beefsteak heirloom with a squat shape, deep lobes, and prizewinning flavor.

'Fourth of July' is an exceptionally early producer of tasty 4-ounce fruit.

'Sungold' produces sweet, bite-sized orange-yellow fruit in grapelike clusters; it has excellent flavor.

'Supersweet 100' bears sweet, 1-inch, red globes.

GARDEN COMPANIONS
Tomatoes are generally grown in rows in the vegetable garden. Grow compact varieties in a large container, such as a half-barrel interplanted with parsley or basil.

Seasonal Chores

You don't have to be an obsessive planner to recognize the virtues of a checklist of seasonal chores. In gardens, what happened last year is very likely to happen again, which is why I've logged the gardening questions that come into my office in the Horticulture Department here at Virginia Tech. Here's what to do, and when.   —ALAN R. McDANIEL

Spring

PLANTING

PLANT BARE-ROOT AND CON-TAINER PLANTS. Plant bare-root plants, such as cane berries, fruit trees, grapes, roses, and strawberries, in late winter or early spring as soon as the soil is workable. Plants that don't tolerate bare-root transplanting, such as rhododendrons, azaleas, and some conifers, are sold in containers. For tips on planting both kinds of plants, see pages 258 and 259.

PLANT SEEDS OR SEEDLINGS OF ANNUAL HERBS, such as basil, cilantro, and dill. Deadhead them regularly to keep fresh foliage coming, or don't so that you can harvest seeds.

SOW SEEDS OF LETTUCES AND OTHER COOL-WEATHER CROPS like peas, spinach, and cabbage in early spring. Plant beans, corn, pumpkins, and squash after the soil has thoroughly warmed.

The combination of naturalized daffodils at peak bloom underneath an aged, blooming flowering cherry forms an iconic image of springtime in the Mid-Atlantic.

PLANTING A ROSE OR OTHER BARE-ROOT SHRUB

1 Make a firm cone of soil in a planting hole wide enough to fit the roots. Spread the roots over the cone, positioning the plant at the same depth that (or slightly higher than) it was growing in the field. Use a shovel handle or yardstick to check the depth.

2 Hold the plant upright as you firm soil around its roots. When backfilling is almost complete, add water. This settles the soil around the roots, eliminating any air pockets. If the plant settles below the level of the surrounding soil, gently pull it to the proper level while the soil is saturated, and firm it in place with soil.

3 Finish filling the hole with soil, then water again. Take care not to overwater while the plant is still dormant, because soggy soil may inhibit the formation of new roots. When the growing season begins, build up a ridge of soil around the planting site to form a basin that will keep water from running off; water the plant whenever the top 2 inches of soil are dry.

START SEEDS OF SLOWER-GROWING VEGETABLES INDOORS under fluorescent lights by early April (6 to 8 weeks before outdoor planting time). Choose both early-maturing varieties, such as 'Early Girl' tomato, and later-ripening types, like 'Brandywine' tomato, to extend the harvest over a period of several months.

PLANT SUMMER-FLOWERING PERENNIALS AND ANNUALS IN THE GARDEN as soon as the soil is warm and workable and there's no danger of a late frost. Pinch back leggy plants to encourage bushier growth.

MAINTENANCE

PRUNE APPLE AND PEAR TREES in late winter or very early spring before the buds begin to swell. Avoid making many small cuts, which encourages leaf growth, when cutting off a larger branch will do.

SPRAY FRUIT TREES AND ORNAMENTALS. Before buds swell, apply horticultural oil to fruit trees and flowering trees and shrubs with previous insect problems to kill pests before the growing season starts.

PRUNE MOST ROSES BEFORE LEAVES EMERGE by cutting out dead or crossing canes and weak growth. Prune roses that flower only in spring after flowers fade.

BEGIN LAWN CARE. To thwart crabgrass and other germinating weeds, apply a pre-emergent herbicide, such as corn gluten meal, to your lawn by the time the forsythia is in full bloom. Wait until Memorial Day to fertilize. You can start a new lawn or repair an existing one now, but late summer is a better time.

DIVIDE MOST PERENNIALS when new shoots first appear. Or divide mid- to late-summer bloomers, such as daylilies, delphiniums, phlox, daisies, irises, asters, and rudbeckia once they've finished flowering. Divide peonies, Siberian irises, and other plants with fleshy roots in fall.

FERTILIZE TREES AND SHRUBS that grew poorly last year or suffered winter injury. Use an acidic fertilizer for rhododendrons, azaleas, and blueberries.

PLANTING A CONTAINER PLANT

Place the container on its side and roll it on the ground while tapping it to loosen the roots. Upend the container and slide the plant out. Cut off any badly coiled roots.

1 Dig a planting hole at least twice as wide as the root ball and slightly shallower, and spread the roots out over a central plateau of firm soil. Adjust the plant until it sits an inch or so above the surrounding soil.

2 Backfill with the soil that you dug from the hole, adding it in stages and firming it around the roots with your hands as you work.

3 Mound the soil to create a ridge around the plant to direct water to the roots. The trunk should not be directly exposed to water or it may rot. Irrigate gently. Spread a layer of mulch around the plant, keeping it several inches away from the stem or trunk.

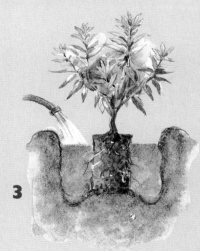

GIVE PLANTS TIME. Don't be too hasty to pronounce a bare plant dead. Some plants, including rose of Sharon, butterfly bush, and some ornamental grasses, are very slow to develop new foliage in the spring. If in doubt, scratch the bark and bend a twig; healthy twigs are pliable and green inside.

FERTILIZE PERENNIALS with a controlled-release fertilizer. Or try this organic formulation: 1 tablespoon fish emulsion and ½ teaspoon liquid seaweed or kelp fertilizer in a gallon of water. Water with this mixture every few weeks during the growing season.

PRUNE EARLY-FLOWERING SHRUBS after they've finished blooming. For light shaping, simply cut back the longest shoots. To rejuvenate large, old shrubs, cut one-third of each shrub's oldest branches to the ground, then cut back the remaining branches to a third of their height.

THIN SEEDLINGS THAT YOU STARTED INDOORS, and gradually acclimate them to the outdoors by placing them in a sheltered location for a few hours a day before transplanting them into the garden.

PREPARE VEGETABLE BEDS by removing weeds and spreading 2 to 4 inches of compost over the surface. When the soil is dry, rototill it to a depth of 6 inches, or turn it over by hand.

PRUNE FLOWERING CHERRY, PLUM, AND PEACH TREES after they have bloomed. To discourage canker diseases, prune when weather is predicted to be dry with temperatures over 60°F/16°C for several days.

GROOM SPENT BULBS. Snap off spent flowers of spring-flowering bulbs, but allow the leaves to wither naturally before cutting those off. This gives bulbs time to store energy for next year's blooms.

PRUNE PINES. Prune new shoots on pines (called "candles") by shortening them by one-third to one-half of their length. This pruning helps to shape the trees and creates denser growth.

USE CAGES OR RINGS TO STAKE BUSHY PERENNIALS, such as peonies, before they bloom. Tie hollyhocks, lilies, delphiniums, and other tall plants with heavy blossoms to bamboo stakes. Plant tall, slender plants next to ones with sturdier stems that they can lean on for support.

OPPOSITE PAGE: *A Yoshino cherry at peak bloom in early spring stops traffic.*
ABOVE: *The fragrant blooms of a peony fill in between the fence and a gold-leaved spirea.*
BELOW: *Long-stemmed daffodils and tulips are framed by a low boxwood hedge.*

Summer

PLANTING

SOW SEEDS OF WARM-SEASON CROPS, such as corn and beans, directly into the garden. Make successive plantings 2 weeks apart or plant varieties with different maturity times to extend the harvests.

START A NEW LAWN. While mid-September is the best time to seed a new blue grass, fescue, or ryegrass lawn, early summer is best for warm-season grasses for coastal and more southern locations. Zoysia is most often started by planting plugs (small plants); sprigs (shredded sod) are used for improved Bermuda grasses.

MAINTENANCE

CHECK RHODODENDRONS, BLUEBERRIES, AND PIN OAKS for signs of iron deficiency (chlorosis). Yellow leaves with deep green veins are an indicator. Spraying leaves with a foliar spray containing iron is a temporary solution. Testing soil pH, and correcting it if necessary, provides long-term results.

CUT BACK EARLY-BLOOMING PERENNIALS. After flowers are spent, cut perennials such as catmint, foxglove, hardy geraniums, and dianthus back by one-third to promote growth of fresh leaves and flowers. Later in summer,

LEFT: *Scarlet runner beans add a vertical accent and red flowers to a garden.*
RIGHT: *A pot of large-leaved, exotic plants adds a tropical look to a patio.*

shear perennials such as purple coneflower, rudbeckia, and phlox after they've finished flowering. This will keep your garden looking tidy and encourage plants to put on fresh growth. Discontinue shearing in early fall.

WATER CONTAINER PLANTS. Keep container plants well watered and fertilized. You may need to water them daily in dry weather. Watering leaches nutrients from the soil, so fertilize at least once a week unless you've applied a controlled-release fertilizer.

STAY AHEAD OF WEEDS. Keep bare spots between plants weeded until plants fill in. Weeds with shallow roots are best cut off at the soil surface with a sharp hoe. Carefully dig out deep-rooted weeds like dandelions with a hand weeder or trowel.

WATCH FOR PESTS. Look for drooping, twisted, chewed, or discolored foliage, which may

Blue-flowered catmint owns the day in an herb garden that also includes thyme, oregano, lavender, and a shaded bench.

indicate an insect problem. Check the undersides of leaves and use a hand lens if the culprit is not readily apparent. Low-toxicity products, such as insecticidal soap, horticultural oil, and neem, control many pests with little environmental impact. Read the label to make sure that the product will control the pest and that it is safe to use on the infested plant.

PINCH PERENNIALS. Some perennials, such as chrysanthemums, border phlox, bee balm, and 'Autumn Joy' sedum, can be pinched or sheared to delay their bloom period and to create a denser plant. Try it with a few to test the results!

DEADHEAD ANNUAL FLOWERS. Remove the spent flowers of annuals such as marigolds to promote reblooming.

STRATEGIZE TO STOP SLUGS. They will congregate during daylight under a board or rock; squash or drown in soapy water any you find there. Gardeners wishing even less contact will find a few drops of isopropyl alcohol dripped on a slug to be very effective. Slugs are also attracted to saucers of beer; they fall in and drown. Bands of diatomaceous earth also will discourage slug travel.

PRUNE ROSES. Climbing and pillar roses can be thinned again in midsummer after the flowers have faded by cutting

1 inch of water per week to flourish in hot summer conditions. If rainfall provides less, irrigate as needed. Conserve water by using soaker hoses and collected rainwater. Water in early morning; evening sprinkling can cause fungal problems.

TREAT POWDERY MILDEW on zinnias, phlox, and bee balm when temperatures are below 85°F/29°C by spraying the leaves with this home remedy: 1 tablespoon each of baking soda and horticultural oil in 1 gallon of water.

STOP FERTILIZING TREES AND SHRUBS by late summer so that new growth has time to mature and develop hardiness before the first hard frost.

LEFT: *In summer annuals come into their own. This planting includes annual phlox, 'Crystal White' zinnia, speedwell (with blue spikes), and silver-leaved dusty miller.*
OPPOSITE PAGE, BOTTOM: *Red 'Dortmund' and pink 'Thérèse Bugnet' roses climb an arbor.*
BELOW: *Upright flowers of bear's breech contrast down-facing petals of purple cone flower.*

out the flowering canes close to the roots. After blooms have died on a hybrid tea or floribunda rose, cut the stems just above a leaf with five leaflets, which will encourage the development of new flowering shoots.

PRUNE SUMMER-BLOOMING SHRUBS, like potentillas and hydrangeas, for shape after they've flowered.

WATER DURING DROUGHTS. Most plants need at least

Fall

PLANTING

PLANT COLD-HARDY ANNUALS.
Pansies, chrysanthemums, and flowering cabbages are excellent for late-season color. Also, cover hardy perennial mums with mulch by late fall.

PLANT TREES AND SHRUBS.
Fall planting encourages root development and lets plants get established before spring. Roots will grow as long as the soil temperature is above 40°F/4°C. Keep new plantings well watered until winter.

PLANT SPRING BULBS such as crocuses, daffodils, grape hyacinths, and tulips in mid-October. If you're planting bulbs in masses, an auger speeds the process of digging holes. Or, excavate the entire bed to the proper depth. Add bulb fertilizer when planting. Mark the locations of your bulbs so you don't mistakenly dig them up, and so you'll know if any are missing come spring. Complete most bulb planting by late October; tulips can go in as late as November, however.

TRANSPLANT DECIDUOUS TREES AND SHRUBS after they're dormant but before the ground freezes hard. Dormant plants are less likely to suffer from transplant shock. Dig as wide a root ball as possible, and stake large trees and shrubs.

MAINTENANCE

FERTILIZE LAWNS. If you only want to fertilize once a year, use a complete fertilizer higher

This classic fall vignette includes rosey 'Autumn Joy' sedum, fountain grass, and yellow 'Moonbeam' coreopsis.

in nitrogen around Labor Day. If possible, make another application with a "winterizer" type fertilizer about the time of your last mowing for the season.

KEEP WATERING YOUR GARDEN as needed as long as it's warm enough to keep a garden hose outside. When temperatures dip to freezing, drain the hoses, store them inside, and turn off outdoor spigots.

GROOM PERENNIALS. Cut down spent perennials that are looking ratty. Leave those with good fall color and attractive seed heads until spring if you wish. Many ornamental grasses look beautiful in winter as well.

DIVIDE PERENNIALS WITH FLESHY ROOTS, such as peonies, Oriental poppies, and Siberian irises, if they show signs of overcrowding. Divide other perennials now, as long as there's a month before the first killing frost so that roots have time to establish before plants go dormant.

MOVE HOUSEPLANTS INDOORS. In the evening, bring in house-plants and tender container plants such as geraniums, tuberous begonias, and fuchsias, as nighttime temperatures may drop precipitously at this time of year.

COLLECT AND COMPOST LEAVES. Compost fallen leaves that aren't used to mulch beds. To use them as mulch, shred them with a lawn mower first so they don't mat together.

LABEL PERENNIALS. Mark the positions of perennials with durable tags so you won't disturb their roots when you plant bulbs in late fall or work in the garden in spring.

LOOK FOR GYPSY MOTHS. Check tree trunks and limbs, outdoor structures, and fences for tan egg cases of the gypsy moth. Scrape off and destroy any that you find.

MULCH FOR WINTER. Once the ground is frozen, add a thick layer of mulch over tender

Jewel-like red leaves of Japanese maple rest on a bed of dark green lily turf in fall.

perennials. This helps keep soil frozen, which prevents plants from being uprooted in a freeze-thaw cycle.

PROTECT ROSES. Tender roses planted in exposed areas are susceptible to freeze damage. Protect them one of three ways: a mound of soil over the crown of the bush; a tar-paper or wire-mesh collar around the plant filled with peat moss, pine bark mulch, or straw; or a plastic rose cone purchased from a garden center placed over the plant.

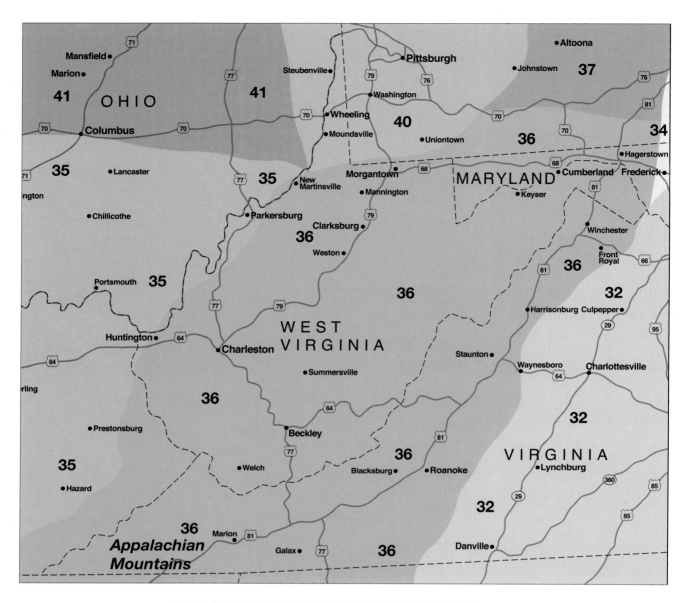

MID-ATLANTIC GARDEN CLIMATE ZONES

It can't be said often enough: Successful gardening depends on choosing the right plant for the right place. The Top 10 plants are among the most reliable performers for Mid-Atlantic gardens, but that doesn't mean each of them will thrive in every corner of this region. A plant's performance is governed by all aspects of the climate: the length of the growing season (days without frost), the amount of rainfall and its timing, winter low temperatures, summer high temperatures, and humidity. The most important limiting factor for permanent plants, such as trees, shrubs, and perennials, is winter cold. For annual vegetables and long-season fruit trees, success depends on heat and the length of the growing season. Sunset's five Mid-Atlantic climate zones take all

these factors into account, and each plant recommended in this book is a reliable performer in one or more of these zones. Here are brief descriptions of the Mid-Atlantic zones. For more information about your climate, check with your local Cooperative Extension Office.

Zone 31, Coastal Mid-Atlantic. Here in the southeast corner of Virginia, the growing season is 240 to 270 days. July temps hover between the 80s and 90s (upper 20s to low 30s C); winter lows dip to 0°F/–18°C.

Zone 32, Heart of the Mid-Atlantic. This is the climate zone that surrounds the Chesapeake Bay and so

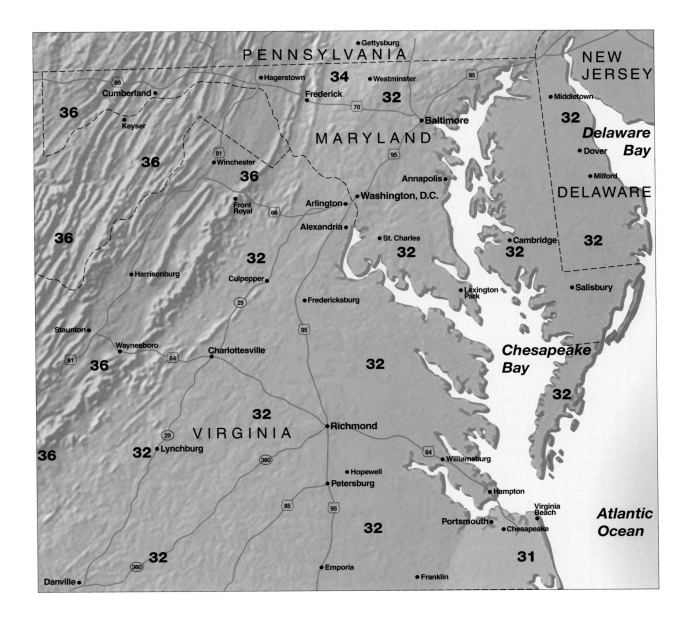

dominates much of the Mid-Atlantic region. Where southern and northern climates blend, gardening here is a delight. The growing season ranges between 180 to 240 days; winter lows reach the 20s (around −4°C) and summer highs are in the 90s (in the 30s C).

Zone 34, North Central Maryland. This sliver of coastal northeastern climate dips into northern Maryland around the cities of Frederick, Taneytown, and Westminster. The growing season averages 120 to 150 days; winter lows are typically in the high teens and low 20s (−7 to −5°C), though arctic air can deliver subzero temps. July temperatures rarely exceed the upper 80s (low 30s C).

Zone 35, Western edge of West Virginia. The mid-continent climate pushes into West Virginia around Parkersburg and Huntington. Summers are hot and humid, often in excess of 100°F/38°C. Winter lows are usually in the teens (around −10°C) but sometimes drop to −20°F/−29°C. The growing season is 150 to 240 days.

Zone 36, Appalachian Mountains. This region includes western Virginia, West Virginia, and western Maryland. Summers are relatively cool and winters are cold, with lows typically below zero. A typical danger to early-blooming fruit trees here are late spring frosts that come after a spell of warm weather. Growing season length is 120 to 160 days.

Index Pages listed in *italics* include photographs.

A

Acer, 178–179, *267*
  griseum, *178*, 179
  rubrum, *169*, *178*, 179
Aesculus
  × *carnea*, 138–139
  flava, 139
  hippocastanum, 138
  pavia, *138*, 139
Alchemilla, 222–223
  erythropoda, 223
  mollis, 223
Alstroemeria, 60–61
× *Amarcrinum*, 62–63
Amaryllis belladonna, 62
Amelanchier
  arborea, *126*, 127
  × *grandiflora*, *10*, 126–127
  laevis, 126
Anethum graveolens, 242
Annuals, 36–37, 264, 266
Arborvitae, *See Thuja occidentalis*
Aster
  divaricatus, 27
  novae-angliae, 26–27
  tataricus, 27
Astilbe
  × *arendsii*, 17
  chinensis, 16–17
  simplicifolia, 16–17
Autumn chores, 266–267
Azalea, *See Rhododendron*

B

Bare-root shrubs, 258
Barrenwort, *See Epimedium*
Basil, *See Ocimum basilicum*
Beans, 236–237
  bush lima, 237
  scarlet runner, *262*
  snap, 237
Beech, *See Fagus*
Berries
  blackberries, 252–253
  blueberries, 238–239
  strawberries, 250–251
Betula
  nigra, *7*, 182–183
  papyrifera, 182
  pendula, 182
Birch, river, *See Betula*
Black-eyed Susan, *See Rudbeckia fulgida*
  'Goldsturm'
Black-eyed Susan vine, *See Thunbergia*
Blackberries, thornless, 252–253
Blueberries, 238–239, 262
Bluegrass, Kentucky, *See Poa pratensis*
Boston ivy, *See Parthenocissus*
Boxwood, *See Buxus sempervirens*
Bridal wreath, *See Spirea*
British soldiers, *See Lycoris*

Buckeye, *See Aesculus*
Bulbs, 58–59, 261, 266
Buxus sempervirens, 152–153

C

Cardinal climber, *See Ipomoea*
Cardinal flower, *See Lobelia cardinalis*
Carex pensylvanica, 227
Catharanthus roseus, 44–45
Catmint, 263
Cercis canadensis, *6*, 130–131
Chamaecyparis
  obtusa, *147*, 163
  pisifera, 162–163
Chard, Swiss, 246–247
Cherry, *See Prunus*
Chionanthus
  retusus, 137
  virginicus, 136–137
Chrysogonum virginianum, 218–219
Cladrastis kentukea, 188–189
Clematis, 198–199
  × *jackmanii*, 199
  montana, 199
  terniflora, *198*, 199
Clethra alnifolia, 120–121
Climate zones, 6–7, 268–269
Coffee tree, Kentucky, *See Gymnocladus dioica*
Coleus, *See Solenostemon scutellariodes*
Compost, 267
Coneflower, purple, *See Echinacea*
Conifers, 146–147, 261
Containerized plants, 259, 263
Coreopsis, *266*
Cornus, *124*
  florida, 134–135
  kousa, *81*, 134
  × *rutgersensis*, *134*, 135
Cosmos, 40–41
  bipinnatus, 40
  sulphureus, *36*, 40
Cotinus
  coggygria, 116–117
  obovatus, 117
Cranberry bush, *See Viburnum*
Crape myrtle, *See Lagerstroemia*
Crinum
  moorei, 62
  × *powellii*, 63
Crocus, 64–65
  flavus, 65
  sieberi sublimis, 65
  tommasinianus, 65
  vernus, *64*, 65
Cucumbers, *11*, 240–241
Cypress, false, *See Chamaecyparis*

D

Daffodil, *See Narcissus*
Dahlia, *59*, 68–69

Decumaria barbara, 201
Design guidelines, 7–10
Dill, *See Anethum graveolens*
Dogwood, *See Cornus*
Dolichos lablab, 204–205
Dryopteris, 20–21
  erythrosora, 21

E

Echinacea, 265
  paradoxa, 31
  purpurea, 30–31
Edible plants, 234–235
Epimedium, 214–215
  × *perralchicum*, 215
  × *versicolor*, 215
  × *youngianum*, 215
Evapotranspiration, 169
Evergreens, 146–147, 261

F

Fagus, 170–171
  grandiflora, 171
  sylvatica, 171
Fall chores, 266–267
False cypress, *See Chamaecyparis*
Ferns, *213*, *See also Dryopteris; Polystichum*
Fescue, *See Festuca arundinacea*
Festuca arundinacea, 227
Flowering shrubs, 102–103
Flowering trees, 124–125
Foster's holly, 154–155
Fothergilla
  gardenii, 104–105
  major, 105
Fringe tree, *See Chionanthus*
Fruits and fruit trees, 234–235

G

Gleditsia triacanthos inermis, *168*, 172–173
Grape hyacinth, *See Muscari*
Grasses
  lawns, 226–227
  ornamental, 28–29
Green and gold, *See Chrysogonum virginianum*
Greens, salad, 246–247
Ground covers, 212–213
Gymnocladus dioica, 176–177
Gypsy moths, 267

H

Halesia
  carolina, 142–143
  diptera, 143
  monticola, 143
Hamamelis, 102
  × *intermedia*, 122–123
  japonica, 122
  mollis, 122
  virginiana, 123

Helianthus annuus, 54–55
Hellebore, *See Helleborus*
Helleborus, 12, 14
   foetidus, 23
   niger, 23
   orientalis, 22–23
Herbs, 242–243
Holly, *See Ilex*
Holly, false, *See Osmanthus heterophyllus*
Honeysuckle, *See Lonicera*
Horny goat's weed, *See Epimedium*
Horsechestnut, *See Aesculus*
Hosta, 4, 12, 24–25
   sieboldiana, 25
Hyacinth bean, *See Lablab purpureus*
Hyacinth, grape, *See Muscari*
Hydrangea, 13
   anomala petiolaris, 200–201
   macrophylla, 113
   quercifolia, 103, 112–113
Hydrangea, wild, *See Decumaria barbara*
Hylotelephium, See Sedum

I

Ilex
   × *attenuata,* 154–155
   cassine, 154
   glabra, 160–161
   opaca, 154, 155
Impatiens walleriana, 42–43
Inkberry, *See Ilex*
Ipomoea
   alba, 208–209
   batatas, 209
   lobata, 209
   × *multifida,* 209
   tricolor, 190, 209
Ivy, Boston, *See Parthenocissus*

J

Japanese pagoda tree, *See Sophora japonica*
Japanese pieris, *See Pieris japonica*
Japanese silver grass, *See Miscanthus sinensis*
Johnny-jump-up, *See Viola*
Juneberry, *See Amelanchier*
Juniper, *See Juniperus chinensis*
Juniperus chinensis, 158–159

K

Kalmia latifolia, 110–111
Kentucky bluegrass, *See Poa pratensis*
Kentucky coffee tree, *See Gymnocladus dioica*

L

Lablab purpureus, 204–205
Lady's-mantle, *See Alchemilla*
Lagerstroemia, 128–129
Lamb's ear, *See Stachys byzantina*
Larkspur, *58*
Laurel, cherry, *See Prunus*
Laurel, English, *See Prunus*
Laurel, mountain, *See Kalmia latifolia*
Lavender, *263*
Lawns, 226–227, 259, 262, 266–267
Lenten rose, *See Helleborus*

Lettuce, 246–247
Leucojum
   aestivum, 74–75
   vernum, 75
Lilium, 72–73
   Asiatic, *58,* 73
   orientals, 73
Lily, belladonna, *See Amaryllis belladonna*
Lily, hurricane, *See Lycoris*
Lily, Peruvian, *See Alstroemeria*
Lily, spider, *See Lycoris*
Lily, surprise, *See Lycoris*
Lily, toad, *See Tricyrtis*
Lily turf, *See Liriope muscari*
Liriope muscari, 228–229, 267
Lobelia cardinalis, 18–19
Locust, honey, *See Gleditsia triacanthos inermis*
Lolium perenne, 227
Lonicera
   × *brownii,* 203
   × *heckrottii,* 202–203
   japonica, 202
   sempervirens, 203
Lycoris, 76–77
   radiata, 77
   squamigera, 77

M–O

Madagascar periwinkle, 44–45
Magnolia
   grandiflora, 184–185
Magnolia
   denudata, 140
   liliiflora, 140
   × *soulangeana,* 140
   stellata, 141
   virginiana, 141
Maiden grass, *See Miscanthus sinensis*
Mandevilla, 206–207
   × *amoena,* 207
   boliviensis, 207
   sanderi, 207
   splendens, 207
Maple, *See Acer*
Marigold, *See Tagetes*
Maypop, *See Passiflora*
Mazus reptans, 212, 230–231
Mildew, powdery, 265
Mina, *See Ipomoea*
Miscanthus sinensis, 8, 28–29
Molinia caerulea arundinacea, 28–29
Mondo grass, *See Ophiopogon japonicus*
Moonflower, *See Ipomoea*
Moor grass, *See Molinia caerulea arundinacea*
Morning glory, *See Ipomoea*
Moss pink, 232–233
Mountain laurel, *See Kalmia latifolia*
Mulch, 267
Muscari
   armeniacum, 70–71
   botryoides, 71
Mustard greens, 246–247
Narcissus, 66–67, 256–257, 261
New England aster, *26–27*
Oak, *See Quercus*
Ocimum basilicum, 242

Ophiopogon japonicus, 229
Oregano, 263
Osmanthus heterophyllus, 146, 156–157
Oxydendrum arboreum, 144–145

P

Pachysandra
   procumbens, 221
   terminalis, 220–221
Pagoda tree, Japanese, *See Sophora japonica*
Pansy, *See Viola*
Parsley, *See Petroselinum crispum*
Parthenocissus, 191
   quinquefolia, 197
   tricuspidata, 196–197
Passiflora
   caerulea, 210–211
   incarnata, 211
   jamesonii, 211
Passion vine, *See Passiflora*
Pennsylvania sedge, *See Carex pensylvanica*
Peony, *261*
Peppers, *234,* 244–245
Perennial ryegrass, *See Lolium perenne*
Perennials, 14–15
   fall chores, 267
   fertilizing, 260
   pinching, 264
   staking, 261
   summer care, 262–263
Periwinkle, Madagascar, *See Catharanthus roseus*
Pests
   gypsy moths, 267
   summer chores, 263
Petroselinum crispum, 242–243
Petunia
   × *hybrida,* 52–53
   integrifolia, 53
Phlox, *213,* 264–265
   divaricata, 233
   stolonifera, 233
   subulata, 232–233
Pieris japonica, 106–107
Pine, *See Pinus*
Pinus
   mugho, 165
   strobus, 164–165
   thunbergii, 165
Plane tree, *See Platanus*
Platanus, 186–187
   × *acerifolia,* 186, 187
   occidentalis, 186
   orientalis, 186
Poa pratensis, 227
Polystichum, 20–21
   acrostichoides, 21
   polyblepharum, 21
Powdery mildew, 265
Prunus, 125, 256–257
   caroliniana, 151
   'Hally Jolivette', 132–133
   laurocerasus, 150–151
   × *subhirtella,* 132, 133
   × *yedoensis,* 132, 133, 260
Public gardens, 8–9

Q

Quercus, 180–181
  alba, 181
  chlorosis, 262
  coccinea, 181
  palustris, 181

R

Redbud, *See Cercis*
Rhododendron, 12
  calendulaceum, 115
  chlorosis, 262
  prunifolium, 115
  schlippenbachii, 114–115
River birch, 182–183
Rosa, 80–81, *264*
  chinensis, 90, 97
  climbing, 80, *81,* 82–83
  fall chores, 267
  floribunda, 84–85
  glauca, 101
  × *harisonii,* 101
  hybrid musk, 86–87
  hybrid species, 100–101
  hybrid tea, *80,* 88–89
  miniature, 90–91
  modern shrub, 92–93
  Noisettes, 94–95
  old garden, 96–97
  planting bare-root, 258
  polyantha, 98–99
  pruning, 259, 264
  × *roxburghii,* 101
  rugosa, 97
  species, 100–101
Rudbeckia fulgida 'Goldsturm', 216–217
Ryegrass, perennial, *See Lolium perenne*

S

Sage, *See Salvia*
Salad greens, 246–247
Salvia
  coccinea, 49
  farinacea, 37, 48–49
  officinalis, 243
  splendens, 49

Sawara false cypress, *See Chamaecyparis*
Seasonal chores, 257–267
Seasons, 5–7
Sedge, Pennsylvania, *See Carex pensylvanica*
Sedum, 15, 266
  'Autumn Joy', 32–33
  ternatum, 33
Seeds, 258
Serviceberry, *See Amelanchier*
Shadblow, *See Amelanchier*
Shadbush, *See Amelanchier*
Shade gardens, 12
Shrubs
  fall planting, 266
  fertilizing, 259, 265
  flowering, 102–103
  planting bare-root, 258
  pruning, 260
Silver grass, Japanese, *See Miscanthus sinensis*
Slugs, 264
Smoke tree, *See Cotinus*
Snowdrop tree, *See Halesia*
Snowflake, *See Leucojum*
Soil building, 12–13
Solenostemon scutellarioides, 38–39
Sophora japonica, 174–175
Sourwood, *See Oxydendrum arboreum*
Spanish flag, *See Ipomoea*
Speedwell, *264–265*
Spiraea, 118–119
  japonica, 118
  thunbergii, 118
  × *vanhouttei,* 118, 119
Spring chores, 257–261
Spurge, *See Pachysandra*
Squash, 248–249
Stachys byzantina, 224–225
Strawberries, 250–251
Summer chores, 262–265
Summersweet, *See Clethra alnifolia*
Sunflower, *See Helianthus annuus*
Sweet potato vine, *See Ipomoea*
Swiss chard, 246–247

Sycamore, *See Platanus*
Symphyotrichum novae-angliae, See Aster

T

Tagetes, 46–47
  erecta, 46
  patula, 46
  tenuifolia, 46
Taxus, 166–167
  baccata, 147, 167
  cuspidata, 167
  × *media,* 167
Thuja occidentalis, 146, 148–149
Thunbergia
  alata, 194–195
  grandiflora, 195
Thyme, *See Thymus*
Thymus, 263
  × *citriodorus,* 243
  herba-barona, 243
  serpyllum, 243
  vulgaris, 243
Time as factor in design, 10–11
Toad lily, *See Tricyrtis*
Tomatoes, 254–255
Trees
  evergreen, 146–147
  fall planting, 266
  fertilizing, 259, 265
  flowering, 124–125
  fruit, 234–235
  pruning, 261
  shade, 168–169
Tricyrtis, 34–35
  hirta, 35
Tulipa, 59, 78–79, *213*

V

Vegetables, 11, 234–235, 260
Viburnum
  carlesii, 108–109
  dilatatum, 109
  opulus, 109
  plicatum tomentosum, 109
Vines, 190–191
Viola, 50–51
  cornuta, 50
  × *wittrockiana,* 50
Virginia creeper, *See Parthenocissus*

W–Z

Weather, 6–7
Wisteria
  floribunda, 192
  frutescens, 192–193
  frutescens macrostachya, 193
  macrostachya, 193
  sinensis, 192
Witch hazel, *See Hamamelis*
Wood vamp, *See Decumaria barbara*
Yellow wood, *See Cladrastis kentukea*
Yew, *See Taxus*
Zinnia, 56–57, *264–265*
  angustifolia, 56
  elegans, 56
  haageana, 56
  peruviana, 56